RISING ABOVE SHAME

RISING ABOVE SHAME

Healing Family Wounds to Self-Esteem

Stanley Wilson, Ph.D.

Launch Press
Rockville, MD

iv

98 97 96 95 94 93 92 91   9 8 7 6 5 4 3 2 1

Library of Congress Cataloging-in-Publication Data

Wilson, Stanley, 1944-
Rising above shame : healing family wounds to self-esteem /
Stanley Wilson.
       p. cm.
Includes bibliographical references.
ISBN 1-877872-02-4 : $12.95
1. Shame.   2. Shame in children.   3. Parent and child.   4. Self
-respect.   5. Adult children of dysfunctional families-
-Rehabilitation.   I.Title.
BF575.S45W54 1990
616.89—dc20   91-19449
                                                 CIP

LAUNCH PRESS
P.O.Box 5629   Rockville, MD 20855
1-800-321-9167

To Debrah and Noelle,

beloved wife and daughter

Contents

Part II   Rising Above Shame   169

Foreword

Rising Above Shame is an excellent continuation in our ever increasing consciousness of the power of shame to create or destroy the very fiber of our being.

Shame's destructive power lies in its silence and its secrecy. Stanley Wilson does an incredible job in making the many shame- inducing behaviors concrete and recognizable. He goes beyond my own work on shame in several ways.

First, he spells out the specific kinds of shame-based belief that result from each species of parental abuse. This has great value in helping a person make their abuse real. We need to understand dearly what happened to us. The negative belief about oneself that results from battering is different than the belief that results from neglect. The former self creates a feeling of being unlovable; the latter a sense of being unimportant. Different behaviors result from the two different beliefs. We can't know what we don't know. Specificity is what we need in treating shame since there are many species of shame. Each is soul murdering in its own way. In order to heal shame we need to embrace it. To embrace it we need to know the unique and cunning way we have internalized shame. Dr. Wilson has done an excellent job in breaking the genus shame into its various species.

Secondly, this book is the clearest I've seen on the family systems role in creating the context for toxic shame. He shows us how the rigid covert family rules and overt roles foster and maintain a shameful sense of self. An he does this in very simple language. Toxic shame loves pedantic clinical language because it is easy to stay hidden in it. Dr. Wilson refuses to be induced by that invitation.

I truly believe that this book, *Rising Above Shame,* takes the next practical step in the current exposition of shame. It is easy to read and would be a next book to read if you've read my book on shame. If you haven't read my book, this book is a great place to start your healing journey. I wholeheartedly recommend it to anyone who wants good self-esteem and self acceptance.

John Bradshaw   9/12/91

Acknowledgments

Many times in the past two years I imagined how wonderful it would be to complete my manuscript, find a publisher, and have the opportunity to acknowledge those who supported me in the writing of this book. That time has happily arrived, and I wish to express my heartfelt appreciation to:

Debrah Wilson, my wife, support and inspiration, for patiently over-functioning so I would have time to write this book, and for providing encouragement when I needed it most (like the time I had a computer malfunction that erased hours worth of writing!).

Noelle Laura Wilson, my daughter, for opening my heart and teaching me to love unconditionally, and for daily instruction in the process of child development. May you be blessed with healthy pride.

Lorin Wilson, my father, for generously supporting my educational goals, and for guiding me along the path of service.

Yvonne Lovejoy, my mother, for modeling compassion, and for telling me as a child that I could achieve whatever I wanted.

Dianne Nicholson, my sister, grammarian extraordinaire, for correcting the final draft of my manuscript, and for offering helpful suggestions to improve the book for lay readers.

John Bradshaw, whose efforts have inspired millions to seek help, for making time in his impossible schedule to write a foreword that really adds something to my book. You are much appreciated, John.

Jane Middelton-Moz, my friend, for volunteering her time to read early drafts of my manuscript, for stimulating discussions on shame and guilt, and for her efforts in getting this book published.

Lorie Dwinell, my friend, for her unflinching validation and encourage-ment, and for making herself available whenever I had a question.

Dorothea McArthur, my former classmate, for explaining her strategy for getting a manuscript into the hands of the right publisher. It worked!

Trip Quillman, Jim Tufts, and Pamela Thaut, my loving friends and colleagues, for the many consultations that have added immeasurably to my understanding of the shame experience and my growth as a clinician.

Greg and Kathy Bates, and all the folks at Northwest Center for Adult Children, for our valued and ongoing affiliation, and for cheerleading me while I wrote on weekends. Special thanks are extended to Claudia Abbey for her creative input, not the least of which was the "rising above shame" metaphor.

Michael Gladych, my beloved friend and mentor, enlightened elder, raja yoga master, for patiently guiding and affirming me over the past eight years.

Dale E. Turner, my longtime friend and former minister, for reading the section on brainwashing and validating my perception that spiritual abuse induces shame in children.

John Lynch and the staff of Launch Press, for believing in my manuscript and for publishing it promptly and skillfully. Your sustained enthusiasm has made the publishing process an unexpected delight.

Terry Kominers, my editor, for carefully reading my manuscript and making changes that made it more understandable to the lay reader.

My clients, who risked exposure and told me their stories, for what they have taught me about the process of healing shame. For a psychotherapist, the greatest knowledge and skill is gained from the actual experience of being in a relationship with clients. Without them, and their courage to "speak the unspeakable," *Rising Above Shame: Healing Family Wounds to Self-Esteem,* would not exist.

Introduction

No emotion has the potential to inform us more about our selves than does shame. Unfortunately, many of us grew up in families where we were exposed to parental behaviors that induced too much shame. In childhood, carefully measured and small doses of shame lead to the formation of conscience and the capacity for emotional growth and integration. This optimal amount of shame is experienced as feeling exposed as someone who is in some way lacking. It is a temporary and tolerable feeling that is released as soon as it is acted upon. Thus, optimal shame can be used to improve ourselves and our relationships.

On the other hand, too much shame is poisonous to the developing child self because it is internalized; that is, it becomes a lasting part of the self. Instead of having useful information about the self that would motivate corrective measures that release shame, the child forms an enduring core belief that says "I'm bad and unlovable," or some variation on this theme. This belief follows the child into adulthood and is experienced as shame—the painful feeling of being inferior, inadequate, or defective as a person. Too much shame is responsible for low self-esteem as well as difficulties in forming and maintaining close relationships.

This book is about how too much shame is induced in children as certain parental messages are taken into the developing self. These negative messages sever the crucial attachment bond between parent and child and thus activate shame. I will explain how these messages are communicated and how each results in a different shame-based core belief about the self. Readers who were subjected to various combinations of such messages will learn how to counter them and create a new sense of self based on positive self-esteem. Specifically, there are twelve shame-inducing messages (with the corresponding pattern of shaming parental behavior in parentheses):

Message One: "You are inadequate!" (Belittlement)

Message Two: "You are worthless!" (Rejection)

Message Three: "You are disgusting!" (Scorn)

Message Four: "You are unwanted!" (Abandonment)

Message Five: "You are unimportant!" (Neglect)

Message Six: "You are nothing!" (Engulfment)

Message Seven: "You are dirty!" (Molestation)

Message Eight: "You are unlovable!" (Battering)

Message Nine: "You are powerless!" (Terrorizing)

Message Ten: "You are sinful!" (Brainwashing)

Message Eleven: "You are deviant!" (Corrupting)

Message Twelve: "You are crazy!" (Confusing)

This book will also describe parental rules that induce and perpetuate shame by denying the child's most basic human rights. We will see how the child learns to follow and be loyal to five unspoken rules, namely: (1) "Don't be," (2) "Don't need," (3) "Don't make mistakes," (4) "Don't express your self," and (5) "Don't separate." The consequences of growing up under such rules will be examined, e.g., how the "no mistakes" rule results in perfectionism. Readers who came from a family governed by one or more of these rules will have a new understanding of how they were transmitted and how they continue to operate in adulthood. From a position of greater awareness, these shaming rules can be challenged, broken, and replaced by ones that affirm our rights and enhance our self-esteem.

I will also explore dysfunctional family roles that indeed fulfill family functions, but at the expense of the child's emotional and social development. These roles are assigned and scripted parts in the family drama that have little or nothing to do with who the child uniquely is. They induce shame by forcing the child to erect a false self and by defeating the formation of a true personal identity. There are eight characteristic roles adopted by children in shame-based families: (1) the overachieving "Impostor," (2) the troublemaking "Bad Seed," (3) the disappearing "Loner," (4) the entertaining "Comedian"/"Comedienne," (5) the virtuous "Saint"/"Angel," (6) the victimized "Little Prince"/"Little Princess," (7) the focused-on "Sick Child," and (8) the role changing "Chameleon." Readers who played one or more of these roles will better understand why they never actualized their deeper potentials, and how they can do it now.

In the final chapter, a model for healing shame from the family of origin will be presented. There are other sources of shame, e.g., peer or cultural shame, but that induced by parents, intentionally or unintentionally, is the most damaging to the developing child self. Furthermore, it is the quality of the parent-child relationship and the child's ability to maintain self-esteem that determine how successfully he or she will deal with sources of shame outside the family, i.e., whether they will be released or internalized. This model is especially intended for the reader who is already involved in or is considering therapy. It is based on my experience that the successful resolution of shame is a six-step process that involves: (1) acknowledging shame, (2) developing an affirming relationship, (3) releasing shame, (4) countering messages, breaking rules, quitting roles, (5) confronting shame-inducing parents, and (6) forgiving or letting go. Completing these steps leads to a rebirth of the true self and the formation of a true personal identity based on positive self-esteem.

This book differs from other books on shame in that it emphasizes a family systems approach to understanding how shame is taken into the self. For our purposes, this means that the family is seen as a system where all parental behavior is considered a form of communication that sends either positive or negative messages to children. It was written for anyone raised in a family system based on shame; that is, a family that is characterized by any combination of the twelve negative messages, five dehumanizing rules, and eight self-negating roles. It will explore the emotional aftereffects or symptoms that result from being raised in such a family, namely: low self-esteem, depression, rage reactions, panic attacks, eating disorders, sexual and relationship problems, and addictions of all kinds. Understanding and healing these shame wounds is the topic of this book.

Our understanding of shame is nowhere near complete, in part because of the cultural tendency, motivated by shame, to hide shame. I believe this book will bring a crucial aspect of shame into the open—one that is potentially ugly and discomforting because it involves parents mistreating their children. Because many of us have blindspots when it comes to our own unhealed shame, and because the concept of shame can be confusing, I have attempted to write a book that can be easily understood. The central task of this book is to make shame more understandable so as to facilitate the process of healing. The first chapter is devoted to learning a language that allows us to distinguish one shame experience from another, e.g., to really understand the difference between shame and guilt. I have tried to avoid technical jargon and clearly define all terms. For example, rather than simply refer to a "dysfunctional family role," I found it helpful to define what a role actually is and explain what makes it dysfunctional. I have also included numerous case examples to make clear the different messages, rules, and roles that induce shame. Like the people who appear in the pages of this book, you can rise above shame and achieve higher self-esteem.

The bad news is that far too much shame is induced in far too many children, and that it is carried into adulthood. The good news is that shame can be healed and that we don't need to pass it on to our children. This book was written for persons who promised themselves they would not repeat their parents' mistakes, but find themselves mistreating and shaming their own children in the same ways their parents did them . . . anyone who is out-of-control with regard to his or her drinking, drugging, eating, or sexual behavior . . . anyone who keeps getting into unhealthy or abusive relationships, or who is in one and can't get out . . . anyone who is burdened by family "secrets" or anxious about exposing who he or she really is . . . anyone who feels fundamentally flawed as a person. This book is for serious readers who want to rise above shame.

ABOUT THE CASE EXAMPLES IN THIS BOOK

None of the case examples presented in this book reflect the life experiences of any one individual. Rather, each case is a composite formed from the lives of numerous clients and families I have seen in fifteen years of practicing psychology. By using composites and altering the stories I have been trusted with, I am protecting each client's right to confidentiality. Any resemblance between a client appearing on the pages of this book and a real life person is a coincidence—one that is based on the similar stories told by clients who were exposed to similar messages, rules, and roles in shame-based families.

I have deliberately omitted the most shocking and horrifying case examples (of which there are far too many) because adults shamed as children tend to invalidate their experiences, e.g., "I have no right to complain compared to what she went through!" If you have been wounded by shame, your story and your pain is no less valid because someone else was wounded worse. You are entitled to feel the way you do!

A note about pronouns. Throughout the book, I use "he" or "she" interchangably to refer to the typical child or adult. Any reference to a hypothetical "he" implies that the same idea is equally applicable to the "she's" in our culture, and vice versa. Using the more modern and generic "s/he" feels unnatural, and writing out "he or she" for every example is unwieldy. Hence, the reader may assume that, unless otherwise stated, any reference to one gender also holds true for the other.

Part I

The Induction of Shame

I had lost nearly thirty-seven years to the image I carried of myself. I had ambushed myself by believing, to the letter, my parents' definition of me.

Pat Conroy, The Prince of Tides

Chapter One

The Shame Family of Emotions

There are numerous words to describe moments of sudden exposure resulting in the feeling of shame. These words make up a shame family of emotions, all describing the inner sense of being defective as a human being. I am including the following as the most important members of this family: shame, guilt, embarrassment, mortification, shyness, and humiliation.

Each of these experiences is different, yet each has at its core the feeling of shame. This causes confusion and these words for shame are used by different people in different ways. Most of us know what it is like to experience guilt, but we cannot say with certainty how this is different from feeling ashamed. Our difficulty in separating different shame experiences makes it impossible to understand them. In order to heal shame, we must learn a language that will allow us to distinguish one shame family member from another.

Such a language will bring shame into awareness where it can be acknowledged and released. Consider this analogy: To escape from a pit you have fallen into, you must first be aware you have fallen into a pit. When shame operates outside of awareness, it is as if we are living in a pit and don't know it. An unconscious filter of shame is superimposed on our experience and we see the world through shame-colored glasses. The way we think, feel, and relate to ourselves and others becomes clouded by shame. Having and understanding a language for the different shame family members allows us to escape from the pit and see our inner and outer world clearly. The following definitions will provide a tool for self-awareness and a way to release and heal these painful feelings.

SHAME

Shame is first an emotion that informs us about our self. As with any emotion, it provides energy and direction for taking action. Although it is always uncomfortable and often painful, shame, in small doses, can help us improve ourselves and our relationships. Just as grief directs us to mourn a loss, and fear directs us to avoid a threat, shame can direct us to change the way we relate to ourselves and to others. Shame is necessary for normal development and is a potential teacher throughout the life cycle. When we understand shame, and come to terms with it, we are able to heal our shame wounds and enhance our self-esteem. All emotions, including shame, have a purpose and offer the potential for growth (becoming more of a person) and integration (becoming more of who we truly are). There are no useless emotions. Shame is useful unless we have too much or too little of it.

John Bradshaw (1988, p.3) makes a distinction between nourishing and toxic shame. Nourishing shame is a healthy emotion telling us we have limitations because we are human. Toxic shame is the feeling of being worthless, a failure as a human being. It is the essence of co-dependency, which he defines as a loss of authentic selfhood. The notion that shame can be healthy has generated a great deal of confusion (Bradshaw, personal communication, 4/17/89).

This confusion can be cleared up by introducing the concept of optimal shame. Optimal shame implies that we experience the right amount of shame, and because shame is so potent, the right amount is a very small dose. A small dose of shame is experienced as a feeling that we are seen as lacking in some way, a feeling that directs us to change ourselves or our relationships. This feeling of exposure is a temporary feeling. Optimal shame is always a brief experience and is released as it is acknowledged and acted upon. It does not become a part of the self. This is what is meant by healthy shame. Too much shame is never healthy because it is internalized and is too intense to be used for self-improvement.

In childhood, carefully measured doses of shame lead to conscience development and serve as a guide for socially appropriate behavior and self-improvement. Too much shame can result in a failure to attach to and identify with the parent. In such a case, the child's capacity to respond with shame is never internalized, leading to poor conscience development (Kaufman, 1989, p.152). The child who has taken in too little shame will act without conscience, that is, he will behave in a self-centered and antisocial way.

On the other hand, larger doses of shame are poisonous to the self of the developing child. The child who is given overdoses of shame cannot shake the feeling of being bad and unlovable. Whereas optimal shame is tolerable and brief, the "I'm bad and unlovable" feeling cannot be tolerated and does not go away. As parents administer repeated doses, shame accumulates and becomes internalized, or taken into the self. The feeling of being exposed becomes chronic and is then experienced as a shamed sense of self—the child feels fundamentally bad, inferior, and defective. This feeling is what is meant by too much shame. Too much shame is not useful because it is so painful that it overwhelms and immobilizes us. When we internalize too much shame as children, we feel unworthy and unlovable as adults.

Internalizing an optimal amount of shame leads to an awareness and appreciation of our own and others' boundaries. We respect ourselves and our right to privacy. This respect is based on the belief that certain thoughts, feelings, and actions should not be exposed to the scrutiny of others. It should not be shameful to sexually pleasure oneself, but modesty demands it be done in private. Self-disclosure is made only when it is appropriate and in our own best interest. With optimal shame we likewise respect the privacy of others. It is intrusive to expect someone to be transparent and disclose the intimate details of his personal life, and one should not expect to enter someone's personal life without an invitation. When someone honors us by disclosing something personal, discretion demands that we protect that confidence.

Optimal shame also implies respect for the rights of others, and the self-awareness to know when one has violated those rights. It thus provides a directing emotion in relationships. Consider the father who acts as if he is perfect and denies his son's right to make mistakes. When the boy breaks his fishing pole, the father strikes his son and calls him a "little shit!" If he could experience optimal shame, and feel temporarily lacking as a person, he could use the feeling to repair the emotional wounds he has inflicted. Reparation would include an acknowledgment of wrongdoing, a mature apology, and a sincere vow not to do it again. It would include an affirmation of his child's right to make mistakes, and require that he drop his arrogant attitude of God-like perfection. A hug, if the boy wanted one, would help mend the severed attachment bond. In this way, an optimal amount of shame directs the father toward a healthier self and more intimacy with his son. Too much shame and the experience of exposure immobilizes him in such a way that he cannot improve himself as a person and repair the damage. Too little shame and he has no awareness of his deficiency and simply justifies his actions.

Optimal shame enables a person to live with humility. Contrary to the dictionary definition, humility does not mean an absence of pride or self-esteem, it means having an awareness and acceptance of one's limitations (this is close to Bradshaw's definition of nourishing shame). A person who lives with humility has no illusions of grandeur. Persons with too much or too little shame often develop a grandiose sense of self-importance. Presenting themselves as special is a defense against feelings of being especially unworthy. Exaggerating their abilities is a protection against the shame of feeling little and unimportant. Grandiosity may show itself in fantasy or behavior, either way it signals the absence of humility. The grandiose person wants to actualize an image of himself as having more worth, more power, more knowledge, more beauty than others. That inflated image is always a compensation for feeling small and insignificant based on messages from a shaming parent.

The person with optimal shame is never contemptuous of others. The expression of contempt, the feeling that someone else is lower, or less of a person, is another example of a lack of humility. Whereas the grandiose person wishes to feel bigger than others, the contemptuous person tries to make others feel smaller. Ronald and Patricia Potter-Efron use a metaphor to explain the difference between grandiosity and contempt. Imagine two people as balloons that are equally inflated. Now imagine overinflating the first one with hot air to the point that it is ready to burst. That is the grandiose person. He or she seeks to compensate for feelings of shame by pumping themselves up with false pride. Now imagine bursting the second balloon by sticking a pin in it. That is what the contemptuous person does to others to hide their own deficiencies. By deflating another person's ego, he or she transfers their own shame to the other and feels superior (1989, p.41).

In the earlier example of the boy who broke his father's fishing pole, the abusive father is both grandiose (self-image of infallibility) and contemptuous (he makes his son feel worthless for being fallible). It would take humility for him to accept he was wrong and apologize for striking and verbally humiliating his son. Acceptance does not imply approval for his abusive behavior. It means he is aware of his limitations as a person and a parent and takes responsibility for them. Optimal shame and a sense of humility would enable him to "lower" himself and sincerely say "I'm sorry." In lowering himself, both he and his son would rise in self-esteem. Optimal shame directs him to move from the position of someone who humiliates to the position of someone with humility.

An optimal amount of shame is an unlikely attribute for anyone raised in a shame-based family. A shame-based family is one where shame is the predominant and organizing emotion, the basic ingredient in parental rules and family roles. Such families are headed by parents who induce shame in children by communicating messages that suggest the child is bad or unlovable. A shame-inducing parent is one who intentionally or unintentionally overdoses his or her child with shame, and then relates to that child in a way that does not allow for reparation of the severed attachment bond. Too much shame is the primary symptom in the shame-based family and is the focus of this book (from this point on, the reader may assume I'm referring to too much shame when the word shame is used by itself).

Shame is the painful feeling of being inferior, bad, or defective as a person. It is the loss of self-esteem that follows a moment of sudden exposure. The experience of feeling exposed results in a compelling need to hide (the word shame is derived from a root that means "to hide or cover up"). When exposed in public, we experience a "loss of face" so disturbing that we avoid eye contact and hang our heads. At the same time, we feel the physical sensation of shrinking, as if we were getting smaller and smaller. It is as though we wish to become invisible, to disappear. "I am ashamed," means "It is too painful to be seen for who I am. I want to hide." Shame causes us to feel psychologically isolated, afraid of further contact, afraid of further exposure. Shame causes us to feel like aliens, and is most intense in the presence of those to whom we feel most vulnerable, i.e., family members. We feel unlovable!

It was once thought that shame needed an audience, but it does not. The shamed person needs no "shamer." During moments of private exposure, the mind's eye turns upon the self and passes judgment. The self then feels "seen" as worthless or flawed. This self-inflicted shame is the result of having taken the bad (shaming) qualities of the parent inside the self. It triggers automatic core beliefs about the self that were learned in childhood, e.g., "I am unlovable!" or "I am worthless!" There is simply no place to hide. Just as public shame results in alienation from others, private shame results in alienation from ourselves. This is the experience of being cut off from our feelings, or having a split within ourself, e.g., a sexual part of the self ("I want to make love with him") in conflict with a repressive internal parent part ("It's sinful to have sex before marriage!"). In the throes of shame, we feel utterly alone and without hope of reconnecting with ourselves or others.

GUILT

Guilt is the painful feeling of self-reproach resulting from a judgment that we have behaved badly or immorally. When we experience guilt, we are aware of having done something wrong that either violated a moral value or injured someone. This awareness of wrongdoing is usually associated with the ashamed feeling that we are lacking in some way, and that we should make amends for what we did, or failed to do, that was wrong. Lying beneath the surface of guilt there is a foundation of shame, hence guilt lowers self-esteem, and is considered a member of the shame family of emotions. Guilt can be thought of as shame that follows moral transgression—it is "immorality shame" (Kaufman, 1989, p.23).

Shame and guilt both reflect our personal values, and both come from an awareness that we are essentially lacking in some way, but they are different. Guilt is a negative feeling about our behavior; shame is a negative feeling about ourselves. "I feel guilty" means "I have done something bad." "I feel ashamed" means "I am a bad person." Consider again the father who struck his son because of a broken fishing pole. If he realizes he has wronged his son and judges his own behavior as bad ("That was a rotten thing to do!"), he is feeling guilty. Guilt here is the result of having gone too far, of having stepped beyond the boundaries of human decency. If he feels exposed by his own abusiveness and judges himself as bad ("What a rotten person I am!"), he is feeling ashamed. Shame here is the result of failing to live up to his self-image as a good person, a decent human being. In other words, his guilt concerns a specific action; his shame is generalized to the whole self.

Wechsler, in "What's So Bad About Guilt" (1990, p.15), notes that Freud used two German words in his many discussions of guilt: "Schuldgefuhl" (guilt feeling) and "Schuldbewusstsein" (consciousness of guilt). This distinction reflects that guilt can be either emotional and visceral, or cognitive and intellectual, or both. Whereas a guilty feeling is a natural human emotion having to do with regret over bad behavior, the cognitive/intellectual side of guilt is more a learned state of mind. As such, it may be used in a manipulative way.

Manipulative guilt lacks the genuine feeling of regret and is expressed for the purpose of getting some payoff. People use it as a way of justifying certain behavior so that they can then continue to do it (Greenber and Safran, 1987, p.180). The father in the above example can continue to strike his son in the future as long as he feels sufficiently guilty in the present. If he lacks genuine feelings of guilt, and has no intention of making amends, he is simply an abusive parent with a "swiss-cheese" conscience. By saying he feels guilty, he manipulates others, perhaps even himself, into believing he has good intentions, when in fact he does not. Now his abusive behavior becomes more acceptable, to himself and others. After all, he has made a guilt payment by beating up on himself, so he should be exonerated. And, by beating others to the punch, he wards off criticism that would shame him.

Optimal shame provides the foundation for internalizing constructive guilt, that is, the ability to judge when our behavior is injurious or immoral, followed by a sincere desire to make amends. Such a judgment is a matter of conscience and is based on limits and values taught by parents and then internalized (Middelton-Moz, 1990, p.57). The optimal amount of shame, very small and carefully measured doses, lovingly teaches the child when he or she is lacking, and what lesson needs to be learned—without severing the attachment bond. The child willingly takes in the parents' value system because he or she needs to protect the relationship from harm, needs to belong, needs to be admired, and needs to be loved. Because guilt is internalized instead of shame, the child is able to realize when his or her behavior is out of line without becoming immobilized.

For example, if a young boy steals apples from the neighbor's tree, he can feel constructive guilt ("I did a bad thing taking Mr. Smith's apples") instead of destructive shame ("I'm nothing but a thief...I'm a bad apple myself!"). There is no way to make amends from the position of too much shame. But, from the position of optimal shame that leads to constructive guilt, the child can make amends by taking responsibility for his wrongful act. He can tell his parents what he did, apologize to Mr. Smith, and make amends by returning or replacing the stolen apples. He could offer to work in Mr. Smith's yard, or help him pick the remaining apples. Both his optimal shame and his constructive guilt are released by his acts of reparation. Too little shame and the child fails to develop a conscience, or develops one with holes in it. He keeps the apples and either doesn't realize or doesn't care that he has broken a rule. Too much shame and the child is immobilized. He may have a guilty conscience, but he cannot use his guilt because he is too afraid to expose himself to another overdose of parental shame ("What kind of son are you, anyway? You should be ashamed of yourself!"). He keeps the apples, makes no amends, and has no way to release his guilt and shame. The entire scenario reinforces his shamed sense of self— that he is bad, unforgivable, unlovable.

EMBARRASSMENT

Embarrassment is an acute attack of public shame due to a social blunder or an error in etiquette. To be embarrassed is to suddenly lose composure and become the center of unwanted attention. Here the experience of exposure is accompanied by a rush of self-consciousness and the characteristic wish to disappear. There is an inspired scene in the film, "The Lonely Guy," that dramatizes this aspect of embarrassment. The main character, played by Steve Martin, is painfully shy and somewhat of a loner. He enters an elegant and obviously expensive restaurant, by himself, and asks a snobby maitre d' for a table for one. He is already embarrassed about being alone when the band stops playing and a hush comes over the room as the maitre d' announces, "Table for one!" A spotlight is then focused on this poor self-conscious fellow and follows him to his table. He is the center of attention and feels impaled by the eyes of every person in the restaurant. His embarrassment is complete.

Embarrassment is often accompanied by a feeling of confusion and self-condemnation, such as, "How stupid can I be?" or "I can't believe I did that!" For example, it would be embarrassing to find your zipper down or blouse unbuttoned at a social gathering. Another real life example happened to a friend of mine who wore a wig to cover stress-related bald spots. My roommate and I were engaged in a hotly contested game of chess, with several other friends watching. Barbara, the wig wearer, decided to sit next to my opponent on a small couch. Directly over the chess table was a hanging lamp fixture. As Barbara seated herself, her wig caught on the lamp, and she sat down without her wig. Instead of retrieving the offending hairpiece, she just let it hang there. She was stunned, immobilized by her embarrassment. All she could say was, "I can't believe this is happening!" Being a good sport, she began to laugh and, believe me, everyone laughed with her. The laughter released her shame, yet I would have to think she has never forgotten this embarrassing scene.

It is moments like these (and we have all suffered them) that cause blushing, the redness in the face from shame experience. Blushing amplifies both the discomfort of being embarrassed and the wish to hide. It calls attention to the face, heightening self-consciousness, compounding shame, and causing us to feel ashamed of shame (Kaufman, pp. 18-23).

Because children need to identify with their parents, and do so strongly, they themselves will experience embarrassment when their parent is socially inappropriate. Children from shame-based families are so often psychologically merged with a parent, it is as if they were the ones who blundered. There are few children of alcoholics who have not suffered embarrassment as a consequence of parental drunkenness. The embarrassment is not only for the parent but for themselves as well. The embarrassment may be even more intense since children so desperately wish to be proud of their parents. Here the wish to hide is multiplied because the child not only wishes to disappear, but wishes the embarrassing parent would disappear as well.

MORTIFICATION

This variation of the shame experience is similar to embarrassment but much more intense. To be mortified is to be mortally wounded by shame. The feeling of shame is so intense during a moment of mortification that we may think "I wish I were dead!" Mortification implies that shame can "kill," indicating the reality that shame can be an overwhelmingly painful feeling (Morrison in Nathanson, 1987, p.287).

Larry, a freshman in college, was referred for treatment of depression by his counselor at school. He had been dating Lisa rather seriously, and decided it was time to take her home to meet his mother. He figured it was safe to stop by in the afternoon because his alcoholic mother didn't start drinking until dinnertime. He figured wrong. They found his mother passed out on a couch, reeking of booze and urine. "When I saw that she'd wet her pants, I just wanted to die! I couldn't face Lisa after that." It didn't matter that Larry himself had done nothing wrong. Like most children of alcoholics, he was psychologically merged with his drinking parent and felt shame by association.

Once activated, it is difficult to escape the feeling of being mortified. The "I could die" experience is followed by seemingly endless instant replays in the mind, each one adding to the momentum of shame and reopening the painful wound. In this regard, the experience of psychological mortification is analogous to that of physical mortification (a discipline wherein religious fanatics inflict pain to their bodies to subdue sexual desire). Mortification of the flesh is motivated by shame about the body and its sexuality, which is experienced as feeling bad to the bone. Mortification of the self is motivated by shame about the self, which is experienced as feeling rotten to the core.

SHYNESS

Shyness is shame in the presence of or at the prospect of approaching a stranger (Kaufman, 1989, p.24). Shyness is also felt in the presence of persons who are not well known. It may be experienced as either a momentary feeling or an enduring personality trait. Shyness is rooted in an approach-avoidance conflict that causes self-consciousness in unfamiliar social situations. There is a wish to be acknowledged and a simultaneous fear of exposure. This clash of opposing impulses ties us in a psychological knot. We are wary of being caught off guard and being exposed. When we feel exposed, whether or not we actually are, we become painfully aware of ourselves as the center of attention. In a state of self-conscious shyness, we are afraid to speak for fear of saying something foolish; afraid to move for fear of appearing clumsy; afraid to feel for fear of losing control; afraid to interact for fear of calling further attention to ourselves.

Wurmser (in Nathanson, p.68) makes a distinction that helps to clarify the experience of shyness. He distinguishes between shame affect, shame anxiety, and shame as a preventive attitude. Affect is behavior that expresses a feeling (in this case feeling ashamed), thus shame affect means "I feel exposed and would like to crawl into a hole and disappear." Shame anxiety means "I am afraid of being exposed at any moment and hence shamed." Shame as a preventive attitude means "I must hide my defective self in order to avoid being exposed and hence shamed." When feeling shy, we experience all three—the feeling of being exposed, the fear of further exposure, and the self-protective wish to hide. They are all experienced in the context of a social situation where we shrink from the notice of others who are not well known to us.

Persons with optimal shame have some degree of shyness. This is healthy in that it protects our privacy until we can decide whether someone is safe for self-disclosure. Too little shyness and we expose too much, too soon, and inevitably to the wrong people. Too much shyness and we dread saying or doing anything that would risk any exposure at all. We become speechless and motionless, immobilized by shame. In this state, our true selves are hidden away and natural expression is suppressed. Any spontaneity is squelched to protect us from exposing too much of a self we believe is defective. Too much shyness and we lose contact with the world. Everyone is a stranger, and everyone remains a stranger.

HUMILIATION

To be humiliated is to be on the receiving end of an "aggressive shaming attack" (Nathanson, 1987, p.4). Whereas public shame, embarrassment, and shyness are experienced in the presence of another, humiliation is experienced at the hand of another. The "shamer" humiliates his victim as a way of establishing dominance and control. He has too much shame and he wants to get rid of it. He projects his shame into his victim, who then feels exposed as weak and disgraceful. Shame has been transferred. The humiliated victim becomes the container for shame that belongs to the victimizer.

The shaming attack is often delivered with an audience present because the victimizer delights in seeing his victim squirm as he once did. The victim may be forced to "eat humble pie," that is, he or she must not only accept being humiliated, but must also apologize for not liking it. One overweight client explained how her father repeatedly criticized her appearance in front of her friends, calling her "fatso" and "lardass." She would then cry hysterically and scream obscenities at him. Later in the day she was expected to say, "What you said was okay, and I was wrong to be angry about it." If she didn't, he would give her the silent treatment, causing her to feel isolated and abandoned. Desperately needing to repair the severed attachment bond, she would give in.

Children are exquisitely sensitive to humiliation, especially when the person inflicting the wound is their parent. Parents are not supposed to attack their child's developing self-esteem, they are supposed to build and nurture it. Children need dependable sources of love and protection in order to thrive. Thus, humiliation destroys the trust that is necessary for the development of a healthy sense of self. If children cannot trust their own mother and father to affirm them as belonging and worthy of esteem, who can they trust?

Humiliation lowers self-esteem and breaks the spirit of a child. It severs the attachment bond and activates primitive impulses to get even with the shaming parent. These impulses are seen in retaliatory fantasies and acting-out behavior, e.g., lying, stealing, school behavior problems, running away, substance abuse, delinquency, etc. Such behaviors are examples of how the child becomes the container for the "shamer's" own shame and then angrily acts it out. They represent unconscious attempts to call attention to the wounded self, as well as attempts to get even. Humiliation defeats the child and always results in the internalization of too much shame.

Chapter Two

Shame-Inducing Family Messages

The Suggestible Child

David Calof, who trained with Milton Erickson (considered the world's foremost authority on hypnosis and trance induction), integrates concepts from hypnotherapy and family therapy. He has identified the "trance dance" as a process that takes place in dysfunctional families (1989). Family members, especially children, are in a "trance" because the central organizing principle in such families is denial. According to Calof, children dissociate (space out) and go into trance because of the discrepancy between what is and how parents talk about what is, e.g., mom and dad abuse their children, yet refer to themselves as loving parents. It is a dance because every family member has his or her own well-defined steps in the ongoing drama. Children must step to the tune of a command that reinforces denial—"See no evil, hear no evil, speak of no evil, and feel no evil!" The child is essentially put in a trance and given the post-hypnotic suggestion, "Don't see, hear, feel, sense, or address what is real, but accept what is unreal!" Thus, reality for children in such families is "plastic and constructed," that is, parents tell their children what to believe—including what to believe about themselves.

John Bradshaw (1988, pp.36-38) has similarly likened the family to a group of individuals in a hypnotic trance. Children make ideal trance subjects because they are bright, trusting, and open-minded. The child mind is psychologically naive and readily influenced by suggestion. When a parent says "Shame on you!" or "You should be ashamed of yourself!" the child is receiving a direct suggestion that induces shame. A parent who angrily asks, "Can't you ever do anything right?" is giving an indirect suggestion that induces shame. The child mind is in a trance-like state of absorption, so parental messages operate like post-hypnotic suggestions (p.36). If a child is repeatedly told she is stupid and lazy, she will become an underachiever. If a child is told he is just like his father and will never amount to anything, he probably won't. If he does, he will most likely feel like an impostor pretending to be a success.

Because of their suggestible nature, children are susceptible to a hypnotic phenomenon called "trance logic." Trance logic is a subjective experience that accounts for the fact that children "buy things that don't add up" (Kroger, 1977, p.29). If we are told we should be ashamed for touching our genitals, we buy it. If it is suggested that we are responsible for mom's drinking or dad's violence, we buy it. If parental messages induce us to believe we are worthless or unlovable, we buy it. The myth of Santa Claus coming down the chimney and visiting the home of every boy and girl on Christmas Eve is a good example of trance logic. It demonstrates how a suggestible child believes whatever he or she is told.

The power of the family trance is effectively dramatized in the rock opera TOMMY. Little Tommy's father is presumed lost at sea. He returns unexpectedly, finds his wife with a lover, and kills him in front of the boy. Mother and father then give Tommy a direct suggestion..."You didn't hear it, you didn't see it, you won't say nothing to no one ever in your life!" (The Who, 1969). This suggestion is repeated over and over. Tommy is commanded to do the "trance dance"—"Don't hear, see, speak of, or address what really happens, but accept what is unreal!" As if struck by lightning, Tommy instantly cannot hear, see, or speak in response to his parents' post-hypnotic suggestions. Only when the trance is broken years later does Tommy experience a "miracle cure" and regain his senses.

The Building Blocks of Personality

Parental messages are essentially direct and indirect suggestions. A message is communicated through the "you are..." statements that define a child's developing self. Messages that suggest the child is loved and valued induce healthy pride and self-esteem, e.g., "You're wonderful!" Shame, on the other hand, is induced when parents convey messages that suggest the child is in some way bad or unlovable, e.g., "You're a pain in the ass!" Messages that shame always lower the child's self-esteem. These messages become internalized through mental images or scenes that are charged with emotion (Tomkins in Kaufman, 1989, p.59). A scene is a recording of visual, auditory, and kinesthetic images that replay experiences as they originally happened (p.59-60). They are like videotapes of our life experiences and are stored in our memories.

The self is the center of the personality, and childhood scenes are the "building blocks of personality (p.60)." Feelings of low self-esteem are stored in childhood scenes wherein a parent induced too much shame. Such a scene may or may not be accessible to consciousness. The earliest and most painfully shaming scenes are the ones most likely to be repressed, that is, pushed out of conscious awareness to avoid feeling over-whelmed. Scenes that are repressed can never be worked through, or mastered, and this is why we tend to repeat unfin-ished business from childhood. Freud referred to this phenome-non as the "repetition compulsion," noting that we are compelled to re-enact traumatic aspects of our relationships with parents.

There are several ways scenes are re-enacted in accord with the "repetition compulsion." In the first, an adult relives a child-hood experience, but changes roles with the parent in the original scene. Here, the scene is said to be recast and re-enacted (Kaufman, p.123). Thus, a father who is consciously or uncon-sciously reliving a childhood scene where he was battered, may re-enact that scene by battering his own child, who is recast as the victim. A variation is the mother who was, as a child, molested by her father. She re-enacts her molestation scenes by marrying a predatory man who eventually molests their daughter, i.e., her child is recast as the victim of incest.

A second way of re-enacting the same scene would be to play the role of the abusive parent and batter oneself (p.123). I have clients who have beaten their heads against walls, tackled stop signs, and injured their bodies by burning or cutting their own skin. All were battered children who were reliving and re-enact-ing scenes involving physically abusive parents.

A third way of re-enacting scenes is for individuals to enter into relationships with someone who will victimize them the way their own parents once did (p.123). Thus, a woman who was battered by an alcoholic father may unconsciously seek out a violent and alcoholic partner. She feels compelled to re-enact traumatic scenes from her childhood, as if the scene can now be mastered in the present. Unconsciously, she believes that if she can earn the admiration and respect of her partner, who is like father, she will be affirmed as lovable. Being affirmed by someone who is stable and respectful won't count because he is not like father. The shamed child within wants to be affirmed by father, or someone who resembles him. Instead, she is revictimized. Her original humiliation and helpless rage are re-experienced and new shame is added on. As with the first two ways of re-enacting scenes, what gets re-enacted is determined by the negativity of the scenes that are taken into the developing self.

A Shamed Sense of Self

The self is the sum total of a person's essential parts at any given moment. The self contains a body part, an interpersonal part, an intrapsychic part, an achievement part, and a spiritual part. The self can thus be divided into different "subselves" that correspond with the five parts: a body self, an interpersonal self, an intrapsychic self, an achievement self, and a spiritual self. Scenes are taken into each of these subselves during the course of development.

The body self is first to develop and is oriented to seek pleasure, avoid pain, and ensure survival. The interpersonal self is next to develop and is formed from experiences with significant others, initially mother and father. It is sensitive to parental evaluations and seeks approval, validation of worth, and a feeling of belonging. Next to develop is the intrapsychic self. Intrapsychic means situated and taking place within the mind. It is the mind's eye view of oneself, the master self that evaluates and relates to the other parts of the self. The achievement self develops as the child seeks to achieve competence and master the environment. Later, this part of the self becomes oriented to setting personal goals, making intelligent choices, and achieving success in one's chosen occupation or career. Finally, the spiritual self is the part that strives to find meaning in life, actualize one's deeper potentials, and connect with a Higher Power or Creator. To fully actualize this self, one must be able to believe in something that cannot be seen (Middelton-Moz, personal communication, 5/22/90). This is only possible when the person has, as a toddler, established object constancy—the capacity to evoke an image of mother when she is not present. Hence, children with insecure attachments to their mothers, or primary caretakers, fail to establish full object constancy and find it difficult to summon an unseen image (i.e., God) to be used internally to soothe or support themselves.

These selves operate in association with one another to form a center for thinking, feeling, and relating—the composite self. Hence, when I refer to the self, rather than a specific part of the self, I am referring to the composite of the body, interpersonal, intrapsychic, achievement, and spiritual subselves.

The self develops as children respond to parental messages by taking in scenes that are emotionally charged. The child acquires a basic sense of self through this process of internalization. This sense of self is the feeling of unique individuality that answers the questions "Who am I?" and "What are my essential qualities?" Thus, a shamed sense of self develops when the child takes in scenes containing messages that he or she is bad or unlovable. Such scenes become stored in memory and may include shame about one's body, one's relationships, one's identity, one's adequacy, and/or one's spiritual being.

These dimensions of shame correspond to the five parts of the self. Shame scenes involving the body self produce body-image or sexual shame — the molested child who feels dirty. Shame scenes involving the interpersonal self produce relationship shame — the rejected child who believes no one likes him. Shame scenes involving the intrapsychic self produce identity shame — the confused child who has no sense of who she really is. Shame scenes involving the achievement self produce adequacy shame — the belittled child who feels inadequate. And, shame scenes involving the spiritual self produce spiritual shame — the religiously programmed child who feels sinful.

Shame can be taken into any one or all of these parts of the self, or in combinations according to the unique combination of shame-inducing parental messages. Instead of experiencing optimal shame that is temporary and useful, and then releasing it, the child internalizes shame scenes that result in an ever-present shamed sense of self. The self is damaged.

Parental Messages and Self-Esteem

The primary function of the self is to strive for and maintain self-esteem, the most important aspect of personality (one's characteristic way of thinking, feeling and relating). Self-esteem is the value one places on the self as a whole and is the basic motivator in human relationships. It is determined by how one evaluates the five parts of the self as either positive or negative at any given moment. This is largely determined by the positive or negative nature of messages given by parents in childhood. Children develop positive self-esteem and pride when they are given positive messages that tell them they are inherently good, lovable, and prized. When parents give negative messages to their children that tell them they are inherently bad or unlovable, their children develop negative self-esteem, a symptom of shame.

Most shame-inducing messages do their damage because they are repeated so often that the child eventually believes them and takes them into the developing self. A few messages are so traumatic they only need to be communicated once to induce deep shame. A child who has just been molested for example, almost always gets the message that he or she is dirty.

In almost all cases, parents do not intend to damage their child's self-esteem, but unintentionally convey messages that do just that. It would be tempting to believe that only the worst kind of parent would damage his child with shame, but even well-intentioned (but unhealed) parents do so because they are compelled to repeat scenes from their own shame-based childhoods. They also internalized too much shame and unintentionally "pass the hot potato" to their own children.

To some degree, all parents convey messages that shame their children at one time or another. However, the shame-inducing parent lacks empathy with the wounded child and repeats the pattern of communicating negative messages. Such parents pass their unfinished business on to their children by unconsciously re-enacting their own childhood shame scenes.

The more respectful parent is aware of when he or she has inflicted too much shame and is able to empathize. They put themselves in their children's shoes and decide to make amends. Thus, they take steps to repair their child's self-esteem so that shame is released rather than internalized, e.g., they offer an apology, or hug, to reconnect the severed attachment bond. Next, they resolve to use shame more carefully with their child in the future.

Self-esteem is determined by how positively or negatively we evaluate the five parts of the self which, in turn, is determined by the scenes taken into the developing self. Scenes play like good or bad movies in the head, depending on whether the scene is charged with positive or negative emotion. Consider two very different scenes: "the time mom held me when I was scared by the thunder," and "the time dad called me a 'jerk' for wetting the bed." The child internalizes the experience contained in each scene along with the feelings that occurred during the experience. A message is then derived from the scene. The message is what is unspoken, but implied by the parent's behavior. It is the child's interpretation of the event, a way to make sense of what happened.

To make matters worse, children take messages personally; that is, they blame themselves for their parents' behavior. In the first scene, the mother implies that her frightened child is valued and that her feelings are taken seriously. The scene is charged with positive emotion. By being emotionally available and providing comfort, the respectful mother conveys a message that enhances her daughter's developing self-esteem. The child feels loved and lovable. In the second scene, the father belittles and scorns his son for wetting the bed. He implies that the boy doesn't "measure up" and that his habit of bed-wetting makes him disgusting. The scene is charged with negative emotion. Name calling is a form of humiliation and conveys a message that lowers the boy's self-esteem. As similar scenes are internalized, the boy develops a shamed sense of self. He takes his father's messages personally and accepts there is something wrong with him, not his dad. He begins to form core beliefs about his self—that he is inadequate and disgusting.

Core Beliefs About the Self

The child takes in scenes and forms a self that is a composite of different parts. The way the parent behaves in each scene conveys a message to the child that either enhances or lowers self-esteem. As messages accumulate over time, they cluster and persuade the suggestible child to form core beliefs. A core belief is a judgment about the essence of the self as a whole, taking into account the five parts of the self. It is a conviction held by the innermost part of one's self about the self as a whole.

To illustrate, consider the scene: "the time dad hit me for breaking the neighbor's window." In recalling this scene, the battered child would replay visual, auditory, and kinesthetic imagery and the feelings that go along with those images. He might visualize events as they happened, hear the window breaking and his father yelling, tense up from the memory of being hit, and feel some combination of fear, grief, humiliation, and retaliatory rage. The father's behavior conveys an unspoken message that implies the boy is unlovable, a source of irritation. This message is personalized—the boy blames himself for breaking the window, not his father for hitting him. As similar scenes are repeated, shame is internalized and a core belief is formed..."I am unlovable."

This core belief is based on a negative evaluation of the interpersonal self ("I feel unloved by my own father") and intrapsychic self ("I don't like myself, either"). It will profoundly affect how he thinks, feels and relates to himself and others. He is induced to feel shame about the self, which he experiences as low self-esteem. Until the family trance is broken, he can never love himself, and he will believe no one else can love him. If he someday has his own children, he will likely identify with his father and re-enact his past by battering them. He is doing the "trance dance" and there is only one way to stop. He must understand how the familial trance was induced, release his shame in the context of an affirming relationship, and separate emotionally from the parent or parents who induced it.

Case Example Involving a Molestation Scene

Ellen, a depressed young mother, entered therapy complaining of low self-esteem and sexual difficulties. She was disinterested in sex and felt "uncomfortable" whenever her husband touched her breasts (sexual shame). I asked her if anyone older than she had ever touched her in an inappropriate way while she was growing up. She disclosed the following scene that happened when she was sixteen. Her father, a respected minister, placed his hand on her bare breast and said, "You don't mind, do you?" In hypnosis, this form of question is called an indirect suggestion, a very powerful and effective way of inducing a trance (especially coming from someone with her father's authority). He went on to misrepresent his action as a healthy demonstration of affection and cited a magazine article to back him up. When I asked her why she thought this happened, she replied, "I must have given him some encouragement." As molested children so often do, Ellen felt responsible and blamed herself. She convinced herself that her father couldn't be at fault because he was a man of God!

This betrayal, by the most important man in her life, induced Ellen to believe she was no more than an object for the gratification of men, a thing, and a sinful thing at that. The scene of being molested was internalized into the self and she formed a core belief "I am dirty!" The intensity of her sexual shame ("My sexuality is bad") and spiritual shame ("My soul is full of sin") outweighed any positive feelings of worth that came from other parts of the self, such as pride in her achievement self because she was a good student.

Ellen formed a "map of the world" (Elkhaim, 1986, p.35), or world view, that "all men are untrustworthy." Not surprisingly, she began to have poor judgment about sexual partners, got pregnant, and had an abortion—all having the effect of intensifying her shame. In spite of her distrust, she found herself attracted to abusive men who revictimized her. Without knowing it, she was re-enacting the original molestation scene with her lovers playing the role of her incestuous father. To her credit, she recognized this pattern and eventually married a man who could be trusted. Still, the parental message operated like a post-hypnotic suggestion and she felt dirty and objectified during sex. When her husband touched her breasts, she would unconsciously replay the incest scene in her mind and feel "uncomfortable."

In therapy she was able to re-experience the original scene, release the shame, grief, and rage it contained, and counter the message that she was dirty. When she was well along in the process of recovery, we invited her parents to a session and she confronted her father. This confrontation had the effect of reclaiming her power and gave Ellen the opportunity to break a family rule by expressing her outrage. She transferred the blame (and the shame) back to her father where it always belonged. In so doing, she broke the family trance and emotionally separated from her parents. Having healed her shame, and regained her self-esteem, her depression disappeared and she bgan enjoying sex with her husband.

Taking Parental "Badness" Inside the Self

Why would Ellen blame herself for her father's incestuous behavior? Why do children prefer to believe something is wrong with them rather than with the parents who shame them? Why do they see themselves as bad instead of seeing their parents as bad? Children obviously personalize their experiences, that is, they blame themselves for events over which they have no control. Thus, they not only internalize messages that induce shame, but also take the bad qualities of the parent inside the self.

There are actually four reasons why children deny parental badness and instead take it inside the self. First, they are highly suggestible and believe what they are told, and they are told, directly and indirectly, that they are the bad ones. Children accept blame passively and then learn to actively blame themselves. This is true for whatever form of mistreatment they endure. Being naive and suggestible, they swallow what their parents tell them, and they swallow it whole. If dad spills his drink it's because "accidents happen," but if they spill their milk it's because they're "careless" or "clumsy." Shame-inducing parents have an inordinate need to be right so they cultivate the impression they are never wrong. They rarely if ever acknowledge mistakes, admit fault, say "I'm sorry" with sincerity, or ask forgiveness. They can do no wrong and their kids can do no right. Children buy this because they don't know better and because they are little and dependent. In order to feel safe, they need to see their parents as bigger and more powerful. Children want infallible parents. Thus, they are set up to accept blame and believe that they are the bad ones.

The second reason for taking the bad qualities of the parent inside the self has to do with the issue of control. Control is a key issue in shame-based families because loss of control causes shame, which in turn causes loss of control, e.g., alcoholism. By taking the badness inside, children preserve a measure of control over their parents' out-of-control behavior. As children take in messages that induce shame, they form an internal bad parent. This internalization gradually becomes experienced as a part of the self. By containing the bad qualities of the parent inside the self, the child believes he or she has some measure of control over the badness (Wood, 1987, p.59). The badness seems more predictable and controllable if it is inside. Consider the child whose parents call her "stupid," an all-too-common form of verbal humiliation. She internalizes her parents' badness and then picks up where they left off. By calling herself "stupid," she beats them to the punch. Her philosophy seems to be, "I'll do it to myself and it'll be over with." (Calof, personal communication, 10/20/87). It gives her an illusion of control over the belittling parent, but at the cost of reinforcing her already shamed sense of self—her belief that she is inadequate.

A third reason for taking the bad qualities of the parent inside the self is that it defends against insecurity. Seeing oneself as bad spares the parent and preserves the fantasy that the parent is good enough. Remember that infants would literally die were it not for parental care. This position of overwhelming dependency is never completely forgotten. To acknowledge a parent's badness is to feel alone, threatened, and insecure. It intensifies the already present fear of annihilation—that the child might not survive the badness. It is less threatening to point the finger of badness at oneself. It is preferable because it feels safer, but "outer security is purchased at the price of inner security" (Fairbairn in Wood, p.55). Now the child is at the mercy of the internal bad parent. Shame-inducing messages come from inside and outside the self and the child's self-esteem is under continual attack.

Finally, seeing oneself as bad is a more optimistic position than to acknowledge the parent's bad qualities. If it is they who are bad, then the child feels truly hopeless. He or she has no chance of changing them and getting the good parent that is desperately needed. However, if the child is the bad one, there is a glimmer of hope. The child can change...get straight "A's" at school, become mommy's little helper, avoid "making waves," or never make another mistake. The child's hope is that if he or she is more acceptable, the parent's bad qualities will disappear and they will give the love and affirmation that is longed for.

In denying parental badness, children become the container for the bad qualities of the parent. They may feel more in control, more secure, or more optimistic, but the feeling of being bad is now experienced on the inside as a quality of the self. The cost is lowered self-esteem due to internalized shame. They now have an "inner shamer."

Twelve Messages that Induce Shame

There are twelve parental messages that induce shame in children. There may be others, but they are likely to be variations of the ones explained below. To review, children are suggestible and easily persuaded by parental messages, as if in a state of trance. Shame is induced when direct or indirect messages suggest the child is bad, inferior, or defective. Such messages may actually be spoken aloud or implied by the parent's behavior. For example, a rejecting mother may actually say "You're worthless!," or she may nonverbally communicate it through an attitude of hostility. A scornful father may actually say "You're disgusting!" or he may say it with a contemptuous look that says "You make me sick!"

These experiences are stored in memory as scenes. Scenes convey messages that are implied by the parent's behavior, e.g., rejection conveys the message that the child is worthless. The self develops as scenes become internalized and core beliefs are formed. The child develops a shamed sense of self, e.g., the rejected child believes..."I am disgusting." Shame becomes the source of low self-esteem and the feeling of being bad, inferior, or defective as a person.

In the remainder of this chapter, twelve messages are explained in terms of how they induce shame. There is a description of what the parent does, or fails to do, to communicate each message. There is also a description of the kind of parent who conveys each message. Examples of scenes that convey each

message are given. The core belief associated with each message
will be explained.

The twelve shame inducing messages are (with corresponding
pattern of shaming parental behavior in parentheses):

Message 1:   "You are inadequate!"   (Belittlement)

Message 2:   "You are worthless!"   (Rejection)

Message 3:   "You are disgusting!"   (Scorn)

Message 4:   "You are unwanted!"   (Abandonment)

Message 5:   "You are unimportant!"   (Neglect)

Message 6:   "You are nothing!"   (Engulfment)

Message 7:   "You are dirty!"   (Molestation)

Message 8:   "You are unlovable!"   (Battering)

Message 9:   "You are powerless!"   (Terrorizing)

Message 10:   "You are sinful!"   (Brainwashing)

Message 11:   "You are deviant!"   (Corrupting)

Message 12:   "You are crazy!"   (Confusing)

Each of these messages induces too much shame because each
results in a severed attachment bond between parent and child.
Kaufman refers to this as "breaking the interpersonal bridge," the
bridge that is formed when the parent convincingly shows the
child they are truly wanted and loved as a unique self (1989,
pp.33-34). Failure to form a secure attachment bond, or severing

that bond once it has been formed, is the crucial parent-child event that induces shame. It is the common denominator of the twelve shame-inducing messages, each of which causes the child to experience himself or herself as inferior or defective. The feeling of being inherently unlovable is at the core of the shame experience.

Rarely does one of the twelve messages exist by itself because shame-based parents specialize in inducing shame. A battered child is always a rejected child. He feels both unlovable and worthless. A child whose essential needs are ignored is both neglected and abandoned. She feels both unimportant and unwanted. Although the twelve messages overlap, each one is different and the emphasis here is to highlight differences. For example, all battered children are rejected, but not all rejected children are battered. All neglected children are abandoned, but not all abandoned children are neglected. Since each message leads to a different core belief, it is important to treat them separately and avoid lumping them together. In reality, children from shame-based families suffer various combinations of these messages. For now, we will examine one message at a time.

Message One: "You are Inadequate!" (The Belittled Child)

The belittled child internalizes the shame-inducing message that she does not measure up to parental expectations and is therefore inadequate. The child grows up feeling not good enough, and does not believe in herself. Even when her performance is outstanding, she feels unacceptable because the belittling parent communicates messages that make her feel deficient in some way. She sees herself as little and incompetent.

Belittling parents are always haunted by their own unresolved feelings of inadequacy. They were typically belittled by their own parents and are "passing the hot potato" to their children. They transfer shame by becoming the belittler rather than the belittled. The parent unconsciously believes that by putting down his child, he elevates himself. By making his child feel little, he makes himself feel big. He conveys the message to "be little" because he needs to feel bigger and more powerful than someone. He seeks to escape his own inadequacy by projecting it elsewhere, and his child is a convenient container. Children are exceedingly vulnerable to put downs and are easy targets for belittling parents. The part of the self most injured is the achievement self ("I see myself as incompetent") as the child internalizes shame over the issue of adequacy.

Healthier, more respectful parents convey messages that tell the child he or she is good enough as they are. Such parents may have high expectations for performance, but the child is warmly encouraged and supported when they fall short. The parental message is "You can do it," and the child learns to believe in himself or herself. Mistakes are considered a part of the learning process rather than evidence of deficiency. Forgiveness is offered when the child screws up. The respectful parent avoids making comparisons to other siblings or peers that would send a "not enough" message. The child develops feelings of competence, confidence, and positive self-regard.

A belittling message is conveyed whenever the parent causes his child to feel inadequate. Belittlement occurs as parents put down their child for not fulfilling expectations. In such families, children are under so much stress and pressure that even realistic expectations are difficult to meet. To make matters worse, the parent typically sets unrealistic expectations and then humiliates the child when he or she inevitably fails. Should expectations be met, the belittling parent would "change the finish line" rather than credit the child.

Two examples. A rather boyish client in his early thirties was goaded by his father into running a marathon (26.2 miles). After training for six months, he ran and completed one in just over four hours, a very respectable time for his first marathon on a hilly and difficult race course. His father's comment was, "It doesn't mean anything unless you come in under four hours."

A slim and fit looking woman told me in our second session, "My whole life my mother hounded me about my weight, so in the last year, I lost seventy-five pounds. Now she says, 'Your butt still sags!'"

Parents who need to belittle their children will either ignore or invalidate their children's accomplishments. A child who has just learned to ride a bicycle wants to show off and be admired. He or she wants mom and dad to share the excitement and healthy pride. When parents don't have time, or disregard the child's newly mastered skill, they inflict another wound to the achievement self.

One client related an incident when as a ten-year-old, she spent all day Saturday cleaning the house. It was to be a surprise for her mother. The place was a terrible mess when her mother left and immaculate when she returned. But her mother made no comment on the transformation. When my client asked if she noticed, she was told, "It's about time you did something around here." Such comments spoil the child's good feelings about her accomplishments, sever the attachment bond, and lower self-esteem.

Another way parents communicate inadequacy messages is to make unfavorable or offensive comparisons. Comparison-making parents always find their children lacking in some way that they consider worthy of esteem. "So you got a pretty good report card. Fred's daughter got straight A's." Or, "I don't know where you got your lazy streak. Stu's son mows and edges their lawn every week, and he does a damn good job to boot!" One client, an attractive woman in her early thirties, was repeatedly told by both parents that her younger sister was prettier. This insulting comparison wounded her self-esteem and caused her to question her femininity. It was only after considerable therapy that she regained healthy pride in her appearance.

Criticism and blame also activate feelings of inadequacy. Overly critical parents break a child's spirit and lower his self-esteem. Such parents are looking for someone to blame whenever anything goes wrong and children are easy targets. Belittled children live their lives on guard, cautious not to make mistakes or offend the disapproving parent. Blaming means accusing the child of being bad for being wrong, of being a disappointment to the angry parent. "Blame activates intolerable shame, shredding dignity and self-respect...there is no way to keep one's head held high" (Kaufman, 1989, p.39). The blamed child cannot escape feeling inadequate, not good enough, diminished as a person.

Name-calling is another way of belittling a child, an all-too-common one. Many clients report having been called abusive names. "Stupid" appears to be the favorite of belittling parents. Names that call attention to any bodily flaw or physical limitation are especially humiliating to sensitive children, e.g., "fatty," "four-eyes." To be called names by someone who is supposed to affirm your sense of worth is devastating to the developing self.

"You are inadequate!" is the shaming message children take in when parents repeatedly belittle them. Such parents set unrealistic expectations, discredit accomplishments, make offensive comparisons, criticize, blame, and call their child abusive names. Scenes where the child was belittled are internalized and a core belief is formed..."I am inadequate." The child is suggestible and swallows the message whole. Because she needs to see the belittling parent as in some way affirming, she takes the parental badness inside the self. Belittling herself gives her the illusion of control. It's less humiliating if she does it to herself. She becomes her own worst critic and invariably strives for perfection as a defense against shame. When a child with high self-esteem fails, she says, "I failed at this task, but I learned something." The belittled child says, "I am a failure." She has internalized too much shame and has formed a shamed sense of self—that she is not measuring up, not good enough, imperfect, incompetent, inadequate.

Message Two: "You are Worthless!" (The Rejected Child)

The rejected child internalizes parental messages that he is somehow unacceptable and does not belong in the family. The rejecting parent directly and/or indirectly communicates an attitude of hostility. This unfriendly attitude pushes the child away and causes him to feel rejected. Whereas belittling parents make their children feel inadequate, rejecting parents make their children feel worthless. Such parents are full of hostility, and act in ways that deny the child's very right to exist.

Parents who are rejecting are typically persons who were never accepted and affirmed as worthwhile by their own parents. They often feel overwhelmed by stress and may be either alcoholic or married to an alcoholic. They marry with the unconscious fantasy that their spouse will provide the unconditional love and affirmation their own parents withheld. Of course this is a fantasy that never comes true. When a newborn arrives they either feel unenthused about parenthood or downright jealous.

Insecurity causes them to resent the attention the child gets from their spouse. They may engage in a form of sibling rivalry with their own child, competing for attention as if they were the oldest sibling. Such parents are frequently emotionally, physically, and/or sexually abusive. Rejecting parents often use their children as containers for their own shame. One client reported that his dad repeatedly called him "stupid" and "worthless." The father, uneducated and unemployed, projected his own unwanted parts into his son, then rejected him for containing them.

By way of comparison, healthy and respectful parents have an attitude of acceptance and good will toward their children. They convey a message that their child belongs and is a valued member of the family. They affirm their child's worth by interacting in ways that tell him he is admired and respected. They convince him that he is prized and genuinely loved. The child is welcomed to the world.

A rejection message is conveyed whenever the child feels pushed away, causing him to feel worthless and ashamed. Some children are rejected in the womb. The pregnancy may be altogether unwanted or inconveniently timed. Sometimes there is an enforced pregnancy where the child is unwanted but carried to term because of religious or family pressures. Once born, infants are rejected by parents who fail to initiate smiles and vocalizations, the behaviors that help form an attachment bond (Garbarino, Guttman and Seeley, 1986, p.25). Or perhaps the parents wanted a child of the opposite sex. Some little Robertas were supposed to be little Roberts. Some little Michaels were supposed to be little Michelles.

At some level of consciousness, all adopted children wonder why their birth parents rejected them, and may mistakenly believe it has something to do with their inherent worth, or rather the lack of it. Children placed in foster homes also may feel this way, regardless of the circumstances requiring the placement. Children of divorced parents often feel rejected by the non-custodial parent, especially when that parent refuses to visit or moves far away. How the child views these different rejections is largely determined by the explanations given by the adults who care for them. For example, adoptive parents who tell their children early on that they are adopted, and who emphasize how much they wanted the child, minimize the potential effects of rejection and convey a message that builds positive self-esteem. Adopted children who find out by accident that their "parents" are not their "real parents," or who are told years after they were developmentally ready to understand the truth, can only conclude that there is something shameful about the circumstances of their birth, otherwise there would be no need for secretiveness and deception. They should be given the information in an open and straightforward way, and be allowed to ask questions and show curiosity.

As a child grows up, rejecting parents actively create distance by refusing to hold him. If a child is physically or emotionally hurt, his parent's refusal to meet his need for holding leaves him feeling unprotected and insecure (Kaufman, 1989, p.69). One client reported that as a five-year-old, in a fit of anger, she screamed at her mother, "I never want you to hug me again." Her mother didn't. The first word this client learned to spell was "pest," because her mother would say, "You are a P...E...S...T, pest!"

Because of our inborn need to be touched and held, any withholding of physical comfort or affection constitutes a painful form of rejection. Not telling a child that he or she is loved is another. I am surprised at how many clients, when asked, sadly report that their parents never once said "I love you." Some pretend it didn't matter, to defend against grief and shame, and to protect the vulnerable and hidden true self from further rejection.

Still another form of rejection occurs when parents fail to make or take quality time to spend with their children. To a needy child, and all children are needy, time is love. One client lamented, "I gave up asking dad to do things with me because I got tired of hearing 'I don't have time right now.'" Such messages are always personalized at some level, that is, the rejected child believes there is something wrong with him, not the parent.

Dave was referred to therapy by his family physician for treatment of depression. He presented himself with a forced smile, as if he were covering over or masking a gloomy mood. After assessing the typical symptoms of depression I asked him, "Do you ever feel so desperate that you think of taking your life?" At this point he burst into tears and said he should never have been born in the first place. This was the message his parents had conveyed and having fully internalized his rejecting parents, he questioned whether he was worth the air he breathed. When parents are hostile and act in ways that question the child's very right to exist, suicide can become an option because it is a way of ending the inescapable pain that permeates every moment of life. This was the case with Dave. He had never been affirmed as worthwhile and didn't see himself as fitting in anywhere. He was able to recall many scenes where his parents responded to him with hatred and he had developed an even stronger self-hate. This is often the case because the hated child will internalize scenes of his parents when they were most hostile. This colors his perception in such a way that he views them as even more hateful than they actually were. The internal bad parent then rejects and hates him in a way that is more toxic and shaming than the real life parents upon whom the internalization is based. I was able to convince Dave that suicide was a permanent solution to a temporary problem and that therapy was a positive alternative. The part of him that wanted to live, the part that got him to this first session, agreed and he made a commitment to long-term therapy, which was successful.

"You are worthless!" is the shaming message children take in from repeated experiences of parental rejection. Because he needs to see his parents as accepting, the child believes there is something wrong with him, that he is the one who is defective, i.e., their rejection messages are taken personally. Scenes where he is rejected are internalized and a core belief is formed..."I am worthless!" He is compelled to re-enact these scenes by playing the role of the hostile parent and internally rejecting himself. It is the interpersonal part of the self that is most injured, resulting in deep shame over the inability to relate to others. Lacking accepting parents, and containing their badness, he is unable to develop or maintain a secure feeling of self-esteem. If his own mother and father cannot affirm him as worthwhile, he cannot help but grow up feeling less of a person. He is left with a shamed sense of self—that he does not belong, that he is not valued, that he is worthless.

Message Three: "You are Disgusting!" (The Scorned Child)

The scorned child internalizes a message that she is disgusting, a disgrace to her family. Scorn is rejection with an exclamation point! The child is more than unacceptable to her parents, she is repulsive. Whereas the rejecting parent communicates a hostile attitude, the scornful parent is positively hateful. In reality, such parents may not actually hate their child, but treat the child as if they do. They communicate an attitude of extreme, often indignant contempt—the child is seen as low, unworthy, and disgusting. They treat her as if she had a foul smell or made them sick to their stomachs.

The parent who is full of scorn is full of shame. Expressing scorn is a way of projecting unacceptable feelings and attitudes about oneself. The hated child becomes the container for the parent's self-hatred. Such parents were humiliated in their own families of origin. Now they re-enact childhood scorn scenes by changing roles with their own parent, and scorning their own child, who is recast as the object of contempt. Putting the child in the victim role represents a momentary triumph over intolerable shame. By looking down on the child, the parent assumes an elevated position. Of course, any relief from shame is short-lived, necessitating regular scorn attacks on the child.

Having scornful parents is almost like having no parents at all. It is frightening to the child because of the dependent position she is in. Children don't need parents to be perfect, but they need parents to show some measure of respect and love. The scornful parent shows neither, and fails to form an attachment bond with their deeply wounded child.

Scorn messages are conveyed when the child feels the parent react with disgust, as if the child was repulsive. Scenes that constitute rejection are played out (e.g., refusing holding), but the intensity of parental hostility is turned way up. And, the reason for the rejection is more obvious—namely, the child arouses a deep aversion in her parents. Thus, the parent not only withholds love and affection, but rejects the child's love and affection, viewing her offerings as offensive.

Some examples. One client reported, "He could make me feel lower than a worm just by the way he looked at me. It wasn't so much what he said, it was how he said it." An adolescent client felt shamed to the core when his father revealed his bed-wetting problem to his peers. Other scornful parents name-call in ways that mock and ridicule. This is similar to messages that belittle the child, but are more contemptuous. To be criticized for being overweight is belittling; to be called "bubble butt" (as was one overweight client) is to be made the object of scorn. Another client was referred to as "it" by her scornful father. He seemed to delight in mocking her, by saying things like, "'it' has a pimple."

While most of the twelve shame-inducing messages are conveyed unintentionally, this wound is inflicted with a purpose. Here, scorn is expressed in order to gain control and transfer shame. The scornful parent must be in control because of his own shame related feelings of inadequacy and vulnerability. His attitude all but destroys the developing self-esteem of the child, who longs for parental acceptance. Like all children, she needs to feel affirmed and unconditionally loved, but feels hated instead. The interpersonal self is particularly damaged and she experiences relationship shame. When the scorn attack is directed at her body (e.g., "fatso") or a body function (e.g., menstruation, body odor), she suffers body-image shame as well. When the scorn attack is directed at her sexuality (e.g., "slut," "whore"), sexual shame results. Scorned children suffer massive overdoses of shame. They become containers for the transferred shame of their parent.

"You are disgusting!" is the shaming message internalized by children who become the objects of parental scorn. The message tells the child that she is deemed low and inferior by one or both of the most important persons in her life. Not only does she see herself as not belonging in the family, she sees herself as disgracing them. Scenes where she was the object of parental scorn are taken into the self and she forms the core belief..."I am disgusting!" She takes it in and she takes it personally. She believes, "There is something wrong with me," even if she also believes there is something wrong with them. By taking the bad qualities of the parent inside the self, she gains some sense of control over future shame attacks. She can predict and control the badness if the attack comes from the inside. But, in the attempt to insulate herself from outside shame attacks, she becomes contemptuous of her self. Her self-contempt matches or even surpasses that of her parent who scorned her. She makes fun of herself, calls herself names, and sets herself up in relationships where someone will scorn her the way her parent did. She re-experiences the verbal and emotional abuse of her childhood, always feeling victimized. At the core of her self, she believes she is disgusting and deserves to be hated. Her parents may not actually hate her, but if they treat her as if they do, how can she expect anyone else to love her? How can she find herself lovable? She can't. She has developed a shamed sense of self—that she is repulsive, a disgusting human being.

Message Four: "You are Unwanted!" (The Abandoned Child)

The abandoned child internalizes the shame-inducing message that she is unwanted. The parent is either physically absent or communicates an attitude of emotional unavailability. Abandonment is similar to rejection, but the child internalizes a different message. Rejecting parents are hostile and actively push their children away. The child feels worthless. Abandoning parents are more self-absorbed than hostile and passively pull away. Their unavailability is due to preoccupation with their own problems rather than active dislike for their children. The child feels unwanted, but not necessarily worthless.

Such parents are typically carrying on a family legacy that has been passed on for generations. Their own parents were emotionally unavailable and, despite good intentions, they replay scenes of abandonment with their own children. Not having internalized an available and comforting parent, they lack empathy and fail at being responsive to their child's emotional needs. They are so preoccupied with their own stresses that they see children as more or less another stress. Most often they become self-absorbed because of emotional, financial, or addictive problems, and simply ignore their children.

By contrast, parents who are emotionally available are emotionally attuned to their children. They convey a message that they are really there for their child, ready to attend to them, hold them, comfort them, and support them. They encourage and then validate their child's feelings and perceptions. They listen and respond appropriately to their child's needs. The child feels supported and wanted. The family is a place of safety and security. Shame is given in very small doses and leads to a temporary feeling that is useful. It is not taken into the self so it does not damage the self.

Abandonment messages are communicated at times when the child needs a parent and the parent is unavailable. In infancy, this happens when the newborn's basic needs to relate and be nurtured are ignored. If an infant is to develop a secure attachment, parents must respond to her cries of distress in a timely and comforting way. An infant needs parents to mirror her emerging developmental competence. This means she needs them to reflect back to her in ways that affirm and support her development. Whether she picks up a rattle for the first time, or learns to recite the alphabet, she needs a parent to be there to reflect excitement and pride over her accomplishments. This lets her know she is noticed and admired, reassures her that someone is available, and affirms her developing self.

Abandonment messages are also conveyed when parents ignore their child's need to be lovingly touched and held. Whereas the rejected child is more actively pushed away, the abandoned child's needs are passively ignored. This in injurious to all children, but especially to those who have not yet acquired expressive and receptive language skills. Pre-verbal children depend on physical contact to form and maintain the crucial attachment bond with parents (Kaufman, 1989, p.36). When it is withheld, they cannot internalize the satisfaction and security necessary for basic trust. Basic trust is the essential building block for emotional development and the key to "a sense of positive identity and self-esteem" (Middelton-Moz, 1989, p.7). The abandoned child is unable to form an acceptable sense of self, always feeling burdensome and unwanted.

As children get older, they experience abandonment when parents fail to take an active interest in play or school activities. Children whose parents have divorced experience abandonment when either parent becomes physically or emotionally unavailable. Adolescents feel abandoned when neither parent is available to provide information and support regarding the physical changes associated with puberty, e.g., breast or genital development, menstruation, or increased sexual drive. These changes draw attention to the self and leave adolescents feeling exposed and ashamed (Kaufman, pp.43-44). It may be even more shaming when these physical changes do not occur, e.g., the teenage boy with no pubic hair or teenage girl with undeveloped breasts. Such children need even more support.

One client, when asked to recall shame scenes from her adolescence, reported that the most shaming event was when she asked her mother for a training bra, and her mother said, "You don't need a bra because you're flat as a board!" This only heightened her self-consciousness and body-image shame. She already felt embarrassed that she didn't "measure up" to her peers, but what hurt most was feeling abandoned and belittled by someone she looked to for support. This client needed to share her embarrassment and vulnerability with a parent who had survived this tumultuous time of life. She needed guidance to deal with her confusing feelings. And, more importantly, she needed validation and encouragement to maintain her self-esteem.

"You are unwanted!" is the shaming message children get when they are repeatedly abandoned by their parents. The child, sensing her parents' unavailability, questions whether they want her and loses self-esteem. She feels burdensome rather than prized. Rather than attribute their unavailability to their deficiencies as parents, she believes it is something about herself. Scenes where she experiences abandonment are internalized and a core belief is formed..."I am unwanted!" "If my own mom and dad don't want me," she decides, "I must be bad." If she is the bad one, there is hope that her parents will eventually be there for her once she proves her goodness. She learns to abandon herself by not asserting needs or sticking up for herself. As she grows older, she is compelled to re-enact scenes of abandonment by co-creating relationships with men who will either be emotionally unavailable or leave her altogether. She will settle for less than she needs because she has a shamed sense of self—that she does not belong, she is unwanted.

Message Five: "You are Unimportant!" (The Neglected Child)

Neglected children grow up believing they are unimportant because their parents fail to provide essential care. Whereas rejecting parents push their children away, and abandoning parents pull away, neglectful parents never seem to engage their children at all. They seem disinterested, as if they don't even notice that a dependent child is living in their midst. To such parents, children are a low priority in the scheme of things.

These are parents who typically have serious emotional problems and lack the inner resources to provide good parenting. Infants born to such parents have a higher mortality rate at birth and in their first year. They may be neglected while still in the womb, e.g., poor nutrition, alcohol and other drugs, no prenatal medical care. Neglectful parents often suffer from chronic depression which can be traced to lack of adequate parenting in their own childhoods. Having no model of a nurturing parent, they neglect their own children.

Poverty is almost always a factor in families that neglect. Too many kids and not enough money creates a debilitating stress. The pressure to make ends meet and survive is overwhelming to parents who can't get good jobs or who have not matured to economic adulthood. Many neglectful fathers choose to leave the family rather than accept the responsibilities of parenthood. Then, they fail their responsibility to provide child support payments. Mothers are young, single, and crushed by their responsibilities. Whereas rejection is an error of commission, neglect is mostly an error of omission. Nonetheless, it is an error that robs the child of a healthy sense of self. The disregard of the child's needs conveys a message that he is unimportant and introduces him to shame.

To compare, parents who are attentive and nurturing do not feel impinged upon by their child's neediness. They are more prepared for parenthood and willingly accept their responsibilities. They are economic adults and their children are more likely to be their highest priority. The child is a "big fish in a small pond." The parents are attuned to his or her needs at any given moment and allow their children to use them to satisfy those needs. They have the resources and the parenting skills to provide essential care.

Children take in neglect messages when parents allow their child's basic needs to go unmet. Infants who are neglected go without proper holding, comforting, bathing, and feeding. They lie unattended in cribs, their stomachs empty, their diapers dirty, their cries of distress disregarded. Neglected infants are understimulated and slow to accomplish the usual developmental milestones. They are more accident prone because no one takes the measures necessary to make their environment safe. One client, a victim of child neglect, would jump from trees with her legs crossed in the hope of injuring herself and receiving some much needed attention and care.

In early childhood, these are the waifs who run unsupervised in the neighborhood. They may be dressed improperly for the weather or be expected to wear filthy or ill-fitting clothes. They may be fed junk food or no food at all. One client described how she and her siblings would be fed biscuits while her parents would eat chicken. The message was that her needs didn't count, her hunger didn't matter.

When neglected children become ill, they may or may not be tended to or taken to the doctor's office. One client described how her younger sister complained of severe stomach pain for several days. Her mother told her to "shut up" and quit complaining. Finally, an older brother demanded that his sister be taken to the hospital, where she was treated for a ruptured appendix. She ended up in an intensive care unit and the physican who treated her angrily told the mother that had she waited a few more hours her daughter would have died.

Many clients have related similar stories of how they were denied much needed medical or dental care. One client was born with a congenital hip malformation that was never treated and another was never taken to a dentist until she was seventeen. It was not for lack of resources that these clients were neglected as children. Both were born into military families and would have received treatment at no charge! Both puzzled over why their parents wouldn't take them to get help, and both concluded it was because their parents had more important things to do. Each felt unimportant. Still another client suffered a childhood seizure disorder that was never treated. Her parents knew she was having seizures, but told her she would grow out of it.

Neglectful parents show little or no interest in school activities, and neglected children are classic academic underachievers. Teachers often consider them learning disabled or "hyperactive" because they are inattentive, impulsive, and overactive. Of course they are overactive; they become self-stimulators to compensate for being understimulated at home. They long for attention and will do just about anything to get it, including misbehave. Such children suffer from an emotional disorder that is a consequence of parental neglect. They are not to be confused with children who have an attention deficit disorder that includes hyperactivity — a neurological problem that is not due to parental mistreatment (although neglect would worsen the problem).

Neglected children sometimes internalize too little shame and thus have poor conscience development. Having never received adequate supervision or effective discipline, they know no limits. Lacking inner controls on their behavior, they feel no guilt over their bad behavior. Having little attachment to their parents, they show little social attachment to others. Even relationships with peers lack any real feeling of bonding. As they get older, their parents disengage even further and by adolescence they are usually left to fend for themselves.

"You are unimportant!" is the message children internalize when they are denied essential care by neglectful parents. The neglected child learns that his most basic needs don't count—he doesn't count. His parents have done little to convince him otherwise and scenes where he was neglected are taken into the self. The victim of neglect feels like a nobody and often has no group loyalties. Also affected is the intrapsychic part of the self resulting in identity shame. Instead of forming a true identity and knowing who they are, neglected children are typically assigned dysfunctional roles, e.g., the acting-out child or the loner. Internalized shame is reflected in the core belief that is formed..."I am unimportant!" The neglect messages are personalized, there is something wrong with him, he feels insignificant. "If I was more important," he decides, "they would take better care of me." If it is he who is at fault, he can preserve the illusion that his parents are adequate. This allows him to hold on to the fantasy that they may some day come through for him and provide satisfactory care. By faulting himself he avoids the frightening realization that he is on his own. When he is old enough to really be on his own, he re-enacts scenes of parental neglect by ignoring his most basic needs. This is the guy who doesn't bathe often enough or brush his teeth every day. Having never internalized a caring parent, he is missing skills when it comes to self-care. This void is a reflection of his shamed sense of self—that he is insignificant, unimportant.

Message Six: "You are Nothing!" (The Engulfed Child)

A child who has been engulfed internalizes a message that she doesn't exist apart from the parent, usually her mother since she is most often the primary caretaker. To be engulfed is to be swallowed up, taken over by an all-powerful being. The child is never allowed to define a boundary that would differentiate her from mother. They are psychologically merged.

The engulfing mother is a shame-based person who does not feel psychologically whole. Her child is everything to her and exists to complete her. If she suffers low self-esteem (and she does), her child must make her happy. If she feels trapped in an unsatisfying marriage (and she does), her child gives her a place to divert emotional energy and a future ally against her husband. Her child becomes her all, her everything, her obsession, her possession. The needy child inherits an even needier mother. The mother reverses roles and her child quickly learns to affirm her mother by making her feel needed and loved. Unlike the alcoholic or mentally ill mother, the role reversal is not obvious because she looks loving and supportive. On the surface, she is attentive and emotionally available, but she is actually overly attentive and overly available. She smothers rather than mothers.

Such a mother has an unconscious desire to keep her child in a dependent state. She treats her child like a helpless infant regardless of her level of development. She impinges on her child and sabotages her efforts at independence in subtle ways, e.g., voice tone, looks, gestures, and unspoken commands (McArthur, 1988, p.10). The child is powerless to escape her sphere of influence, and is punished for attempting behaviors that would achieve separation. She is given an injunction to not grow up.

Father is distant and uninvolved with child rearing and does little to protect his child from being engulfed. He acts in collusion with mother to sabotage the child's efforts at separation and mastery. Having already failed an attempt to repair his wife's self-esteem, he welcomes the child's presence since it allows him to escape the demands of an intimate marriage. This sets up the so-called "perverse triangle" so often seen in family therapy: an engulfing and controlling mother, distant and uninvolved father, and a troubled and symptomatic child. Both parents interact with the child as if she were something or someone other than who she really is, a pattern called depersonification (Rinsley in McArthur, 1988).

By comparison, healthy parents both participate and cooperate in parenting their child. They "pull on the same end of the rope," and what they pull for is the child's emerging developmental competence. By reflecting back excitement and pride when their child learns a new skill, they help her acquire a sense of mastery. The primary caretaker respects her child's need to define a boundary and form a separate and eventually self-governing self. Mother and father want their child to become her own person and value her for whom she uniquely is, not for whom they expect or need her to be. They respect her individuality and reinforce her gradual independence.

An engulfment message is conveyed when the child is repeatedly smothered with attention. This is the opposite of an abandonment message where the parent is unavailable and pulls away. Here, mother is forever available and will not allow the child to pull away, even when he or she wants to do so. At the same time, father is nowhere to be found, so the child is engulfed by one parent and abandoned by the other. Whereas the rejecting parent says, in effect, "You have no right to exist," the engulfing mother says, "You do not exist apart from me!" The child is not permitted to form a boundary that would define a self and feels controlled by the all-encompassing mother. The primary injury is to the child's intrapsychic self, causing the experience of identity shame. Having no boundary to define a separate self, there is no self to esteem.

Engulfment is due to an early parental failure that interrupts the normal process of development. Margaret Mahler's (Mahler, Pine, and Bergman, 1975) model of childhood development is most helpful in understanding this process. Mahler and her colleagues describe successive stages of development that lead to the establishment of a separate self. In the autistic stage (the first two months), the infant responds primarily to internal stimulation and seeks to maintain a homeostatic equilibrium. As the infant becomes more sensitive to external stimulation, she begins the symbiotic stage (the next three months) where child and mother are fused together. They share a common boundary; what is self and not-self are undifferentiated. The image of engulfment at this stage is that of an infant who has been breast fed to the point of satiation, and wants to pull away, but is placed back on the nipple. At approximately six months the child begins the supremely important separation-individuation stage of development. It is here that scenes of engulfment become most noticeable because baby begins to differentiate a separate self. First, she loses some interest in mother and seeks to explore her environment. As crawling and walking develop, the child becomes excited in her ability to do things by herself. The engulfing mother is threatened by her child's emerging independence and freedom. She not only fails to mirror accomplishments, but punishes movements away from her with disapproving looks and voice tones.

I once observed an engulfing client with her year-old son in a playroom. It was as if her little boy was on a leash and a choke-chain. As soon as he went beyond the eight-foot imaginary boundary, regardless of how well behaved he was, he was reeled in and reprimanded severely. Her disapproval of his emerging independence was obvious to the boy, who first threw a temper tantrum and then sulked. When I asked if she could give her son a bit more freedom, she told me, "No, he needs me to keep him close." This was a projection of her need to keep him close and dependent.

An engulfed child senses her mother's withdrawal and, fearing that she will be abandoned, returns in desperation—only to be engulfed again. What the child wants is to be refueled emotionally, but instead expends energy just to ensure her mother's availability. This is energy that should be going into the development of a separate self. She never differentiates from mother, never becomes a self-governing person, and is always excessively vulnerable to fears of engulfment and/or abandonment in relationships.

As the child grows older, engulfment messages are conveyed when the child is prevented from doing things that would give a feeling of competence and a sense of mastery over the environment. Mother overfunctions and is always there to dress her, tie her shoes, comb her hair, or help her assemble the puzzle. The training wheels stay on the bicycle long after the child is capable of riding without them. Mother is overprotective during play with preschool peers and conditions her child to be fearful. If her child is a boy, he will be seen as "mama's boy." In fairness to the mother, this is at least as much the father's responsibility for his distance and lack of involvement. He is rarely there and even when he is, he abdicates his role and underfunctions.

When it comes time to begin school, the engulfed child is likely to show excessive separation anxiety. In fact, it is mother who is most anxious about the separation but it is her child who displays the symptoms. Here we see the effects of the "perverse triangle," namely, a child with debilitating psychological and physical symptoms. These symptoms include morbid fears of some harm befalling mother, clinging to and shadowing mother, sleep difficulty with nightmares that involve separation themes, excessive distress in anticipation of or following separation from mother, psychosomatic complaints on school days, and outright refusal to attend school (DSM-III-R, 1987, p.61). The engulfing mother is overreactive to these symptoms and reinforces them. She rescues the child from the stress of separation and in so doing strengthens the dependency and fearfulness that prevents her child from defining a self.

Although periods of separation anxiety are likely to wax and wane over the years, the child is likely to become an overachiever in school. Since she feels herself to be an extension of mother, and since both parents need and expect her to excel academically, she obliges. However, she gets no real self-satisfaction from her accomplishments because she has no self to feel good about. Besides, mother typically takes the credit ("You're such a bright girl. I'm so glad I insisted on your going to a private school").

Upon reaching adolescence she is subtly discouraged from dating since it is a movement toward separation (eventually she will either be discouraged from marrying or mother will choose a spouse or partner who will not threaten their relationship). She will graduate from high school and make plans, but she never quite reaches the "age of emancipation," a time when she is supposedly free from mother's control over her life. Even if she leaves home to take a job or go to college, she never really leaves home psychologically.

This kind of feeble separation was illustrated in a recent Ann Landers column (11/10/89). A fifty-year-old woman writes and complains bitterly about being dominated by her eighty-year-old mother. She lives with her mother and is "guilt-tripped" if she tries to do anything alone. She concludes her letter by pleading with Ann not to indicate where the letter came from, because if the mother figured out she had written it, she would be crucified! Moving out will not solve this woman's problem. She was engulfed, is still engulfed, and feels like a nothing. Until she defines a separate self, she can not become a psychological adult and heal her shame.

"You are nothing!" is the shaming message children internalize when they feel swallowed up and controlled by their mother. The engulfing mother perceives her child as an extension of herself and the distant father supports this view. This sets up a "perverse triangle" with an over-involved mother, uninvolved father, and undifferentiated child. The child gets no respect for her individuality. In other words, she never becomes her own person, never forms a boundary that would define a separate self, and suffers shame over her lack of identity. Scenes of being engulfed are internalized and she forms a core belief..."I am nothing!" She is too dependent to risk acknowledging the bad qualities of her engulfing mother. To do so would be disloyal and mother would once again withdraw and punish her. Any move towards separation is shamed so she gives in and stays symbiotically merged with mother. When she asks herself the question, "Who am I?," she draws a blank. She has low self-esteem because she has no self to esteem. Engulfment has resulted in a shamed sense of self—that she does not exist as her own person, that she is nothing.

Message Seven: "You are Dirty!"
(The Molested Child)

A molested child is a girl or boy who is a victim of sexual abuse prior to the age of eighteen. Child sexual abuse is defined as any sexual contact that takes advantage of the child's powerlessness. This is a broad definition that includes both obvious and disguised forms of sexual abuse (I prefer these terms to overt and covert because overt sexual abuse implies that it is not hidden, and molesters almost always attempt to conceal their actions). Obvious forms of sexual abuse are any behaviors that involve:

1. Penetration of the child's vagina or anus

2. Oral-genital contact

3. Sexualized kissing

4. Sexualized touching (fondling)

5. Masturbating in the presence of the child

6. Simulated or "dry" intercourse

Disguised forms of child sexual abuse are behaviors that involve:

1. Exposing genitals for the purpose of sexual stimulation

2. Watching children bathe or undress for the purpose of sexual stimulation

3. Photographing children for the purpose of sexual stimulation

4. Allowing children to observe adult sexual activities

5. Sexual advances that are not acted upon

6. Assigning the child a family role that is emotionally incestuous, e.g., surrogate spouse

When sexual abuse is perpetrated by a parent or relative, or anyone in a familial role, it is considered incestuous. Parent-child incest is the worst kind of "You are dirty!" message, and is the topic for consideration here. Another type of message occurs when the sexual abuse is extrafamilial (outside the family).

Both incest and extrafamilial sexual abuse are epidemic in our society, and have been for many generations. Nearly one girl in five is a victim of incest, and nearly one girl in twenty is incestu-ously abused by her father (Russell, 1986, p.60). Nearly two girls in five are victims of either incestuous and/or extrafamilial sexual abuse before the age of eighteen (p.61). Boys are also molested although it appears they are more likely to be abused outside the home than within the family (Courtois, 1988, p.5). Most children are molested more than once and each molestation reinforces the message that the victim is bad and dirty. One researcher found that for 92% of female victims who were abused more than once, the abuse lasted over one year. It lasted over three years for 79%, over six years for 59%, and over nine years for 28% (Jehu, 1988, p.9).

The incestuous parent is typically a heterosexual male. Finkelhor and Russell (in Russell, p.308) concluded that about 95% of all sexual abuse of girls and 80% of all sexual abuse of boys is perpetrated by men. The personality of the incestuous father is characterized by low self-esteem, poor impulse control, im-paired empathy, and a "swiss-cheese" conscience. Such men typically have a severe personality disorder, that is, a firmly fixed and unhealthy way of thinking and relating to others. Before they actually act out their incestuous impulses, such men fantasize about molesting their daughters and may develop a plan. A typical strategy is to get drunk just before molesting. This lowers their inhibitions and provides an excuse if they're caught in the act, or confronted someday. Alcohol is for such men a license to act shamelessly, and a way to bypass guilt. Many victims who confront their incestuous fathers are told, "I must have been drunk out of my mind. I don't remember it." They all read the same book!

What kind of father would exploit his child and commit the ultimate betrayal? What would motivate a man to step over the line and break the incest taboo? Justice and Justice (1979) de-scribe most incestuous fathers as either symbiotic, sociopathic, or pedophilic. The "symbiotic father" (80 to 85% of all molesters) had emotionally unavailable parents who frustrated his need for closeness, i.e., he was abandoned. He learns to get his need for closeness and comforting met through sex. His wife is at first a source of sexual gratification and closeness, but she eventually withdraws because he is unavailable to meet her needs. He then feels cut off from his only source of closeness and begins to sexualize the relationship with his daughter. He may rationalize his incestuous behavior as harmless ("She likes it") or educational ("Better she learns from someone who loves her"). He may be a tyrant who controls family members by intimidating or terrorizing them. Molesting his powerless child is an expression of contempt for women in general and makes him feel more powerful and in control.

The "sociopathic father" molests his daughter because it is exciting and physically stimulating. He has never attached to anyone and couldn't care less about the emotional damage he inflicts. Aggressive and cruel, he may actually take sadistic pleasure in the suffering of his victims. He either internalized too little shame and has no conscience, or internalized an overdose of shame and is acting-out rage over his childhood failure to attach to a parent figure.

The "pedophilic father" is an immature and incompetent man who feels threatened by grown-up women and adult sexuality. He turns to his daughter while she is young because she is little and nonthreatening. In one study, pedophiles were asked to draw a man and woman. Whereas normal men drew the man larger than the woman nine times out of ten, the pedophile drew the woman larger six times out of ten. The implication was that they see women as bigger, thus more threatening. Many pedophiles molest their young sons as well as daughters and most do not restrict their pedophilic behavior to their own children.

While all types of incestuous fathers may appear to be shameless, the act of molestation is most often motivated by the internalization of too much shame. The molester is driven to re-enact his own childhood scenes of humiliation. He may or may not have been a victim of childhood sexual abuse, but he is always from a shame-based family. He recasts his daughter in the role of the victim, and temporarily frees himself of shame by defeating and humiliating her (Kaufman, 1989, p.125). Sexual gratification is less a motive than is the transfer of shame.

The mothers of incest victims likewise often come from shame-based families and were often molested themselves. Some co-create a relationship with a man who would someday molest their daughters and thus unconsciously re-enact their own molestation scenes (Kaufman, 1989, p.25). A combination of low self-esteem, morbid dependency, and intense abandonment anxiety renders such women unable or unwilling to seek healthier relationships. They marry for the wrong reasons and find themselves in a submissive position to their controlling and sexually deviant husbands. Their lack of power undermines any ability they would otherwise have to protect their vulnerable daughters. Because they are economically dependent and have limited resources, they feel helpless and trapped.

My clinical experience is that many mothers of incest victims are inadequately bonded to their daughters. As young girls age, and especially around the vulnerable ages of ten to thirteen, they are more likely to be molested and more likely to need a protective mother. Instead, the mothers either passively or actively act in collusion with their incestuous husbands. I suspect that those victims who have more supportive and protective mothers do not so often end up in therapy. In other words, a victim of father-daughter incest would be more likely to end up in therapy if she also felt betrayed by an unsupportive mother. If there is such a thing as a typical incest family, it is made up of an emotionally needy father with poor conscience development and a submissive, powerless mother. They come from and re-create a shame-based family system that conveys a "You are dirty!" message to their children. Shame is transferred to the next generation.

The molested child feels betrayed by the incestuous father and again by her mother if she colludes with the molester. Another betrayal occurs when the child discloses sexual abuse, incestuous or extrafamilial, but does not get the validation and support she needs. The victim desperately needs to hear that she was induced into the victim role, and that what happened wasn't her fault. She is quite powerless to resist given the exercise of adult (male) authority, threats of violence, or physical force—all of which intensify her humiliation. Some fathers bribe their daughters or misrepresent the sexual activity as a game or sex education. These inducements contribute to the sense of betrayal and she cannot help but feel used, violated, dirty.

The demand of secrecy by the molester allows him to escape detection and continue acting-out. The victim is too ashamed and frightened to tell her mother what happens when daddy comes into her room at night. Secrecy isolates the victim and perpetuates her belief that she is to blame, that she is the dirty one. She is too ashamed to tell anyone outside the family and feels different from peers. Most victims keep sexual abuse secret for years because they are afraid of being disbelieved, blamed, or shamed. Others maintain secrecy out of loyalty to their fathers or out of fear that he would become violent if they told. In Jehu's (1988) study, only half of the victims disclosed abuse experiences prior to the age of seventeen, and those who did disclose to their mothers were met with overwhelmingly negative reactions (p.13). The least common reactions by mothers were anger toward the molester and guilt over failing to protect the victim (p.14)! Thus, many victims are first betrayed by their fathers and then betrayed again by their mothers when they break secrecy. The second betrayal reinforces the message that they are dirty, otherwise mother would act on their behalf.

A molestation message is conveyed whenever the incestuous father exploits his child's innocence and powerlessness to transfer shame and gratify himself sexually. He violates the child's body in such a way that she feels impure, unclean, or dirty. The molestation scene contains the visual memory of what was done to her, the auditory memory of any sexual sounds, and a kinesthetic memory of any physical sensations experienced during the molestation. These scenes are charged with emotion and are replayed like a bad movie in her head—a horror film! The message conveyed is that she is dirty.

She is most likely to feel shame during and after the molestation, but there is also helpless rage, fear, and eventually grief. For no apparent reason she may find herself replaying a molestation scene and re-experiencing these disturbing emotions. Without warning, she may have a "flashback," as if the experience was actually happening again. Clients report lying in bed at night and vividly re-experiencing physical reactions such as nausea, shock, pain, and/or "creepy sensations." Many report that "it was the only time he ever paid attention to me" or that "it felt good." Some molesters go to great lengths to physically pleasure their victims so they can rationalize their behavior ("She enjoyed it."). This only intensifies the victim's shame ("If it felt good, I must have wanted it").

Sometimes the molestation scene appears in nightmares so disturbing the victim becomes afraid to go to sleep. Or the victim learns to avoid reminders that might trigger a replay of the molestation scene. One client, molested by her father on her thirteenth birthday, dreaded subsequent birthdays because of a yearly anniversary reaction of shame and helpless rage. Many victims of incest report an aversion to being touched where the molester touched them. Instead of experiencing sexual pleasure and gratification, they replay the molestation scene and feel used or dirty. Hence they ask their partners to avoid touching certain parts of their bodies, avoid certain activities (especially oral sex), and/or avoid certain positions during intercourse. Needless to say, this can cause sexual dysfunction and relationship conflicts. Many others dissociate (space out) during sex, a defense that enabled them to cope during the original scene. Some develop such an aversion to sex they avoid it altogether.

Many adults molested as children never have intercourse during the course of their lifetime. I treated a severely depressed nun who joined a convent as a young woman because of her aversion to sex. Any thought of being sexual triggered an immediate replay of molestation scenes and an intolerable feeling of being dirty. After keeping the secret of incest for fifty years, she continued to feel ashamed (time does not heal incest wounds). Unfortunately, she withdrew from therapy after disclosing the molestation scene with her father, apparently overwhelmed and immobilized by excruciating shame.

In short, the victim of sexual abuse suffers from chronic post-traumatic stress disorder (PTSD), a characteristic set of symptoms that follow the extreme stress of being molested as a child. These symptoms involve disturbing replays of molestation scenes, avoiding reminders of molestation scenes, and/or a numbing of overall sexual responsiveness. Thus, PTSD occurs as victims of incest replay molestation scenes, complete with fear, powerlessness, and shame.

"You are dirty!" is the shaming message children take in when they are molested by a parent. The victim has been exploited and feels like an object, a thing, and a filthy one at that. The violation of her body boundary is a betrayal, and father-daughter incest is an ultimate betrayal. A second betrayal occurs if she discloses sexual abuse but is disbelieved, blamed, or shamed by her mother. This reinforces the message that she is dirty, bad, deserving of abuse. So does the demand for secrecy. Her ability to trust is shattered when she realizes that she was used by someone she depended upon, and not supported by someone who was supposed to protect her. A molestation only has to happen once to have its shaming effect. A single dose is an overdose! Scenes of being molested are internalized and a core belief is formed..."I am dirty!" The body, interpersonal, and intrapsychic parts of the self are all damaged and this is why incest is so devastating. The victim is left with body-image and sexual shame, relationship shame, and shame about her identity. She typically blames herself for the molestation, as if she had the power to say no, or as if not saying no was the same as choosing to participate. The molester has transferred his shame to her and she takes his "dirtiness" inside. By containing his badness, she gains some measure of control, but at the cost of feeling like dirt. As an adult, she is prone to chronic depression and suicidal impulses, phobias and panic attacks, mood swings and rage reactions, eating disorders and addictions, sexual and relationship problems, psychosomatic symptoms and chronic pain. These behaviors make sense when we see them as symptoms of post-traumatic stress and realize that being molested is the most shaming message of all. Untreated, the victim of incest has a deeply shamed sense of self—that she is bad, unclean, dirty.

Message Eight: "You are Unlovable!" (The Battered Child)

The battered child internalizes a parental message that he is unlovable, a source of frustration to his parents. Like sexual abuse, physical abuse is epidemic in the United States. It is difficult to estimate its incidence because researchers disagree as to how broadly or narrowly it should be defined. Battering is here defined as any form of physical violence that would include slapping, hitting, kicking, whipping and spanking.

Those who spank their children and were spanked as children will likely object to thinking of spanking as battering. Spanking as a form of discipline is the norm in most families. Can so many parents be battering their children? To batter, according to Webster's New World Dictionary, is "to strike with blow after blow," and that sounds like spanking to me. It may be the least severe form of battering, but it is striking children with repeated blows. The intent of the parent may soften the blow, but it is a blow nonetheless. A loving parent who spanks her child for running into the street may do so with the best of intentions, but the child is still being hit and may learn to associate love with physical abuse. One client, whose mother claimed to spank "out of love—not anger," associated love with violence and married a man who threatened to kill her if she declined his proposal. She explained, "If he'd go that far, he must really love me."

Spanking is usually carried out under the guise of discipline, and some parents quote scripture to justify their actions ("Spare the rod, spoil the child"). They fail to realize that the biblical rod was for guiding wayward sheep back into the flock, not striking them. If an adult strikes an adult, it is considered assault. If a parent strikes a child it is justified as being for the child's own good. Although it is considered discipline, it is really a way through which the powerful vent frustration at the expense of the powerless. A child should no more be hit with a hand than a paddle or anything else. It hurts, physically and emotionally. It may or may not result in physical injury, but it always results in an emotional injury with the bruise on the inside. It is humiliating to be spanked and, if it happens often enough, leads to a shamed sense of self. Many of my clients have argued that they were spanked and they turned out okay. Of course, many of them didn't turn out okay, but that's not the point. The point is that if they are okay, it is in spite of the spankings their parents inflicted, not because of them. Their "okayness" is the result of the good-enough parenting they received, not the humiliation.

Spanking is also poor modeling and teaches children that it is okay to hurt others as a way of resolving conflict. It is a lesson that says violence is a solution to problems. Granted it may establish momentary control over some misbehavior, but at a cost of shaming the child. The humiliated child becomes an adult with low self-esteem. The rationalization, "I deserved to be hit or spanked," is a reflection of shame and low self-esteem, i.e., "I was a bad child." It is also a defense against the urge to retaliate against the shaming parent.

The more respectful (and more informed) parents give positive reinforcement for desirable behavior rather than spank for misbehavior. They catch their children doing something right, and then praise or reward them. They use an approach that emphasizes the "natural and logical consequences" of behavior, knowing it is far more effective than spanking because the

discipline is logically related to the misbehavior. A child who
draws crayon pictures on the wall needs to be disciplined. He
will learn more from parents who reason with him and model
self-control than from parents who vent their frustration and
spank him. A spanking has no connection with the misbehavior,
but taking his crayons away and making him help clean the wall
does. The consequences approach implies the child's behavior
is unacceptable. Setting limits leads to the internalization of
constructive guilt. The punitive, spanking approach implies the
child himself is unacceptable, resulting in the internalization of
too much shame. A battered child is unable to separate his
behavior from his identity.

Children learn internal control over their behavior by observing parents control their own behavior. They cannot learn self-
control from parents who model loss of control. A child will not
accept correction from a parent who resorts to bullying tactics.
Such tactics only humiliate children and convince them that they
are bad and deserve to be hit. It matters little whether the parent
hits with a hand or a hanger, either way the child feels unloved
or unlovable. Rudolf Dreikur, the famous child psychologist, was
once asked if he believed in spanking. "Certainly I believe in
spanking," he thundered. "I believe parents who spank their
children should be spanked."

Whenever I give workshops on shame and childrearing, someone always asks something like, "Dr. Wilson, you really have
strong feelings about not spanking children. Were you spanked
a lot as a child?" The truth is, I had one spanking in my life. The
scene took place in our bathroom and I was about seven or eight
years old. I remember my dad saying, "This is going to hurt me
more than you." He turned me over his knee and struck my rear
end (I was wearing jeans) maybe eight times. It didn't hurt
physically because he didn't hit me hard. What I will never forget
is how humiliated and enraged I felt. I cannot for the life of me
recall for what I was being spanked. I don't think I could say I'm
glad it happened, but I'm convinced that had I not got that
spanking, I couldn't possible imagine how such a widely accepted practice could be so shaming.

Obviously, spanking is mild compared to other forms of battering, such as hitting with a fist, whipping, or throwing a child
across a room. The more severe forms are more humiliating and

thus more damaging to the child's emerging sense of self. This is because the self is made to feel more shame (the child feels more unloved and unlovable). When a child is battered by both parents, his shame is doubled. If one parent attempts to buffer the child from the battering parent, some self-esteem is preserved because the child feels more worthy of love and protection. If one batters and the other fails to protect him, or if the non-battering parent sets up the child ("Wait until your father gets home and I'll tell him about this!"), it reinforces the message that he is unlovable. The part of the self most affected by battering is the intrapsychic self. The battered child develops identity shame and sees himself as fundamentally flawed and unlovable. He also develops relationship shame, finding it difficult to trust and be intimate.

Parents who act-out the more severe forms of battering share certain character traits. They are aggressive, immature, lacking empathy, and low in self-esteem. Most were battered by their own parents and are continuing a family legacy of violence towards children. A combination of low frustration tolerance and poor impulse control causes them to be explosive. All children frustrate their parents, but for such parents frustration triggers a response that leads to violence, especially under the influence of alcohol or other drugs. At the moment of losing control, they relive (unconsciously) their own childhood scenes of being battered. But, they relive them from the perspective of the parent who battered them and now play the role of the victimizer (Kaufman, 1989, p.123). The roles are recast and now it is their child who is the victim. Inflicting a black eye or bloody nose may activate shame in the victimizer, but it is either too little, too much, or too late.

Lacking optimal shame, the victimizer never makes reparation to his child and never takes responsibility for controlling his aggressive impulses. Instead, he blames the child for frustrating him in the first place. If the child hadn't "talked back," or "asked for it," he wouldn't have hit him. By blaming the victim, the victimizer justifies his behavior and at the same time wards off intolerable shame.

The victim learns both roles during a battering. He may eventually become a victimizer through "identification with the aggressor," a defense that leads to "an active assault on the outside world" (Anna Freud, 1966, p.116). This strategy rids him of the feeling of helplessness and allows him to transfer the shame of being humiliated to someone else. It is better to make someone else feel unloved. He also learns that violence is a way to control others and a solution to problems. If he is feared, he feels less vulnerable, and thus less exposed to future shame attacks.

Occasionally, violence is turned against the unlovable self, and all kinds of self-destructive behavior result. There will be approximately 6,000 teen suicides in the U.S. this year. Therapists know that a disproportionate number of these suicides were battered children. Battered teens are too afraid to express their retaliatory rage to the parent who abused them. I am convinced that some kill themselves to prevent themselves from killing their parents. Such suicides are acts of retaliation that say..."See what you did to me!" They act out their revenge fantasies by destroying what the parents have created, their possession. This ultimate act of self-destruction is one of rage turned against a self that already feels destroyed. They have, in effect, received a fatal dose of shame.

It may be that parents who batter more severely, lack information about child development and that this leads to both unrealistically high and unrealistically low expectations of their children. Twentyman, Rohrbeck, and Amish (in L'Abate, 1985, pp.909-910) propose a four-stage model of physical abuse based on this informational deficit: In Stage 1, a lack of information leads to unrealistic expectations regarding appropriate child behavior; in Stage 2, the child behaves in a way that is inconsistent with the parent's expectation; in Stage 3, the parent wrongly attributes the child's behavior as willful disobedience; and finally in Stage 4, the parent is aggressive toward the child.

This information-deficit model helps to explain how battering conveys the message to a child that he is unlovable. The battered child, handicapped by inappropriate expectations, has no way to satisfy his parents and get their approval. The slightest violation of parental rules triggers a battering. He concludes that there is something wrong with him, that he is defective in some unexplainable way. He learns to see himself as an irritant, a source of frustration, rather than a valued member of the family. He can not help but develop a shamed sense of self—that he is bad, unlovable, and deserving of abuse.

"You are unlovable!" is the shaming message parents convey when they inflict any form of battering. Spanking is the mildest form of physical abuse but nonetheless severs the parent-child bond, thus lowering self-esteem. The more severe forms of physical abuse cause a child to feel hated and absolutely undeserving of love. If your own mother and father don't love you, how could anyone else? The humiliation of physical abuse stimulates the child's urge to retaliate and he gets even in ways that invite further battering. It's a vicious circle perpetuated by shame and rage. Abuse causes humiliation, which causes retaliatory rage, which leads to more abuse, which causes more humiliation, and so on. Scenes where the child was battered are internalized and a core belief is formed..."I am unlovable!" Again, the child takes the bad quality of the parent inside and convinces himself he is only getting what he deserves since he is an irritating troublemaker. Many battered children learn the scapegoat role and show defiant rage as a defense against feeling helpless and ashamed. This role actually stabilizes the shame-based family by distracting attention from other parts of the system that are dysfunctional, e.g., an unsuccessful (often violent) marital relationship. Others become loners and avoid the trauma of physical abuse by withdrawing and being "good." Regardless of his role in the family, the battered child has internalized a deeply shamed sense of self—that the self is fundamentally bad, defective, and unlovable.

Message Nine: "You are Powerless!" (The Terrorized Child)

The terrorized child internalizes a message that she is powerless and is at the mercy of a parent who arouses intense fear. Garbarino, Guttman, and Seeley (1986), consider terrorizing a form of "psychological battering" and define varying degrees of severity. A parent using scare tactics to discipline would be a "mild" form of terrorizing, e.g., "Do it or else!" In its "moderate" form, terrorizing involves direct threats that undermine the child's sense of security, e.g., "You get to your room now or I'll blister your butt!" When parents make or carry out extreme or psychotic threats, it falls into the "severe" category, e.g., one client witnessed her mother kill her puppy for allowing the dog to lick her crotch (p.25-26, examples mine).

In my clinical experience, the most common forms of terrorizing involve threats of violence, deliberately provoking fear, and/or exposing children to frightening situations. Threatening a child with a severe battering is terrorizing, as is allowing a child to witness violence, e.g., the physical abuse of a sibling. Terrorizing induces shame because the child feels both powerless and unloved. The parent-child attachment bond is severed and the parent makes no attempt to repair it.

When children are shamed for expressing fear, shame and fear become bound together (Kaufman, 1989, p.62). To illustrate, if a child is ridiculed or scorned for being afraid of spiders, fear and shame become associated, and all subsequent experiences of fear automatically activate shame. Likewise, the experience of powerlessness induces shame because it becomes associated with weakness and the inability to control one's life. The part of the developing self most damaged is the interpersonal self—the terrorized child feels shame in relation to others. He or she never learns basic trust and is unable to form the positive and satisfying attachments that build self-esteem.

It is not unusual for children to fear their parents at one time or another, but this is a by-product of the parent's inherent power, not the intention of their behavior. Terrorizing usually implies a deliberate intent to frighten the child through threat, but also includes situations where parents fail in their responsibility to buffer their children from scenes that should be recognized as too frightening.

The husband of a client liked to watch terrifying and graphically violent horror movies (e.g., "Nightmare on Elm Street," "Halloween") with their four-year-old daughter. The "payoff" was that the terrified little girl would sit in his lap and cling to him for comfort, making him feel manly and protective. Predictably, she began having nightmares and became preoccupied with violent images as reflected in play with dolls, e.g., "I cut your head off!" and "I kill you!" He blamed these problems on his wife and me for calling attention to the potential harm he was inflicting. Blaming is here a defense against shame by removing it from himself and sending it to someone else. He declined an invitation to come in and discuss the issue, so I informed my client that unless the practice stopped immediately, I would report both of them to Children's Protective Services for psychological mistreatment. The terrorizing stopped, but my client, bowing to pressure from a controlling husband who now "hated" me, terminated therapy prematurely.

This father, like most parents who terrorize their children, was re-enacting frightening scenes from his own childhood. He was regularly forced to fight as a youngster, and beaten and shamed by his father when he lost. On an unconscious level, he was giving his daughter what he desperately needed as a child, namely protection and comfort. However, in order to re-enact his childhood scenes, he first had to terrorize his daughter. He did so by exposing her to frightening movies, a way that allowed him to preserve his image as a good father. His childhood scenes were re-enacted with his daughter recast in the role of the frightened child, while he pretended to play the role of the protective parent. By switching roles, he temporarily freed himself of fear, and shame over feeling fearful.

Fathers are far more likely to terrorize their children than are mothers. Men resort to such tactics because it is a way to establish dominance and control, and because men are socialized to be more aggressive. Terrorizing is a means to an end, namely getting the child to do what he wants. Such fathers are not mature men, but frightened little boys in the bodies of grown men. Their shame is fueled by feelings of impotence and insecurity. They are typically rigid, suspicious, easily slighted and quick to respond with anger that is way out of proportion to the situation. By using terrorizing tactics they make themselves feel more secure about their manhood, as if to say "I am not weak and afraid, I am fearsome."

Men who terrorize often batter their children as well, but this is not always the case. Like the parent who batters, he will often feel secondary shame about stimulating fear in a defenseless child. This does not stop him, but instead generates more shame and thus the need to transfer more shame through more terrorizing. By making the child feel powerless and out of control, he feels powerful and in control, e.g., free of the shame he associates with his own weakness and vulnerability. His wish to feel invulnerable is a wish to avoid further encounters with shame.

Women are characteristically more empathic and respectful of boundaries, and therefore mothers are less likely to terrorize their children. However, some mothers will marry a terrorizing spouse and fail to protect their children because of an unconscious emotional payoff in seeing her child victimized. This happens when the victimization is a re-enactment of her own childhood. Then, her childhood scenes are recast with her child in the role she once played and her husband playing the role her terrorizing father once played. By being passive, she can jump in and comfort the child after the psychological wound is inflicted.

In the "drama triangle," her husband is the persecutor, her child is the victim, and she is the rescuer. She is compelled to repeat the drama of her own family of origin, but does so in a way that preserves her self-image of being a good mother. By rescuing her frightened children, she is likely to be seen as the "good guy," or favored parent. Parenting alongside a husband who terrorizes can make any mother look good, and such women are looking for a way to bolster their low self-esteem. In fact, her passivity makes her a silent partner to the terrorizing father she pretends to oppose.

I once did family therapy with a terrorizing father, passive mother, and their three teenage sons. The father relied on threats and intimidation tactics to control his sons, and had on several occasions battered them. He was a big man with a booming voice and must have seemed like a fearsome giant to his children as they grew up. In the initial interview, I asked him if anyone had ever accused him of being a bully. He acknowledged that his need to be in control had isolated him from everyone, his sons in particular. There was a clear and stable cross-generational coalition in the family between mother and sons, with father on the outside looking in. He looked powerful to his sons, but was not. In reality, the only power he had was his ability to get the boys to do menial chores, and he had to rant and rave like a fool to get them to do that. He felt trapped in a powerless position and wanted out. He realized that making his sons feel powerless did not increase his power; it increased his isolation. His family history revealed that his own father had terrorized him with threats of violence, and beat him regularly. Over time, he was able to see the multi-generational legacy of terrorizing in his family, how he was passing it on to his sons, and how they would likely pass it on to his grandchildren someday—unless it was stopped. He was able to release enough shame so that he experienced an optimal amount, which led to a vow to change his behavior.

After several months of family therapy, he made a sincere and tearful apology to each of his sons and asked them to forgive him. Each son hugged him and it felt like the beginning of a new way of relating, a way based on forgiveness and love rather than grievances and shame. I felt privileged to be in on this very touching reconciliation, and was thinking how well things were going until I noticed his wife's facial expression. To say she was displeased would be an understatement. She immediately tried to sabotage the reconciliation by changing the subject and interrupting the flow of what was happening.

At the next session the couple arrived and at the insistence of the wife-mother, the three sons were left at home. She began by stating that the last session was a "complete waste of time." Her reaction was essentially a resistance to change in the family organization. As her husband moved out of his previous role as persecutor (bad parent), she lost her role of rescuer (good parent). Before this change occurred, she had joined her sons in a coalition that effectively isolated the husband-father. She needed to become a partnership with her husband and stop pulling her sons across the generational boundary that should separate the parental and sibling subsystems. The work shifted to focus on her unresolved childhood conflicts so she would no longer need to re-enact her family of origin scenes in her current family. In time, the couple strengthened and really supported each other in parenting their sons. The three sons, who had been aggressively in conflict with one another, began to bond in a positive way. The terrorizing stopped altogether.

Some clients report having been terrorized just upon awakening from sleep and before they were oriented and alert. At such times, the feeling of defenselessness is more acute. One client's initial complaint was awakening from sleep screaming and in a state of panic, a condition called "sleep terror disorder." She related the following: "My father was a cop and he liked to scare us kids when we were asleep. Several times I woke up looking down the barrel of a gun. I was so scared I couldn't move, couldn't scream...I knew he was crazy enough to kill me."

A male client prone to dissociation ("spacing out" as a defense against feeling overwhelmed), described the following scene that took place when he was six years old. "I woke up because I heard yelling coming from the kitchen. I went to see what was happening...and saw my dad threatening to kill my mother. He had his hands around her throat and was choking her. I was kind of in a daze and I couldn't believe my eyes! He saw me but he was so drunk it didn't even slow him down."

A woman, who suffered a recurrent nightmare that a threatening man was in her house, reported this childhood scene. "I was in bed with a high fever. I must have been about five years old. While I was sleeping, my dad hung one of those life size Halloween skeletons on my bedroom door. As soon as I woke up I saw it. I didn't really know what it was, but I was petrified with fear!" This was not an isolated incident of poor judgment, but a deliberate pattern of intentionally stimulating fear. The same father once sneaked up on his children while they camped out and threw beer cans against a chain-linked fence to make them think a stranger was stalking their tent. The children ran into the house terrified. Another time, he forced his children to run up and knock on the door of a "haunted" house, despite their earnest belief that a witch lived inside and would get them.

Animal phobias (morbid fear of dogs, snakes, rats, spiders, etc.) almost always begin in childhood, and in many cases the phobic sufferer had at least one terrorizing parent. The implication is that the fear of the parent is displaced, or redirected from the parent to a less threatening object. This idea is supported by the finding that most phobics cannot recall a traumatic event that would explain their intense wish to avoid the dreaded object (Barlow, 1988, pp.225-226). In other words, most people who are phobic about snakes are unable to recall a bad experience with a snake where they would have learned to be so frightened. Somehow, the terror that is experienced in the presence of the threatening parent becomes associated with snakes, perhaps symbolically. The frightened child may be enraged at her father for terrorizing her, but it would be suicidal to rage at him. She feels powerless to control this part of her life and displaces her fear onto snakes (all children hear that snakes can be dangerous). The snake internally represents the fear of her rage and consequent fear of her father's reaction if she expressed it. This displacement lessens her feelings of powerlessness because snakes are seen as less threatening than her father. She has greater objective control regarding the feared stimulus (snakes) because, unlike the feared parent, she can avoid them (Middelton-Moz, 1989, p.80). The learned fear of snakes is less intense than the terror of her father because it can be predicted, controlled, and avoided (this is the unconscious intention of the defense of displacement).

Phobias involving specific situations can often be traced to direct traumatic conditioning that involves a terrorizing parent. One client who was deathly afraid of water was repeatedly thrown into a swimming pool by her father. He justified his actions by saying that she had to learn to swim and, by God, he learned by being thrown into the Mississippi River. Another client, afraid of heights, was held upside down by her father and dangled over the Grand Coolee Dam. It was only during the course of therapy that she learned he did the same thing to her siblings—it was a deliberate pattern of terrorizing. Still another woman, phobic about driving in a car, was taken on wild high speed rides by her father whenever he was angry with her mother.

Persons suffering form phobias feel intensely embarrassed about their fears. This leads to shame anxiety, or fear of being exposed and hence shamed. Shame anxiety in turn leads to shame as a preventive attitude, hiding out in order to avoid being exposed and hence shamed. This is nowhere more apparent than in cases of agoraphobia and social phobia, and a disproportionate number of persons suffering from such anxiety disorders were terrorized children. The agoraphobic is afraid of being in situations where escape might be difficult or embarrassing, e.g., being outside the home alone or in a crowded public place. Many become housebound for fear of having a panic attack in public, and thus embarrassing themselves. The social phobic fears doing something that could result in humiliation or mortification in a social situation, for example, being unable to continue speaking while in public. Phobics of all kinds attempt to avoid the dreaded object or situation in order to minimize the experience of being exposed and shamed. The root cause of this association of shame with fear is too often the terrorizing parent who first stimulated fear and then shamed the child for being fearful.

"You are powerless!" is the shaming message children internalize when a parent deliberately provokes fear, actively exposes
a child to a terrifying scene, or passively fails to buffer the child
from a terrifying scene when able to do so. The impact on a child
is to make her feel powerless and out-of-control. Having no
control over one's life causes a feeling of helplessness which is
experienced as a weakness, a source of shame. It reminds the
child of the terrifying helplessness of infancy, a time when one
would literally die were it not for parental care. In a state of
terror, the child re-experiences a primitive state of helplessness
and feels at the mercy of a parent who abuses power. In the
presence of a parent who is out-of-control, she may actually fear
for her own life or someone else's. Scenes that are supercharged
with terror are taken into the self and a core belief is formed..."I
am powerless!" Indeed, the child has no power, and is taught to
equate being powerless with being weak, thus generating shame.
As an adult, she comes to know herself as a victim—it is a part of
her identity. Without power, she develops a shamed sense of
self—that she is small, vulnerable, and powerless.

Message Ten: "You are Sinful!"
(The Brainwashed Child)

The brainwashed child is programmed to believe parental
religious beliefs that are dogmatic; that is, they are handed down
by authority and taught as if they were true and indisputable.
Brainwashing is here defined as the practice of indoctrinating
children so intensely and thoroughly that they uncritically accept
parental religious beliefs. This practice is not limited to back-
woods religious sects where the faithful are handling snakes,
rolling their eyes, speaking in tongues, and quoting scripture
from sunup to sundown. It happens to children whose parents
are dogmatic Protestants, Catholics, Jews, Mormons, etc. Brainwashing children is the practice in all religions that make their
belief system into something that is rigid, judgmental, and negative toward the natural self-expression of feelings and sexuality.
The effect of brainwashing is that the child feels inherently bad
and sinful.

Parents who brainwash their children were often indoctri-
nated into the same religion and consider it their sacred duty to

pass it on to their sons and daughters. Such parents were typically overcontrolled as children and are re-enacting childhood scenes by overcontrolling their own children. This attempt to get their power back, coupled with a desire to make their lives feel more predictable and secure, results in a desperate need to feel in control. They become, in the words of Swiss psychoanalyst Alice Miller, "poisonous pedagogues." A pedagogue is a dogmatic teacher, and brainwashing parents teach and demand unquestioning obedience in a conscious attempt to break the child's will. The rules to be obeyed are that parents are always right and God-like and that children are undeserving of respect. These rigid rules give the parent the illusion of being in control, but at the expense of the child's normal development. The child learns that being emotional is unacceptable, and that being sexual is immoral. These life-negative messages leave children with the belief that they are bad, unloved, and sinful.

By comparison, more respectful and flexible parents wish to introduce their children to a religious belief system, but one that is more tolerant of different beliefs. Their God is presented as more loving and forgiving than the brainwasher's God, who is fearsome and judgmental. They have no need to indoctrinate their child into any particular religion, or any religion at all. They affirm their child's right to express himself and allow him to question their personal beliefs. It is okay for the child to doubt that Moses really parted the Red Sea or that Jesus walked on water. The child is secure in knowing that he will be "seen and heard," and that his need for information about God or spirituality will be met. When the information is in, the child is allowed to decide for himself how he will practice his own spirituality, or eventually raise his own children. The parents are accepting of the possibility that he may choose a belief system that is different than theirs. The child is affirmed as basically good and taught that being fallible is what makes us human. I am reminded of a night, after saying a bedtime prayer with my four-year-old daughter, when I asked her for her thoughts about God. "God is a woman who lives in a motor home in the sky and eats carrots," she answered. To tell her she was in any way wrong would be arrogant and shame-inducing.

Parents are sources of information and children need to identify with them in order to establish their sense of belonging in the family. This need gives the parents enormous power to teach and transmit their own beliefs to the impressionable child. Brainwashed children are not allowed to challenge their parents over religious matters. And what is taught in brainwashing families is religiosity rather than religion. "Religiosity" is the quality of being excessively and unreasonably religious. Such families make a show of being religious for the purpose of managing other people's impressions, especially the minister and congregation. What others think is of paramount importance and brainwashing parents expect perfect adherence to unreasonable rules of "moral" conduct, e.g., "Always honor your parents" or "Never masturbate." Religiosity becomes an obsession, and religion becomes too much a part of the family identity. The show of being religious can serve as a mask behind which one can hide deep shame.

Religiosity and dogmatism encourage the child to see the world in black and white, e.g., "Our religion has the absolute truth and all you poor, misguided others are in deep trouble on the Judgment Day." This arrogant attitude is actually another defense against shame. It says "I'm righteous, and you're not." Religiosity polarizes and alienates by separating people into antagonistic groups. Instead of practicing love for one's fellow man, and tolerance for different beliefs, it cultivates an "us versus them" consciousness. It is not surprising that brainwashed children feel isolated and different. Many are actually prohibited from playing with children from families of different religious persuasion. Compare this attitude to that of the Sufi mystics who teach that all religions are like different beads on the same string, or different notes in the same divine orchestra.

Robert Trask gave a presentation appropriately entitled "God's Phone Number: Repairing the Effects of Religious Fanaticism" (US Journal, 6th Annual Regional Conference on Adult Children of Alcoholics, 7/28/89). He spoke of fulfilling his mother's wish and entering the seminary at age thirteen to become a Catholic priest. As an example of religious fanaticism he related the following story: On his fifteenth birthday, he accidentally killed his fourteen-year-old cousin in a hunting accident. His cousin was Baptist so, "Like a good Catholic, I took water from the stream and poured it over his bleeding head, and I said, I baptize you in the name of the Father, Son, and Holy Ghost." Only then did he know his dying cousin's soul was saved and would go to heaven instead of hell or purgatory, because he was now a Catholic. He went on to say that as crazy and fanatical as that now sounded to him, there was a part of him that still believed it—"It becomes a part of you...a part of what you are." This is the essence of being brainwashed. The dogma becomes a part of your identity.

A belief shared by most brainwashing parents, regardless of religion, is that sex is bad and immoral. Any expression of sexuality by the child is especially bad. The healthy exhibitionism that is important to the development of the young child is squelched and replaced by shame about the body. The child learns to be pathologically modest. It is sinful to either expose his nakedness or see another's nakedness. The message is clear. The body is a bad thing and is to be hidden to avoid shame. If the child is caught touching his genitals, he is shamed for masturbating. Exploring or pleasuring himself in such a way is strictly forbidden and usually met with a message such as, "Shame on you!" If the child is caught in normal, age-appropriate sex play with peers, punishment is swift and shaming. He quickly learns to equate sexuality with shame and experiences a "sex-shame" bind, i.e., whenever he feels sexual impulses he will automatically feel ashamed. As he matures and experiences strong biological drives, his shame is intensified. Sexual impulses that are too strong to suppress will result in self-disgust. He has an approach-avoidance conflict. There is a split in his self. Part of him wants to be a saint and another part wants to be a sinner. He feels sexual and spiritual shame. This is a troubling time and he needs support and information. But sex education is a taboo subject because it is embarrassing to the parent. The message is that sex is so shameful it can't even be discussed. Such parents rarely inform their teenage children about birth control; they rely on shame and fear as deterrents to sexual activity.

It is hard to believe, but fathers who are excessively religious often act-out incestuously with their daughters, especially when the family is socially isolated. They may thunder against those who sin, but this is a defense against the disowned part of themselves that wants to sin. As they deny their own sexual impulses, the internal pressure builds and they become child molesters. They are the worst kind of hypocrites. They preach the need to resist sexual temptation and the evil of sex outside of marriage, then molest their own children. This may be due to: (1) how repressed and sexually needy they are, (2) an expression of their need for obedience and power, (3) a re-enactment of their own childhood scenes, or (4) some or all of the above. Regard-less, the combination of brainwashing and molestation is one of the most confusing and shaming messages a parent can inflict. Remember Ellen, whose father, a minister, fondled her breasts. When asked to use three adjectives to describe herself, she gave "bad, confused, and empty." In a letter to her father, she de-scribed her life after incest as a "living hell," and added, "I resisted a faith if you are to be a representative of God. I want no part of it."

When children are molested in "religious" families, they often feel both spiritually shamed and abandoned by God. Some de-velop an aversion to religious life. Others may become even more religious than their families in an unconscious attempt to atone for what they believe to be sexual sins. They may develop a religiously based aversion to sex and become sexually dysfunc-tional or even celibate in adulthood.

"You are sinful!" is the shame-inducing message children in-ternalize when parents program them with dogmatic religious beliefs. The child's need to identify with the parent and belong in the family gives the parent absolute power to teach and transmit the dogma. Excessively religious parents are rigid, over-controlling, and negative to the natural expression of feelings and sexuality. The message to the child is that he is bad and full of sin. Children are easily convinced of their sinfulness because they are psychologically naive and highly suggestible. They take in scene after scene that conveys the message that they are fundamentally (pun intended) bad and sinful. Eventually, they form a core belief about the self..."I am sinful!" This belief is deeply ingrained and resistant to change because their indoctri-nation has been so intense and thorough. As a result, the inter-nalized spiritual self is so punitive that the sexual self is completely split off and disowned. This split within the self is one aspect of the deeply shamed sense of self—that the self is wicked, immoral, full of sin.

Message Eleven: "You are Deviant!"
(The Corrupted Child)

The corrupted child internalizes a parental message that he is no good, deviant. He is "mis-socialized" by the corruptive parent who reinforces antisocial behavior, especially in the crucial areas of aggression, sexuality, and/or substance abuse (Garbarino, Guttman, and Seeley, 1986, p.28). By not setting limits or modeling socially acceptable behavior, the parent creates a deviant. This can occur as the result of either too little or too much shame. Too little shame and the child never knows when he is lacking, never knows when he has injured another person or morally stepped out of line. His parents model behavior that reflects a "swiss-cheese" conscience, and that is what he internalizes. He acts shamefully and appears devoid of guilt over his bad behavior. Too much shame and the parent-child attachment bond never forms, leaving the child ashamed, enraged, and rebellious. He does not identify with his parents and refuses to take in their limits and values, assuming they set limits and uphold values. For some children, society can substitute for family and provide conscience development where parents have failed. But for the corrupted child with too much shame, there is such intolerable shame and bottomless rage that he wishes to gratify no one. He is mad at the world and wants to get even. Revenge becomes his reason for being.

Corruptive parents typically have problems with control of impulses and aggressive behavior. There is likely to be a multi-generational family legacy of substance abuse, juvenile delinquency, and criminal behavior. The hidden agenda of such parents, usually the father, is to transfer his shame to the child rather than socialize him. The child is encouraged to show deviant behavior, and when he does, he becomes the container for parental shame. The shame has transferred from father to son, from "outlaw" to "outlaw-to-be." The mother is also irresponsible and participates in the mis-socialization process. She is often from a shame-based and antisocial family and re-enacts childhood scenes with her children recast in the role she or her siblings once played.

Other parents, who are less overtly antisocial, encourage their children to act-out their own disowned parts. A father who is covertly aggressive might subtly encourage his son to initiate fights or show physical cruelty to animals. When his son acts-out his disowned part, the father gets vicarious satisfaction and relief from his own shame. He may feign disapproval, but also gives subtle encouragement, e.g., "Boys will be boys!"

In other words, a parent who appears to act in socially acceptable ways may induce their child to act-out their own unacknowledged parts. One client shamefully disclosed how she, as a high school girl, "pulled a train" (a slang expression for having intercourse with multiple partners in one night). She lived in a small town and decided to tell her mother before she found out through the "grapevine." To her surprise, her mother was far more curious than upset, and even seemed excited by her daughter's promiscuous behavior. The gist of her response was, "I'd have never had the nerve to do that. Tell me what it was like." This corruptive mother induced her daughter to act-out her own secret and unconscious desire to be promiscuous. My client got the reputation of being "the town slut" and, believing herself to be "damaged goods," was extremely vulnerable to sexual revictimization. She was regularly raped on dates and eventually became a prostitute. This completed the process of becoming the container for her mother's unacknowledged and unhealed sexual shame.

Corruptive parents lack internal boundaries and this results in repeated violations of their children. Such parents have a low tolerance for frustration and a high need for excitement. The combination leads to the defense of acting-out. By acting impulsively and without regard for negative consequences to their children, they become terribly abusive. Acting-out aggressive or sexual impulses is a way of humiliating others and transferring shame. When such a parent loses control of aggressive impulses, he uses his child as a whipping post. When he loses control of sexual impulses, he exploits his child as a sexual object. Hence, the corrupted child is often battered and/or molested as well. Unlike children who are battered and/or molested, but not corrupted, the corrupted child is a much higher risk to become a batterer or molester himself, especially if that child is a boy.

Boys who are victims of physical or sexual abuse are far more likely than girls to re-enact abuse scenes by acting them out. Typically, this will take the form of playing the victimizer with another person recast in the victim role. In this way, the once innocent victim is transformed into a deviant victimizer. Boys more often identify with the victimizer as a defense against anxiety and shame, thus they are more likely to develop deviant behavior. Girls more often defend themselves by making a sacred vow not to be like the person who victimized them. The shadowy part of the self that unconsciously wants to victimize others (both roles are learned) is disowned, hence their magnetic attraction to men who victimize. In this way, they have a relationship with, and often attempt to control, an unwanted and disowned part of themselves. They re-enact childhood abuse scenes, not by victimizing, but by entering into relationships with someone who will revictimize them, or victimize their children, the way their parent once did. For every girl with deviant behavior, there are probably five boys with deviant behavior. Adoption studies show that there are genetic factors at work here and this may help account for the preponderance of deviant or antisocial behavior in males.

The damage to the self of the corrupted child is primarily to the interpersonal part, resulting in shame over relationships. As he grows up, he becomes a con man who can be as superficially charming as he needs to be. He treats others as short-term suppliers of his needs and sees manipulation and counter-manipulation as a way of life. As he uses and abuses others, his shame accumulates. He typically acts self-centered and entitled, i.e., "What's in it for me?" and "The world owes me a living." His parasitic attitude and lifestyle alienate him from the society at large. He realizes he is a misfit who is disliked even by people who don't know him. Deep down, he feels he is a social defect. Deeper down, he may even feel spiritual shame regarding his lack of a moral value system.

A corruption message is reinforced when the child is allowed or encouraged to act in antisocial or deviant ways. These messages lead to early behavior problems, at home and at school. He lies, steals, vandalizes, skips school, runs away, starts fires, and starts fights. He grows up believing he is exempt from the rules of society. He observes the corruptive parent and has no idea of what would constitute socially acceptable behavior. He becomes unfit for normal interpersonal relationships because he has no guilt, no internal controls. As his behavior begins to deviate from social norms, he is labeled deviant by teachers,

peers, police, even the parents who corrupted him. Once labeled, a self-fulfilling prophecy is set in motion. He is treated like
a deviant, and expected to act like one, so he does. His lack of
socialization leads to deviant behavior in the areas of aggression,
sexuality, and substance abuse.

Aggression is learned young because his parents rely on physical punishment to control him—they don't really discipline, they
retaliate. It is their excessively punitive attitude that humiliates
him. He is caught in a bind. His parents model and encourage
deviant behavior, then inflict pain or suffering when he acts-out.
One client told me how his father ordered him to "beat the shit
out of that 'nigger' boy on the football team!" Too afraid to defy
his father, he did and was expelled from school. For getting
expelled, his father made him choose a willow branch and then
whipped him with it. Confused and full of shame and rage, my
client learned to use aggression as a way of controlling or humiliating others.

A number of male clients have described how they were
encouraged to engage in sexual behavior before they were anywhere near ready. This corrupts a child. When they then get in
trouble for their sexual behavior, usually molesting little girls,
they are labeled deviant. This form of acting-out is an attempt to
resolve a sexual conflict, more often due to overstimulation than
to being victimized. One client described how as an eleven-year-
old he had access to his father's collection of hard-core porno-
graphic magazines. Looking through these magazines
overstimulated him to the point that he became obsessed by
images of naked men and women engaged in sex. He became a
compulsive masturbator and, as a teen, molested several young
girls. He eventually became bisexual and felt deeply shamed
about his sexual self.

A client who became a prostitute told how as a ten-year-old
she was allowed in her parents' bed during sex. Their lack of
boundaries was a form of disguised sexual abuse and she became
preoccupied with sex. She learned no sense of modesty and
began dressing provocatively to call attention to her precocious
sexuality. By age thirteen she saw her sexuality as a commodity
she could barter for attention, affection, drugs or money. Boys
would fondle her breasts in the hallways of junior high school
and give her marijuana for performing more intimate sexual

favors. In modeling herself after her parents' deviant behavior, she developed deviant behavior herself.

Other parents corrupt children by allowing them the use of alcohol and other drugs before they are mature enough to make responsible choices. A client who kicked a heroin habit told how she was regularly given alcohol as a preschooler and would entertain her parents with drunken puppet shows. Another client told of parents who made no attempt to hide their marijuana smoking and how she would get "high" from being in the same smoke filled room. As an adolescent she saw drugs as the only way of dealing with stress. Since her parents had modeled no effective coping skills, she coped in the only way she knew how. In her words, "I got a bad reputation as a druggie in high school, but that only made the problem worse." Shame is less painful when one is anesthetized or mood-altered.

The corrupted child who becomes a substance abuser often stabilizes their shame-based family. His drinking and drugging may serve to regulate another part of the family system that is not working. For example, substance abuse may detour, that is, distract attention from his parents' unsolvable marital problems. The child is triangled into the marriage in order to defuse tension. Family therapists know that young substance abusers in recovery are often sabotaged by parents who need him to continue acting-out. Many such families even get "high" together, especially when the drug of choice is alcohol.

"You are deviant!" is the shaming message children internalize when their parents reinforce behavior that is considered antisocial by society at large. The corrupted child is never given the controls over aggression, sexuality, and substance use that would make him a good citizen. He begins to act-out to defend himself against anxiety and intolerable shame. As he violates social norms, he is labeled deviant. He is always in trouble, so he believes it and plays the part. The deviant label is taken into the self and a core belief is formed..."I am deviant!" This belief is reinforced whenever he is confronted with his socially unacceptable behavior. But confrontation does not motivate him to change his ways—it intensifies his shame. There is no conscience to plug into. And, there is hidden pressure from his corruptive parents not to change. Antisocial behavior stabilizes such families so his parents are invested in his not changing. So he continues to act-out which precipitates more shame and alienates him from the community as well. Knowing he is seen as an outcast, knowing he is disliked, he has very low self-esteem. It is not just that his behavior is unacceptable—he feels he is unacceptable. He develops a shamed sense of self—that he is bad company, no good, deviant.

Message Twelve: "You are Crazy!" (The Confused Child)

A child who is regularly confused by parental communication internalizes the message that he or she is crazy. The confusing parent verbally and nonverbally communicates in ways that create conflict and uncertainty. The most confusing communications are: (1) the double-bind, (2) mixed messages, (3) invalidating perceptions and feelings, and (4) offering contradictory versions of reality. Children rely on parents to make sense out of their experience, but each of these forms of communication does the opposite. They are confusing at best and crazymaking at worst.

Parents who repeatedly confuse their children are typically communicating in the same way their parents communicated to them. Such parents are inconsistent and unpredictable and create a chaotic environment for the child. Like most shame-inducing parents, they are overly invested in being in control and unaware of the conflicts they create. By making their child the carrier of the confusion and the craziness, they pass on their own shame.

By comparison, parents who communicate clearly and consistently produce children who have a good take on reality and an ability to understand themselves and others. By allowing and validating their child's feelings, they instill trust and a willingness to self-disclose intimate feelings without undue anxiety or fear of being shamed. Their children know where they stand, and if they don't, all they need to do is check it out. They are encouraged to ask questions, and are not afraid to ask for support.

A double-bind is the most crazymaking form of communication. In fact, it was developed as a theory of how parents induce schizophrenia in their children (Bateson, Jackson, Haley and

Weakland, 1956). A double-bind creates an unsolvable conflict. When a child is given contradictory commands by one parent, or when one parent contradicts the other parent's command, a double-bind occurs. The communication is confusing and anxiety-provoking to a child because he is put in a no-win predicament. The child is bound because he is helpless and dependent and cannot leave his parents.

Here is an example of a double-bind. A young boy gives his mother a big kiss on the mouth before going to bed. She pulls away from him and makes a face, nonverbally communicating her disapproval. The following night he withholds his kisses and she says, "What? No kiss tonight? Are you angry with Mama?" He responds by looking puzzled and hurt, to which she says, "Don't be so oversensitive!" The boy is caught in a double-bind. If he offers a kiss, she pulls away as if he has done something wrong. If he withholds his kisses, she is critical. He can't win. He is bound because she is his mother and he needs her love. Parents in double-binding families cannot accept their own shame-based feelings so they hide them. In the example, the mother may be embarrassed by the level of intimacy offered by her son, however innocent it is. Rather than acknowledge such feelings to herself, and communicate her limits to him, she hides behind the disguise of the wounded mother. At first he feels confused, then anxious and angry, because he is bound and can't win. If the pattern is repeated often enough, he will eventually feel so conflicted and controlled that he experiences himself as crazy. The double-bind severs the attachment bond and thus activates shame.

Another confusing form of communication is the mixed message. It too is a contradiction that creates an unsolvable conflict for children. For example, "Stick up for yourself" but "Don't talk back," or "Next time ask me for permission," but "Don't bother me." A variation on this theme is the parent who teaches the "Do as I say, not as I do" message. What is a child to think if his parent says, "Smoking will kill you" and then lights up, or "Drugs are bad for you" and then pours a drink? How about, "If you hit your little sister again, I'll whack you good!" It is confusing to be a child and hear your parent say "Grow up!" just before he or she throws a temper tantrum.

One client told how her parents emphasized, "All we want from you is the truth!" but then would proceed to lie about her age to get her into the movie theater at a reduced price. Another client, a teenager, was urged by her mother to be more open and confiding. When she confessed a minor violation of the family rules, her mother grounded her for a year. Still another client found herself giving mixed messages to an ex-boyfriend and couldn't end the relationship which was abusive. I asked her to recall a scene from childhood where her parents gave her a mixed message. She recalled a time when she was ten years old and her parents told her they were divorcing (which they did). I quote..."Mom was sitting on dad's lap and they were kissing and hugging. Then, they told me they were going to get a divorce."

Mixed messages are not the same as double-binds because the child can choose to obey one message and disobey the other, or even point out the contradiction (Nichols, 1984, p.25). Still, the mixed message is confusing and when repeated often enough can cause a child to feel crazy. A client with a history of binge-eating followed by self-induced vomiting grew up with the following mixed message—her family believed that a plump child was a healthy child. In the rural Mexican culture, having a plump child was considered to be a sign that the parents were good providers and that their child was well cared for. She was encouraged to overeat and "clean her plate" and by age eight had become quite obese. Suddenly the message changed and she was no longer esteemed for being chubby. Now, she was placed on a strict diet and was constantly criticized for being overweight. Not surprisingly, she developed an eating disorder and her shame drove her to the brink of suicide. She felt confused and out of control during episodes of binge-eating, not realizing that this behavior was a symptom of a problem and not the problem itself. Although the consumption of food felt soothing and comforting to the child within, she felt totally confused and deeply shamed afterwards. She described herself as a "crazy maniac that should be put away!" One session we worked on a dream in which her body became so swollen she feared she would burst and die. She became intensely emotional and left the session embarrassed and a bit shaken. I offered a supportive hug which she accepted and seemed to appreciate. The following session I asked what the hug meant to her and she replied, "You think I'm okay, not crazy." Clearly, this was her greatest fear and her association with being emotional.

Another confusing form of communication occurs when parents invalidate the child's perceptions and feelings. Children can be talked out of what they see and hear and feel because they are suggestible and influenced by the family trance—trance logic allows them to believe things that don't add up. However, when children perceive what is happening and are told something else is happening, they experience total confusion. When they are not allowed to express "negative" feelings, or even have "negative" feelings, the confusion intensifies. The child learns not to trust his perceptions and invalidates (talks himself out of) his true feelings.

This form of communication is most evident in the alcoholic family system, where addiction and shame are inseparable. One client told how his drunken father would tumble down the stairs about once a week. The official explanation was that the top step was loose and poor dad fell. He bought it until he got much older and realized that no one else ever fell, nor did anyone ever attempt to repair the offending step.

Another client, Phil, watched his alcoholic mother's car weaving down the street before smashing into a tree. His mother got out of the car stumbling and looking disoriented. He knew she was drunk and walked her home so she wouldn't get ticketed for driving under the influence (codependent and enabling at age ten!). Later, both parents told him the brakes had failed and he began to doubt his first impression. He decided he must have been wrong; she must have been dazed in the accident. On other occasions, Phil would come home from school and find his mother on the verge of tears. She would verbally deny anything was wrong, but would continue to behave like she was very depressed, possibly even suicidal. If he persisted in drawing her out she yelled, "Leave me alone!" If he left her alone, he was criticized for being "selfish and self-centered." In our first session, Phil described himself as "certifiably nuts!"

Alcoholic parents invalidate their child's perceptions and feelings in order to maintain denial. Denial perpetuates the illusion of being in control and allows behavior that is out of control, such as heavy drinking, to continue. Problems that don't exist don't have to be changed. This denial is a house of cards. If one problem is acknowledged, the entire house comes crashing down. So the alcoholic parent is strongly invested in maintaining the denial and imposes his or her distorted reality on the child. At some level, the child knows there's an "elephant in the living room." But when no one validates that it can be seen, heard, and felt, he becomes hopelessly confused. If this pattern is repeated often enough, the child experiences intense conflict and begins to think of himself as crazy.

A final confusing form of communication occurs when parents give children contradictory versions of reality. In this instance, one parent tells the child that "ABC" happened while the other tells the child it was really "XYZ." The event that is being argued is always important to each parent's self-image and emotions are running high. The child is hopelessly caught in the middle.

Here's an example involving a family that was referred to me because of communication problems.

Don

Don came home late and found the front door locked. Believing his wife Marilyn had done it to spite him, he broke in the door. A loud and drawn out fight ensued that awakened their only child. It ended with Marilyn pointing a gun at Don and calling the police. When the police arrived the child overheard each parent present diametrically opposite versions of what had happened. The child didn't know who to believe and became hopelessly confused. The police didn't know who to believe so they arrested both parents for domestic violence. When I heard their opposite versions of what happened, I didn't know who to believe either. Both were very convincing and I felt quite confused myself.

This form of confusing communication is used by parents who need to be right in order to avoid the shame of being wrong. Blaming is one of the cornerstones in crazymaking families and serves to protect each parent's self from shame. If the other parent is always to blame, the self feels righteous and vindicated of wrongdoing. Children are pressured to form coalitions with each parent against the other. The child is caught in the middle. He experiences a conflict of loyalties and feels pulled apart at the seams. If he sides with one parent, he is at odds with the other. It's another no-win predicament. When parents repeatedly contradict one another's reality, the child loses his reality-testing. He never learns to objectively evaluate and judge people around him.

He cannot trust either parent, nor can he trust what he perceives with his own senses. He experiences his distrust as feeling crazy.

"You are crazy!" is the shaming message children take in when their parents repeatedly confuse them. The child feels caught by messages that conflict and is bound in a no-win predicament. Children lack the psychological sophistication to understand that their parents are double-binding them, giving mixed messages, invalidating their perceptions, or offering contradictory versions of reality. The child has no clear or consistent reality coming in, no way to make sense out of his experience. All he knows is that he feels confused and torn by conflict. Scenes of being confused are internalized and a core belief is formed..."I am crazy!" Strange as it may seem, this belief provides a way to finally make some sense out of what is happening. "Of course I'm hopelessly confused," he reasons, "I'm crazy." There is some added security in thinking that he is the crazy one, not his inconsistent and unpredictable parents. Not surprisingly, some confused children quite literally go crazy and lose their ability to test reality, e.g., they hallucinate or form delusional (false) personal beliefs. But, for the most part, the confused child simply refuses to trust or make himself vulnerable in relationships. Relationships are too confusing and only further lower his self-esteem. Isolating himself makes perfect sense when we consider the damage to the interpersonal part of the self. He feels shame about relationships because he is disconnected from himself and others. Avoiding intimacy protects the confused and hidden true self from further shame and harm. He has developed a deeply shamed sense of self—that there is something radically wrong with him, that he is crazy.

Chapter Three

Shame-Inducing Parental Rules

Families are governed by rules or regulations that determine how people act and interact. Families need rules in order to function and children need rules to develop a conscience and social skills. Family rules and parental rules are not always the same because parents may or may not follow the rules they set for their children. In many shame-based families the norm is "Do as I say, not as I do." For example, a parent may be allowed to express angry feelings, whereas his or her child is expected to squelch anger and stay silent.

Parental rules control what children believe, how they feel about themselves, and how they relate to others. Parents who induce too much shame typically have an inordinate need to control their children. Imposing and enforcing the rules gives them an illusion of being in control, and thus being powerful. This need is a reflection of massive insecurity and unresolved shame. Being in control allows the parent to transfer shame to the child and feel less vulnerable to further shame experiences.

In the shame-based family, shame is the organizing emotion, the common ingredient in all the rules. The rules discussed in this chapter are based on shame, induce shame, and perpetuate shame. Because they are continually in effect, rules that shame result in accumulations that are poisonous to the developing self. The child is overdosed and internalizes too much shame.

Parental rules may be spoken or unspoken, conscious or unconscious. Children are aware of spoken rules and generally unaware of unspoken rules. Spoken rules are conscious, that is, they can be reflected upon and challenged. Unspoken rules are usually unconscious, that is, they operate outside of awareness where they cannot be thought over and challenged. Both spoken and unspoken rules have the potential to induce shame by severing the attachment bond between parent and child, and by blocking the development of a healthy self.

Consider a common parental rule, "Don't be selfish." This rule is usually spoken aloud and is conscious in the child's mind, but some parents communicate it in a way that makes the child feel selfish anytime she places her needs first. It induces shame because it tells her she is bad, thus severing the attachment bond. If it is repeated often enough, she will develop a shamed sense of self—that she doesn't deserve to get her needs met. If she denies her own neediness in order to follow the rule, she is likely to become a caretaker. Then she will project her unacceptable neediness into others and care for them. Caring for others will make her feel needed, thus compensating for low self-esteem.

Because they are never processed, unconscious rules are especially harmful. They are followed blindly out of fear and misguided loyalty. Consider the unspoken rule, "Don't reveal family secrets." Although some children are told aloud..."Don't air your dirty laundry in public," this rule is usually unspoken and unconscious. A child who is taught to guard family secrets will believe that his family is bad, that there is something to hide. He feels shame by association. In order to keep the secrets, he must isolate himself, because getting too close to others might mean revealing something he shouldn't. Unable to ask for help, he can never get the support he needs to release his shame. He is stuck because he never reflects upon or challenges the rule.

Parents transmit rules through role modeling and by communicating shaming messages. Children learn rules by observing their models and by taking in shaming messages. Recall that a shame-inducing message is a suggestion that defines the child self in a negative way. A shame-inducing rule is a command that controls the child's emerging repertoire of behaviors in a way that damages the child self. Shaming messages become, in effect, commands to give up certain behaviors. A crying child, who is ignored, feels abandoned (shaming message) and learns to inhibit expressions of distress in the presence of his parent (shaming rule). The abandonment message makes him feel unwanted, and the "Don't express yourself" rule commands him to give up his right to self-expression.

Another example. A young boy observes his mother withdraw in silence rather than express her differences with an alcoholic husband. If this is a pattern, he may learn a rule that says..."Avoid conflict at all costs." He learns (by observation) that conflict is dangerous in his family and that differences are not allowed. This means that breaking the "avoid conflict" rule involves taking a risk. Suppose he confronts his drunken father for not taking him to the baseball game as promised. This violation of the rules is likely to elicit one of the twelve parental messages that induce shame, e.g., "You're gonna learn to keep your mouth shut!" followed by a slap to the face. The "You are unlovable!" message that goes along with being battered becomes a command to follow the rule. His emotional and physical wounds represent painful lessons that teach him how to interact in the family. Eventually, he will follow this and other rules to minimize the risk of being shamed in the future. It is shame anxiety, the fear of being exposed and humiliated, that prevents him from facing up to the conflict. However, learning to avoid conflict by concealing his feelings perpetuates his shame. He is likely to become an unassertive adult who sacrifices himself and ends up with no self to esteem.

The Denial of the Child's Rights

Children struggle to affirm basic rights in accordance with their natural life force and goal of survival (Johnson, 1985, p.25). What are these rights, and how do they become associated with parental rules? They are the right to be, the right to need, the right to make mistakes, the right to express oneself, and the right to separate. In a healthy family, where parents are respectful of children, these rights are affirmed. The parents say, in effect, you have a right to be, have needs, make mistakes, express yourself, and separate from us.

The affirmation of these rights leads to a set of clear, positive, and flexible rules. The rules are functional in that they bring about the development of a healthy sense of self in the child. For example, respectful parents convey messages that their child's feelings are valid and taken seriously. He is convinced his parents are emotionally available and that what he expresses will be attended to and acted upon. Expressing himself gets him what he needs, e.g., to be held, comforted, supported, forgiven, etc.

As he takes in scenes where his parents affirm his right to self-expression, he learns a rule that encourages him to express himself. He is being taught how to relate in a way that leads to effective coping and positive self-esteem.

In a shame-based family, these basic human rights are not extended to the child. The parents not only fail to affirm these rights, but actually deny their existence. The child interprets this denial as a command to give up his rights. For example, an angry little girl whose demand for attention is ignored gets the message that she has no right to express her feelings. The parent may feel impinged upon or threatened by her daughter's natural expressiveness. Regardless, the abandonment message severs the attachment bond and thus activates shame. The girl feels disappointed and frustrated and protests in ways that healthy parents would recognize as a signal to change the rule, but her parents are either unable or unwilling to do so. If they learned the "no expression" rule as children, it is likely to be the one they pass on. They ignore her feedback and continue to deny her right to self-expression. In time, she will be too afraid to risk further abandonment and will therefore deny her own right.

Being Loyal to Dehumanizing Rules

The child is caught in a no-win situation. He can continue to assert his rights and elicit the shaming messages that follow, or give up. He gives up as a matter of survival; it is self-protective. Unfortunately, in so doing, he becomes loyal to rules that dehumanize him. These rules deprive the child of basic human rights (e.g., self-expression) and human qualities (e.g., self-esteem). Somehow these rights impinge on the shame-based parent who then denies them, one by one, with unspoken rules. The five rules that induce and perpetuate shame are:

1. Don't be
2. Don't need
3. Don't make mistakes
4. Don't express yourself
5. Don't separate

There are many parental rules that are not on this list. However, they are likely to be variations of these five. For example, consider the rules named in the previous discussion. "Don't be selfish" is a variation of the "Don't need" rule; "Don't reveal family secrets" and "Avoid conflicts at all costs" are variations of the "Don't express yourself" rule.

The five main rules operate to some degree in all shame-based families, although different parents emphasize different rules. Which rules are emphasized is determined by which shaming messages are being communicated and which rules were handed down from the parents' families of origin. Consider an engulfing and belittling mother who views her daughter as an extension of herself and then demands perfection. She would be most likely to transmit the "Don't separate" and "Don't make mistakes" rules. This would be especially likely if the child's presence allows a rejecting father to escape the demands of an intimate marriage. In pushing his daughter away, he unintentionally pushes her toward the mother, who looks accepting and available (looks can be deceiving). If this combination of rules is a family legacy for either or both parents, they are even more likely to be emphasized. Both parents demand loyalty to the rules.

To review, parents shame their children not only by communicating shaming messages, but by imposing and enforcing one or more of the five shaming rules. Messages are suggestions that define the child's self and rules are commands to control the child's behavior. These rules reflect the negative messages that parents convey through their behavior. If the child breaks a rule, the parent responds with a shaming message. For example, a hungry child who is asking to be fed can be perceived as making a demand on the parent and breaking the "don't need" rule. The parent, who may lack the parenting skills to respond appropriately, may simply ignore the child and continue about his business. This is clearly neglect and as a result, the child takes in a "You are unimportant" message. When rule violations are followed by shaming messages, the child learns not to break the rules. Following the rules minimizes (but does not eliminate) the likelihood of being shamed, and protects the developing self against further harm. Children become loyal to parental rules because their emotional survival depends on it. Their loyalty is motivated by shame anxiety, the fear of exposing the self to a shaming attack. Remaining loyal to any of the five rules perpetuates shame.

Rule One: Don't Be

The "Don't be" rule is communicated when parents are hostile to the child's existence. It is the most shaming of the five rules and is most often communicated through either verbal or physical abuse. For children who are abused in both ways, the feeling of being unloved and unlovable is amplified. They have bruises on the inside and outside. It is usually an alcoholic or drug-addicted parent who communicates this rule, but may be the codependent parent who displaces the frustration and resentment they feel with their spouse onto their child. In any event, the transmitting parent is almost always handing down a rule that applied in his or her family of origin.

This rule is not communicated by all shame-inducing parents, only those most hostile to the child's presence in the family. Some parents who invoke other shaming rules would never think of transmitting this most harmful rule, but do just that under sufficient stress. Then it is seen in the parent's failures to provide essential care, in their lack of emotional availability, or in their efforts to sabotage the child's attempt to define a separate self. It may be unintentional, but it nonetheless denies the child's right to be.

The "Don't be" rule deprives the child of his very right to exist on the planet. It goes hand in hand with the messages conveyed by rejection, scorn, and battering. Such messages become, in effect, commands to disappear, in the form of an unconscious parental rule. We have seen how these messages induce shame and the "Don't be" rule does likewise. It is as if the parent tells the child, "I wish you weren't here. You have no right to be!" The child, needing acceptance as a valued member of the family, feels worthless and unlovable instead. His presence is a source of tension because he is unwelcome. If he cries, he is mocked or ridiculed. If he asks for help with his homework, he is ignored or refused. If he screws up, he is slapped, hit, or whipped. He can only conclude that his very existence is a mistake.

The Suicide Solution

It is not easy to follow a rule that says "Don't be". Since the child cannot really follow the rule, he tries to avoid breaking it by becoming invisible and not making demands on his parents.

He survives by becoming hypervigilant, ever watchful and alert for any trouble. He learns when and how to stay out of the way of the hostile parent. By doing a kind of disappearing act, he can, in effect, cease to be. However, behavior that is acceptable today might make waves tomorrow and the child cannot stay out of the way all the time. As a result, the child cannot altogether avoid the hostile parent and feels hated.

The child's reaction to the cold, hateful parent is shame in combination with rage. He fears that he will be annihilated (put out of existence) if his destructive rage is expressed directly (Johnson, 1985, pp.55-56). For this reason, rage is often turned back on the self, resulting in self-destructive behavior. Because he questions his right to be, and lives with unbearable pain (deep shame and hostile parents), the wish to die may outweigh the wish to live. He begins to contemplate suicide as a way of escaping from life and solving his problems. Teen suicide is almost always a loyal response to the "Don't be" rule.

This was clearly the case with a middle-aged client who had struggled with suicidal impulses from early adolescence. He recognized that his mother had been harsh and rejecting, but denied that she was hostile to his existence. Then, at a Christmas family get-together she told him..."You know, you were really a monster when you were an infant. I couldn't even get baby-sitters to stay with you. I used to lie in bed nursing you and thinking of how I could kill you. You're damn lucky to be alive today!" As he told me of his mother's disclosure, there was terror in his eyes, and he repeatedly emphasized that she was absolutely serious. Suddenly, his long history of suicidal behavior made perfect sense.

This is not an isolated example of a sick parent who felt murderous toward her child. At one time in my practice, I was treating two women and a man whose parents actually tried to kill them during childhood. One was thrown from a bridge, another strangled with an electrical cord, and a third suffocated with a pillow. Although each survived physically, all were emotionally scarred by these "Don't be" commands, and all three, at one time or another, attempted suicide. Two were able to recall the traumatizing scene, one had no recollection. She only knew about the incident because it had recently been described to her by her mother, who claimed to have rescued her at age two. She refused to believe that her father could do such a thing, and steadfastly maintained that it was a lie intended to turn her against him. She had always looked on her father as a "perfect parent," which made her mother jealous. In the course of therapy, she did a family of origin interview with her father who admitted the story was true. In the throes of a psychotic depression, he wrapped an electrical cord around her neck with the intent to kill her.

In such cases, and in ones where the "Don't be" rule is invoked less dramatically, the part of the person that wants to kill himself is a "stand in" for the parent who was hostile to his existence. The hated child is filled with rage, but instead of directing that rage to its source, he turns it back on himself. The suicide solution is a loyal response to the parents' "Don't be" rule and a way of ending a life of intolerable shame.

Robert

Robert laughed as he recalled his mother's motto—"If you want to be happy, don't have children!" He had heard it a million times and learned to laugh to hide his grief and shame. In his own words, he felt that "If I hadn't been born, mom wouldn't be unhappy, so I shouldn't be." His mother's inability to touch, comfort, or say "I love you" seemed to deny his right to exist. He failed in his attempts to be funny and win over his rejecting mother. He was regularly hit with a newspaper (as was the family dog, he joked). His mother constantly criticized him for being in the way. He was repeatedly told to "get lost" and, not surprisingly, he became a chronic runaway. He took street drugs with other runaways to numb the pain and get some sense of belonging. A family therapist might view his repeated attempts to run away as a loyal response to the parental rule, a misguided attempt to restore his mother's happiness. Juvenile court saw it differently and labeled him incorrigible.

By the time he was entering the difficult period of adolescence, the "Don't be" rule had left Robert feeling like an intruder in his own home. He had no sense of belonging or of being a valued family member. He contemplated suicide, but claimed he "didn't have the guts to do it." Seeing this as evidence of cowardice, he felt even more ashamed. At seventeen, he married as a way out of the home. He vowed never to have children, not because he wished to take his mother's advice, but because he didn't trust himself to be a good parent. When his young wife gave birth to a child a year after they married, he found himself saying "...Why on earth did I have a kid?" and sowing the seeds of shame in his own son. As his son grew up, he found himself hitting him with a rolled-up newspaper, re-enacting battering scenes from his own childhood. The "Don't be" rule was a multi-generational family legacy, and, like it or not, it was Robert's turn to pass it on.

Marie

Marie referred herself to therapy because of "no self-esteem," and "thoughts that I would be better off dead!" When I asked why she had come to therapy now versus a year or two ago, she reported that she had recently abused her young son by whipping him with a belt. The "Don't be" rule was also a legacy in her family and she wanted to stop it. Marie was a battered and terrorized child. Her alcoholic father used threats of intimidation and violence to control family members. Her attempts to stay out of dad's way (not be) were unsuccessful. He beat her for no good reason and humiliated her in the presence of her friends.

I asked Marie to draw a shaming scene from her childhood. It showed an imposing adult male whipping a little girl with a belt. I asked her what the little kid in the drawing was feeling and thinking. Her answer clearly reflected her abusive father's "Don't be" rule. She said, "I feel like I should never have been born," and burst into tears. It was the first time I had ever seen Marie cry. She recalled another painful scene where her father humiliated her at a poker party he was hosting. In front of his drinking buddies, he introduced Marie as "the only mistake I ever made."

In the next few sessions, she was able to understand how she was re-enacting childhood scenes with her own son, and how her abusiveness was fueled by shame. We focused on releasing her shame, and working through the grief and rage that accompanied it. She began to feel an emerging compassion for the shamed child inside herself and affirmed her own right to be. She also made a commitment to end the "Don't be" rule with regard to her son and to make amends for the harm she had already inflicted. A follow-up session three years after ending therapy showed that she had ended the family legacy and never battered him again.

Aftereffects of the "Don't Be" Rule

The "Don't be" rule reflects a family environment that is powerfully "depressogenic." Adults who learned this rule as children demonstrate what Seligman calls "learned helplessness" (1981). They expect others to mistreat them, believe they can do nothing to prevent being mistreated, blame themselves for the mistreatment, and internalize more shame each time they are mistreated. Their depression is tinged with despair and is characterized by the so-called "cognitive triad," that is: (1) they evaluate themselves in a negative way, (2) interpret their ongoing experiences in a negative way, and (3) have a negative view of the future (Beck, Rush, Shaw, and Emery, 1979, p.11). It should not be surprising that this combination of shame and helpless-hopeless depression often leads to suicidal ideas and behavior.

The impulse to take one's life follows the "Don't be" command of the internalized parent who was most hostile to the child's existence. The adult who makes an unsuccessful suicide attempt is turning unexpressed rage back on the hated self and, at the same time, is saying "Screw you!" to his parents. The suicide may be a fantasy solution to the problem of protecting the unloved and hidden true self from any further humiliation. In this way, the impulse to take one's life may actually come from a sympathetic or compassionate part of the self.

In cases where the "attempt" did not involve a lethal plan and where there was a high probability that someone would intervene, it is clear that the distressed person is making a plea for help. For example, one client took approximately twenty aspirin at a family get-together and locked herself in the bathroom. In her family, this was the only acceptable way to express that she desperately wanted help. In the "Don't be" family, it may be the only way to communicate the extent to which the self has been harmed.

Those who complete a suicide have several characteristics that can be directly attributed to the "Don't be" rule. First, they feel helpless and hopeless about healing the shame that has been internalized. Not only do they believe that they are beyond help, but they also believe they are undeserving of help. They don't see themselves as worth saving. Second, shame induced by parental hostility brings about losses that they believe cannot be retrieved, such as loss of childhood, family membership and self-esteem. As a result of the failure to form loving attachments, they see relationships as depriving and the world as a hostile place. They are pessimistic about getting back what was lost in the past or getting what they need in the future. Third, they want to pull the plug on awareness because it is simply too painful to tolerate any longer. All attempts to turn off the source of pain have failed, including alcohol, drugs, promiscuous sex, and other compulsive behaviors. There is typically a final blow to their self-esteem. It is often a divorce or loss of a job, and a feeling that every waking moment is filled with shame and helpless despair. Suicide begins to look like the only option that will work, the only way to end the misery. In the end, shame-motivated suicide is a misguided but loyal response to the rule that denies one's right to exist.

Although "Don't be" is the rule most associated with suicidal behavior, most adults who grew up under this rule merely withdraw inside the self and become indifferent or ambivalent about social relationships. Feeling unlovable, the adult who grew up with this rule neither seeks nor seems to enjoy close relationships. He believes that by getting close, especially romantically, he is setting himself up for more rejection and humiliation. Having been mistreated by his own parents, he cannot risk being vulnerable to strangers. Instead, he denies any longing for closeness and convinces himself that it is better to be alone. Unconsciously, he continues to follow the "Don't be" rule blindly, still in the family trance and still trying to be invisible. He is stuck in his shame because he feels too unworthy to be loved and too unsafe to ask for help. He sees the world as a hostile place, and he is cautious not to interact in ways that might confirm his shamed sense of self. He finds it difficult, if not impossible, to trust, and keeps others at a distance to protect himself. He is seen as cold and introverted, always withdrawing inside himself to defend against shame. Should he enter into a romantic relationship, or marry, the relationship is likely to be unstable, ambivalent, and distant. Emotionally, he keeps one foot in and one foot out, never wholeheartedly investing himself in the relationship. This strategy, which Guntrip called the "schizoid compromise," allows him to have just enough relatedness to avoid total isolation, and just enough distance to avoid any further damage to the self (Wood, 1987, p.79). This is usually interpreted as a fear of intimacy. It is not. He longs for intimacy. It is a fear of what might happen should he become intimately involved. It is a fear of exposing the needy, dependent, and hidden true self to further mistreatment. It is a fear of making the self vulnerable to more shame.

When parents fail to affirm the right to be, the shame wound that carries into adulthood is a deep one that requires extreme defensive measures. One such measure is the expression of rage. Rather than withdrawing inside the self for protection, the enraged person discharges uncontrolled anger in every direction, creating a protective boundary around the self. The best defense is a good offense! Rage becomes a part of the character armor that protects that person against further humiliation, and he is always on the lookout for a place to dump it. Jane Middelton-Moz calls this defense the "fire-breathing dragon boundary." It is effective in keeping people away, but at the cost of further alienating the "fire breather."

Paula

Paula, whose abusive parents communicated the "Don't be" rule, repeatedly became enraged with me, launching into tirades about what an incompetent therapist I was. I was stupid! I was sexist! I couldn't possibly understand what was going on in her life! She demonstrated a remarkable ability for locating my emotional buttons, and then pushing them. These attacks on my character represented an attempt to transfer her shame to me. Getting rid of her unwanted parts (e.g., feeling incompetent) allowed her to feel less exposed and ashamed as she revealed herself in therapy. She attacked me in the same venomous way her mother had attacked her and, at the same time, incuced me to become angry with her (thus becoming the "bad" mother). This defense, called projective identification, showed me how it felt to be her when she was a child. Because I took her anger without counter-attacking or abandoning her, that is, without inflicting more shame, Paula became convinced I really cared. She stopped attacking me when she understood that it was a self-protective, but self-defeating way of communicating how incompetent and unlovable she felt. It was extremely difficult for this deeply shamed woman to drop her defensive rage and allow me access to the vulnerable and hidden child self within.

Rule Two: Don't Need

The "Don't need" rule is transmitted when parents are unresponsive to their child's inborn and ongoing neediness. Infants need to be fed, held, diapered, dressed, bathed, soothed, and played with in order to survive. A nurturing parent is available on request. They are preoccupied (in a healthy way) with child care and prepared to meet the child's need for dependency. Such a parent is perceived and internalized as satisfying. The child's needs change as he or she passes through the different stages of development, but the satisfying parent is still there to meet them. These include the needs to be dependent, to be intimate, to be productive, to make sense out of the world, to be affirmed as unique and valued, and to experience choices in making life changes (Harper and Hoopes, 1990, p.41). When these needs are met most of the time, the child's basic right to need is affirmed.

The shame-based parent does not respond satisfactorily and his children are left with chronically unmet meeds. The child's extreme dependency and constant neediness impinge on such parents, who are either emotionally unprepared for the responsibilities of parenthood, overwhelmed by life stressors, or both. The "Don't need" rule is invoked and enforced to give the parent an escape from the child's dependency. It simply denies the child's right to have needs. This rule operates in most shame-inducing families, but is emphasized by parents who communicate neglect, abandonment, and rejection messages. These messages are, in effect, a command to stop being needy and stop making demands. The "no need" rule perpetuates the shame these negative messages induce. If "parents are conflicted about, threatened by, or chronically feel inconvenienced by their children's need for dependency, children believe that they are a nuisance, which leads to their feeling worthless. They experience doubt about their identity, worth, and value as people" (Harper and Hoopes, p.26).

Unmet dependency needs not only undermine the child's sense of satisfaction and security, but block normal development. The process of development is contingent upon parents meeting the child's ongoing needs for attention, approval, support, comfort, protection, discipline, and unconditional love. In order to develop a healthy sense of self, a child must believe: "I have the right to be dependent, express any and all needs, request that my needs be met, and expect my parents to satisfy me." This belief never takes hold when parents deny the right to need. These parents fail to impart to their children a healthy sense of entitlement, i.e., the child does not feel entitled to have needs met. This prevents the formation of a secure attachment bond with the parent and reinforces a shamed sense of self.

Shame-based parents cannot accept their child's neediness in part because they are so needy themselves. They are unable or unwilling to give what their own parents withheld from them so they deny the child's right to need. This denial frustrates the child, who protests to no avail. These protests are communicated through crying spells, temper tantrums, a propensity for accidents, and various forms of attention-seeking misbehavior. Healthier parents would understand these protests and change their responses in ways that would satisfy the child. But the shaming parent does not understand and continues the pattern of frustration and deprivation. They feel impinged upon and respond in ways that, in turn, impinge upon their child. The child's expression of dependency needs begin to elicit messages that transmit the rule—"Don't need."

It is too frustrating to continue asserting unmet needs, so the child eventually stops. Better to give up than to experience oneself as an imposition on the depriving parent. She gives up the right to have her needs met in exchange for the right to survive (Middelton-Moz and Dwinell, 1986, p.33). By choking off her neediness, she unconsciously wishes to become more acceptable and less vulnerable to neglect and abandonment. If she is not so demanding, then her parents are not so depriving, and she can maintain the fantasy of having the nurturing parents she desperately needs. To adjust to the loss of parental availability and nurturance, she decides: "I am not needy. I am needed" (Johnson, 1985, p.31).

The "Gifted" Child

The emotional abandonment of needy children by needy parents is what Alice Miller (1981) calls the "drama of the gifted child." The drama begins when parents, who were themselves deprived as children, look to their own children to meet their needs. What they really need, a nurturing parent, could only have been provided by their mothers and fathers during the critical period of their own childhood. However, this does not deter them from seeking gratification from their children. They discover in their own children what they failed to find in their parents; namely, someone who is attentive and willing to be used, who will never abandon them, and who makes them the center of their universe (p.35).

During early childhood, the "gifted" child becomes sensitive to her parents' needs and adapts to those needs. For example, when she protests her own unmet needs, she senses her mother's withdrawal. Abandonment messages, in effect, command her to back off. Mother is unconsciously transmitting the "no need" rule and her child is unconsciously learning it. At some level of consciousness she recognizes, "If I am needy, mother will withdraw love from me." To avoid being abandoned, she chokes off her need for dependency and adapts to her mother's need for no demands. To see her mother as unavailable induces shame and anxiety, so she tells herself, "I don't need...I will be loving and giving" (Johnson, p.31). She gives up her need for parenting, in the true sense of the word, and instead "parents" her needy mother and/or father.

This perverse role reversal promotes the development of a false self in the child. The false self is a collection of behaviors presented to the parents to protect emotional survival. It is an attempt to cope with parents who are unresponsive to her needs, or parents who force submission to their own needs (Wood, 1987, p.25). A young girl who is expected to meet her parents' needs cannot afford to present her true self. Showing her neediness and true feelings would threaten her insecure parents. Their punishing and abandoning responses would shame her and further harm her true self. For safety's sake, she becomes compliant and pretends not to be frustrated or deprived. She learns to act as if she is the daughter they want. She learns to hide her dependency. She becomes independent and "licks her own wounds." This false adaptation of the self hides the unacceptable true self and protects survival. There is always the hope that the true self may re-emerge and blossom in the context of a future relationship that is responsive and healing (p.38).

We see how the "gifted" child learns the "Don't need" rule out of necessity. The needy and vulnerable part of herself is disowned in order to avoid abandonment. She becomes a substitute parent to her own parents. This is more damaging than parenting her siblings because it constitutes a more complete abandonment by her parents. She supports her parents when they're needy, encourages them when they're depressed, and soothes them when they're anxious. If she does have siblings, she will relieve her parents of their responsibilities for them and take care of them too. As she crosses the boundary between her own and her parents' generation, her childhood is stolen from her. She loses her childlike spontaneity and natural self-expressiveness. She forfeits the carefree existence to which she is entitled. She is forced to hide behind a mask of responsibility and pseudo-maturity. She has no choice but to become a pseudo-adult, who takes care of herself and others. Her parents have transmitted a rule that has her believing she is more needed than needy.

Such parents may love their child, but for the wrong reasons. They love her because she is everything that their parents were not. They love her because she is loving, attentive, and respectful, and because the deprived child in them desperately needs her. Their love is conditional. The condition is that she renounces her true self and adapts to their needs (Miller, p.14). The false self she develops for protection is experienced as a shamed sense of self—she believes she is unlovable as she truly is, needy and dissatisfied.

A "Gifted" Child in the Making

Consider the unborn child of an expectant couple referred for marital problems. This firstborn child-to-be will enter an alcoholic family system and be parented by two persons who are themselves exceedingly needy. It is unlikely that this couple will be able to affirm their unborn child's right to need. The father-to-be, Tom, is a thirty-year-old practicing alcoholic. Gail, in her mid-twenties, is a codependent enabler and compulsive overeater. It is a fact that alcoholic and codependent parents are typically preoccupied with alcohol and the problems that result from drinking. They fail to develop the healthy preoccupation with child care that is characteristic of parents who satisfy their child's need for dependency.

Gail welcomes treatment because she wants Tom to stop drinking before their child is born. Both come from families with the "Don't need" rule; his was alcoholic, hers was dysfunctional due to father's workaholism and mother's depression. Neither had a parent who was consistently available, and both were clearly deprived. Tom expects Gail to make up for what his parents didn't give him and recently left her because she failed this impossible task. He returned because he "couldn't function without her." What this really means is that he is morbidly dependent on his wife. Between the lines he is saying, "I prefer to underfunction and need her to overfunction and take care of me." In a sense, Gail already has a child—Tom. She is a caretaker and he is a "bird with a broken wing."

This marriage is based on an "unconscious deal" (Framo, 1982) that goes: "I'll mother you, if you'll promise never to leave me. You act weak and needy, so I can feel strong and needed." To act out this reciprocal arrangement, Tom is irresponsible and unemployed, although he is bright and employable. Gail works, is overly responsible, and handles everything. The defense of projective identification is at work here. It allows Gail to get rid of her unwanted dependent parts which are projected into Tom. Tom projects his strong and competent parts into Gail for safe-keeping. He unconsciously fears that his self-destructive (bad) parts will destroy the good parts of him. Gail's parents shamed her for being needy and needed her to be strong. Tom's parents shamed him for being independent and needed him to be little and dependent. Thus, each recreates their family of origin and engages in behaviors and roles that are familiar.

In our first session, I asked Tom..."What will happen if Gail becomes preoccupied with child care and neglects you?" He responded, "I'm already jealous because I'm about to become number two. I'm being displaced by the baby." His tone is that of an angry little boy who will greet the new addition as a sibling rival. Tom is rejecting his unborn child while it is still in the womb, and he is likely to communicate an unfriendly, if not hostile, attitude as the child is being raised. The child's neediness will clearly impinge on him. Gail is so deprived and depressed that I question how responsive she can be to the child's needs.

After four sessions Tom and Gail announce they have decided to terminate treatment and do so against my advice. Tom has struggled through a shaky month of sobriety and assumes an "Everything's okay now" attitude. This is more than denial, it is a "flight into health," that is, a form of resistance to facing the shame and grief that underlies his alcoholism. Heavy drinking for Tom is a way of self-medicating to anesthetize intense emotional pain. It is both a symptom and an attempted solution to the unfinished business of his alcoholic family of origin. There is no way Tom would consent to individual therapy, so I strongly urge him to attend Alcoholics Anonymous. He flatly refuses.

I recommend that Gail start individual therapy to work on core emotional issues, primarily low self-esteem, fear of abandonment, over-responsibility, and placing her needs last. Her refusal is related to a fear of exposing and experiencing intense emotions, particularly shame and rage. She also fears that if she begins to recover, Tom will abandon her. I suggest she attend Al-Anon and Overeaters Anonymous to get some support, but this too is rejected. I promise her a follow-up call which I make several months after a baby girl is born. Tom has resumed drinking and is home about one week a month. Gail has returned to work full time at a day care center and is functioning as an overwhelmed single parent. She cares for the little kid in Tom and everyone else's children. No one cares for her, including herself. In her words, she is "exhausted and burned out." Tom and Gail's newborn daughter will more than likely learn to choke off her neediness and become a "gifted" child.

Aftereffects of the Don't Need Rule

Adults who learned the "Don't need" rule remain loyal to the rule by becoming caretakers and neglecting their own needs. Caretaking as a career is a misguided attempt to save the deprived parent and master their own experience of deprivation (Middleton-Moz and Dwinell, 1986, p.9). The caretaker is re-enacting scenes where she was forced to choke off neediness and parent her own parents. The caretaker says, in effect, "I will care for you in the way I longed to be cared for as a child, but wasn't."

Her unacceptable dependent parts are projected into others, and then cared for.

When childhood expressions of need are shamed (e.g., by eliciting parental abandonment or rejection), adult expressions of need automatically trigger shame. Kaufman (1989, p.66) calls this a "need-shame" bind. The need is bound by shame because it cannot be expressed without re-activating shame. For this reason, some caretakers become fiercely counter-dependent, that is, present themselves as if they have no needs and are unwilling to rely on anyone for anything. The counter-dependent person often believes herself to be the only competent person in the world, an arrogant attitude that defends against shame. In fact, she is unwilling to show her neediness or depend on others for fear she will again be abandoned. The rule has taught her that needs are bad and that she is unacceptable when she shows her needy parts. She projects these unacceptable parts onto some-one who needs her, and takes care of them. Caretaking is thus consistent with her fantasy that she is not needy but needed.

A caretaking woman, whether dependent or counter-depen-dent, is likely to attract a needy man (caretaking men find needy women) and then try to restore him to emotional health. She becomes a "woman who loves too much," obsessively caring for someone who is all take and no give (Norwood, 1985). She settles for a vicarious sense of gratification since she has never had her own needs met and does not feel entitled. In all relation-ships, she presents a false self out of fear that she will be rejected and abandoned if she asserts her true needs and feelings. The result is a persistent feeling of emptiness, deprivation, and resent-ment. She suffers low self-esteem because she has never been loved for who she truly is. She gets some feeling of worth because she is needed, but her relationships are based on a pretense, her false self. To the extent that she hides her true self, she cuts off her real source of power. And she must hide her true self because to expose her shamed sense of self would mean certain abandonment. She remains loyal to the "Don't need" rule because it is unconscious and because showing her neediness would lead to abandonment and shame.

Adults who were raised in a "Don't need" environment often remain dependent on others. Unless the right to need is affirmed in childhood, the adult can never truly be independent. The achievement part of the self is underdeveloped and has never been validated. Having never developed a sense of mastery, the dependent person sees the self as incompetent of independent living and must cling to others (the fantasy parents they never had) for survival. In relationships, they are passive and indecisive and elicit an overprotective attitude. They suffer an inordinate fear of abandonment and feel helpless if they are left by the person upon whom they depend. They have learned to be helpless because they see themselves in a no win situation. If they affirm the right to need and assert their independence, they will be abandoned. If they deny the right to need and continue clinging, they will be deprived.

Another aftereffect of the "No need" rule is to become prone to addictive states of all kinds. Deprivation in childhood sets the stage for addiction in adulthood. Having never internalized a need-satisfying parent, the deprived child is likely to develop an addiction in an attempt to either stimulate or comfort the self. The addiction is a substitute for what the child didn't get from the parent (I once worked at a drug abuse agency where addicts referred to heroin as "mother"). It is a substitute relationship. As one client, a compulsive overeater, explained, "Food was there when mom and dad weren't." If the child was ignored and understimulated, an activity addiction will most likely develop. He or she will then become compulsive in the areas of masturbation, sexuality, gambling, shoplifting, spending, or drug use (especially cocaine or other stimulants). If they were denied comforting and soothing, an ingestive addiction will most likely develop. The adult will then abuse food, alcohol, or drugs, (especially marijuana or narcotics that numb pain). Such addictive behaviors were often modeled by parents as the way to cope with shame, anger, fear, grief, or any negative feeling.

The addictive state is not the problem itself, it is an attempted solution to the problem, a way of escaping intolerable feelings. Being addicted is thus a symptom and a defense. The real problem is the inability to either stimulate or soothe oneself and cope with intense negative feelings. Addicted people feel desperate and driven because they have never internalized a need-satisfying parent and don't know what else to do. People have let them down. Since no one has proved to be dependable, they depend on some "thing" they can count on. To be addicted is to move away from people and toward something that is available and satisfying. Expecting to be disappointed and shamed in relationships, addicts turn to behaviors that make them self-sufficient. The compulsive behavior becomes the all-important way to fill the emptiness inside. Drinking, drugging, overeating, and other compulsions ward off depression, anxiety, rage, and shame that would otherwise be intolerable. They are also an attempt to protect the wounded and vulnerable true self from further harm.

Not all addictions are based on shame, but there is always a shame component that blends with other feelings, e.g., shame and grief in the alcoholic, shame and rage in the compulsive overeater. Obsessing over booze or food is a way of avoiding the deeper and more painful issues that motivate the addictive behavior. It is a way of keeping intolerable shame out of awareness. Unfortunately, the addiction reinforces the already shamed sense of self because the out-of-control person feels weak and inferior. She also feels exposed as bad and defective, especially if her addictive behavior is evident, e.g., the compulsive overeater who is noticeably overweight.

Rule Three: Don't Make Mistakes

The "Don't make mistakes" rule is found to some degree in all shame-inducing families. It is self-explanatory. If a child makes a mistake of any kind, he or she is immediately shamed. For example, the rule is transmitted when a parent says, "How could you be so stupid?" to a child who has just spilled her milk. The "no mistakes" rule leads to an overly cautious attitude and an inner sense of badness and incompetence. Since children cannot avoid making mistakes, enforcement of the rule represents a continual assault on their emerging self-esteem. Every mistake is evidence of deficiency, rather than an opportunity to learn or master a skill. Mistakes are unacceptable and the child who makes them is taught that he or she is unacceptable. The child never develops self-confidence or feelings of mastery. In their place are pervasive feelings of deficiency and a shamed sense of self—that they are not good enough.

The Parent who is Always Right

The "Don't make mistakes" rule is primarily enforced by the parent who is most invested in being right and making others wrong. A closer look will show that there is much that is wrong in his life, and that he is defending against shame. His intolerance of mistakes is an attempt to feel adequate and in control. He is a black and white thinker who sees two ways of doing things—his way and the wrong way. His eyes are God's eyes and he rigidly insists there is a "right" way to do everything. When his children do something the "wrong" way, he "puts them down." This expression aptly describes what happens to the child's self-esteem when the right to make mistakes is denied.

To the "no mistakes" parent, errors and mistakes cannot be corrected. They constitute violations of the rule and justify his criticism and blaming. He is known for expecting too much of his children, and the denial of their right to make mistakes is the most unreasonable expectation of all. He expects them to act like perfect little adults and labels them "bad" when they do otherwise. This places enormous pressure on the child and he or she learns to be cautious and serious. In a futile attempt to be loyal to the rule, and thus minimize the frequency of parental shame attacks, the child learns to squelch the true self. It is too risky to be spontaneous and have fun because such behavior may precipitate a mistake. It is impossible to really follow the rule because to be human is to make mistakes, but the child tries to minimize mistakes by presenting a false self that is overly responsible and perfectionistic.

Linda

I first saw Linda in 1980. My impression of her was that she had the look of shame. Her head was hanging, her eyes looked down, and her shoulders were slumped, as if she had been defeated by some unknown enemy. She was a small woman and her way of walking (tiny steps) made her appear even smaller, like a young girl. She had a history of repeated suicide attempts in her late teens and early twenties, some twenty years before, but she was again thinking about ending her life.

I administered the Minnesota Multiphasic Personality Inventory (a true-false test of personality and coping style) to determine suicidal risk and possible need for antidepressant medications.

In addition to severe depression and marked anxiety, her test profile showed her to be (1) overwhelmed by feelings of unworthiness and inadequacy, (2) insecure and self-critical, (3) likely to respond to shame by developing physical symptoms (she suffered migraine headaches and ulcers), and (4) from a family of origin that she perceived as critical and depriving of love and support. The test accurately described her deeply shamed sense of self as well as the source of her shame.

After only three sessions, she quit treatment (by phone) for reasons that were unclear to me. A month or so later I wrote Linda a letter saying: "I regret that in the sessions we had nothing really changed in regard to your self-esteem and depression. I don't believe I was of much help to you and I understand why you have discontinued your treatment. If you choose to re-enter treatment at some point in the future, I hope you know the door is open." I now realize Linda quit because she felt overwhelmed by shame anxiety and was terrified at the prospect of being exposed and shamed. She felt naked in the light of the personality test and my intrusive questioning. In my zeal to be helpful, I went much too fast, and this very private woman felt she was "seen" as defective. Thus, she did exactly what was needed to protect herself from further exposure; she hid her shamed sense of self by terminating therapy.

Five years later (to the day) Linda returned. After listening to her reasons for re-entering treatment, I explained that psychotherapy is an intrusive process and that feelings of exposure were good "grist for the mill" (something that could be used for personal growth). Then I admitted my mistakes with regard to our first round of sessions. I told her that I had learned a great deal about the experience of shame in the past five years and that this time I would be more respectful of her defenses and pace the work more sensitively. I told her that I would still make mistakes and might unintentionally activate shame, but that we could talk about such experiences and learn from them. My admission of making mistakes stunned Linda. She said she had grown up in a family where no one ever admitted to making mistakes and where one was expected to be perfect. The number one rule in her family was "Don't make mistakes."

The work focused on how she took in shaming messages in her family of origin. Linda described an overly responsible childhood where she was expected to act as a parent and care for four younger siblings. Like many firstborn, she learned to carry the family's need for high performance and perfection. The atmosphere in her family was so tense and stressed that the slightest mistake was often "the straw that broke the camel's back." At such times, both parents would seek refuge in the bottle so Linda had an understandable desire to eliminate mistakes from her repertoire of behaviors. Her mother, in particular, belittled her at every turn and caused her to feel inadequate. She was constantly criticized for the most minor infractions of family rules, e.g., "no elbows on the table." When something went wrong with the care and feeding of her younger siblings, or when one of them misbehaved, she was blamed and held responsible.

Linda reported a scene from childhood that encapsulated the "no mistakes" rule in her family. "I was six when something happened that convinced me I could never do anything right. It was a hot summer day and my best friend and I had a great idea. We made lemonade and sold it to some construction workers who were building a house in the neighborhood. The workers were really appreciative and paid us what seemed like a lot of money. I went home with a handful of nickels to show my mom. I was really proud of myself. Instead of praising me for what I'd done, she said, 'If you'd done it by yourself, you could have gotten all the money!'"

Little Linda felt deflated by her mother's comment and was convinced she had done something terribly wrong. The attachment bond between her and her contemptuous mother was broken and she felt ashamed. Without knowing how or why, she had broken the "no mistakes" rule. Based on this and similar scenes, she decided that mistakes were evidence of deficiency, proof positive that she was flawed in some fundamental way. She began to strive for perfection, not so much to earn parental love, but to escape criticism and avoid shame. Perfectionism became her primary defense against shame, an attempt to feel adequate. She learned the rule and denied her own inalienable right to make mistakes. Of course her perfectionism did not prevent her from making mistakes or feeling inadequate. It only made her more self-critical and perpetuated her shame.

Aftereffects of the "Don't Make Mistakes" Rule

Striving for perfection in adulthood is an unconscious attempt to compensate for a self that feels fundamentally flawed, inadequate, and inferior. The perfectionist becomes his or her own worst critic in a misguided attempt to protect the wounded and hidden true self from further harm. The parent who transmits the "Don't make mistakes" rule is taken inside the self. This happens because the child's mind is suggestible and listens to an endless stream of deficiency messages. Also, by containing the critical and unforgiving parent inside the self, the child gains an illusion of control. "If I am perfect and avoid making mistakes," reasons the perfectionist to be, "I will be less likely to be shamed in the future." A child trying to be perfect is not a child. They not only lose their spontaneous and creative true self, but childhood as well.

In families where love is conditional and based on parental expectations of superior achievement, children will strive for perfection in order to get validation and support. As a teenage anorexic explained to me, "If only I could measure up, mom and dad would stop putting me down and start loving me." Of course this strategy doesn't work because the reason such parents withhold love has nothing to do with their child's performance, or lack of it. It has to do with unfinished business, primarily unhealed shame from the parents' own childhoods. They expect their children to make up for their sense of inferiority by becoming what they aspired to be. If the child can win the spelling bee or hit a home run to win the game, the parent feels pride rather than shame. There is nothing wrong in taking pride in your child's accomplishments, unless that child is being pushed and used to make up for low self-esteem. In such cases, the child is burdened by the weight of the parent's grandiose fantasies and gets no validation for who he or she uniquely is.

Perfectionism is a curse that dooms the perfectionist to further failures and an even greater sense of inadequacy. It is a set up to fail because no one will ever attain perfection. Then, when they fail to meet unattainable expectations, the internal critic goes to town. One client, a perfectionist accountant who came from a "no mistakes" family, explained how he botched a client's tax return. I asked him for his first thought, his automatic reaction to making this mistake. It was..."You stupid son of a bitch!" I asked him whose voice this was, who was it he had on his back. He knew it was his father and recalled scene after childhood scene where his father had humiliated him for making mistakes. Like most adults whose parents denied the right to make mistakes, this man didn't know the difference between making a mistake and being a mistake. He had never taken in a forgiving parent and would castigate himself whenever he broke the "no mistakes" rule. Despite his obvious success as a professional, he felt like an impostor. Whenever he failed to meet his own perfectionist standards he would tell himself, "I am a failure!" A person who was more self-forgiving would say, "I failed at this task. What can I learn from this?"

Striving for control in adulthood is another aftereffect of the "no mistakes" rule. When a child is shamed for doing something so unavoidably human as making a mistake, he learns to distrust others. He also learns to distrust himself, since he sees his deficiencies get him into trouble. He learns that by being in control he is less vulnerable, less likely to be humiliated. The child mind reasons, "If I'm not in control, someone else is, and if someone else is, I'm about to be criticized or blamed." As he is shamed for making mistakes, he learns the role of victim (humiliated child) and victimizer (humiliating parent). As an adult, he may re-enact childhood scenes by playing the parent's role and criticizing the imperfections of others. By making others wrong for making mistakes, he makes himself right and feels in control. By controlling everyone and everything, he unconsciously wards off the next shame attack.

Feeling in control of self and others is a way of avoiding vulnerability. He sees others as trying to control him (even when they're not) and becomes a skilled manipulator in order to regain control. As he manipulates and controls relationships, he feels less vulnerable. At some point in time, he has made an unconscious decision that by avoiding vulnerability he can minimize the possibility of being further wounded by shame. Controlling others gives him an illusion of security and allows him to repress the shame of feeling weak, insecure, and frightened. To feel out of control is to feel like a vulnerable and dependent child, and must be avoided at all costs. He becomes fiercely counter-dependent. He develops a need to be in control that is ultimately a reaction to childhood experiences of feeling powerless. Control is an intoxicant that renders him invulnerable to further shame attacks.

In many shame-based families, the controlling parent is prone to episodes of loss of control. It is generally true that the more out-of-control the parent, the greater the need to control the children—providing the illusion of being in control. It is thus the substance-abusing or emotionally unstable parent who typically shows the most inordinate need for control. Yet these are the same parents who are the most inconsistent and unpredictable, so the child must assume control in order to survive. He becomes expert at avoiding positions of vulnerability and must therefore avoid close, intimate relationships. If he could not trust his own parents with his feelings, how could he trust someone else? He anticipates criticism and expects to be shamed in relationships, therefore he shields himself in the protective armor of control. Although striving for control and perfection are both defenses against shame induced by the "no mistakes" rule, both perpetuate shame.

Rule Four: Don't Express Yourself

Denial of the child's basic rights to expression is typically the central rule in the shame-based family. It is a confusing rule because parents typically give themselves permission to be self-expressive. The child sees his parents being expressive, at times inappropriately, yet he or she is told to be "seen and not heard." This is the rule on which the other rules turn and depend since it prevents a discussion of the rules, regardless of how nonsensical, dysfunctional, or shame-inducing they are. In other words, the "no self-expression" rule implies a rule about rules, namely, don't discuss them. It is similar to the "don't talk" and "don't feel" laws spelled out by Claudia Black in her pioneer book on children of alcoholics (1981). It is an all-encompassing rule that makes it impossible for the child to freely express thoughts, desires, needs, values, emotions, problems, and other facets of the self. Enforcement of this rule obviously severs the attachment bond that links parent and child, thus inducing shame in the frustrated and disappointed child.

The "no self-expression" rule is transmitted in several ways. First, the parent may object to the child's natural self-regulation, e.g., crying to show distress, and either withdraw from or punish the expressive child. A crying infant may be ignored or spanked, whereas an older child is told to "shut up" or face a spanking. A second way the rule is transmitted is through observational learning. Here, the child observes his or her parents avoiding expression when expression is called for. Children are perceptive and know when there is tension in the air that calls for expressive communication. When an immediate problem is avoided rather than confronted, the child learns to stifle expression. A third way of learning the rule is by deciding not to be like the shaming parent. Here the child observes a parent being expressive in a way that provokes shame, fear, and disgust. What is learned is a reaction to the parent's inappropriate behavior ("If I express emotions, I'll become like him"). It is a refusal to identify. For example, mom confronts dad about too many beers after work and gets her face slapped. Not only does the child learn to keep quiet, but he or she makes an unconscious decision to "never be like dad." After all, dad is being "expressive," and if this is what being expressive looks like, it is better to be non-expressive. The child confuses being expressive with being abusive, and follows the rule in a misguided attempt to avoid identification with the disrespected parent.

The Silent Victim

Each time the "no self-expression" rule is enforced it severs the attachment bond between parent and child, causing the child to feel cut off, unloved, and ashamed. This repetitive shame experience becomes associated with the expression of any and all emotions—anger, sadness, anxiety, etc. The angry child is counterattacked or told to "shut up," the sad child is ignored or called a "crybaby," and the anxious child is treated like a disappointment or a disgraceful weakling. Eventually, with enough repetition, expression of feelings becomes associated with the shame that follows expression, and the child is caught in an "affect-shame bind" (Kaufman, 1989, p.62). Affect is behavior that expresses a feeling, so this means feelings become bound by shame, i.e., "As soon as I feel something, I automatically feel ashamed for feeling it" (p.62).

This is easily understood when we consider gender differences and the fact that certain feelings are unacceptable. Little girls are typically shamed for expressing anger and are put in an "anger-shame bind." It is no surprise that adult women often feel ashamed and afraid of their anger and learn to inhibit its expression. Little boys are shamed for expressing sadness and are thus put in a "distress-shame bind." This explains why so many adult men report feeling embarrassment or mortification when they cry, especially if they expose this "weakness" in front of others (Kaufman, p.62). They learn as young children to squelch expressions of distress that show vulnerability. Not surprisingly, they appear "cut off" from their feelings. These "affect-shame binds" ensure the child's silence and protect the parent from feeling exposed. The child becomes a silent victim of the parents' rule.

The "Don't express yourself" rule also restrains children from calling attention to what is wrong in the family. This means there is no way to resolve conflicts or deal with messages that induce shame. If the child could tell either parent, "I feel so alone when you won't talk to me," or "I'm really scared when you yell like that," or whatever, there is a chance of improving the parent-child relationship. The rule maintains the status-quo and again protects the insecure parent. The parent who invokes and enforces this rule feels threatened by the child's expressiveness. A child who has the right to point out parental failures or talk openly about parental problems will trigger shame. Such a parent feels exposed by the child's feelings and reactions and, therefore, denies the child's right to self-expression. Thus, as the parent avoids shame, the child takes it in, because anything that can't be expressed must be bad. To the child mind, it is bad to be angry at one's parent, regardless of how appropriate that anger is. It is bad to think that mom is alcoholic, or that dad is a jerk, regardless of how true it is.

The "no self-expression" rule applies inside and outside the family unit. Any discussion of family problems or parental deficiencies outside the family is absolutely forbidden. It is considered a supreme act of disloyalty because it exposes the shame-based parent to the scrutiny of others. Revealing the parent's inappropriate behavior causes them to "lose face" and activates intense public shame. Loyalty to the rule means maintaining secrecy about any evidence of family dysfunction. Family secrets often involve addictive behaviors such as alcoholism or drug abuse, extramarital affairs, illegitimate births, mental illness, and shameful (or shame-inducing) parental behavior—especially incest and physical abuse.

It should be apparent that this rule isolates the child from friends as well as adults who could be supportive. The child must become proficient at looking good, or pretending everything is "okay," and they do. They become great pretenders who are unaware that other people are potential resources. They feel overwhelmed trying to cope with monumental problems on their own. Those who break silence by sharing family secrets outside the family, face severe consequences when their parents find out. These consequences always inflict more shame, such as name-calling, physical abuse, or worse. These shaming messages are, in effect, commands to give up self-expression. One woman client was literally disowned by both parents for reporting her incestuous father to a school counselor. The child part of herself felt orphaned and even more isolated than before. Another client was shunned (as an adult) by his mother and siblings for suggesting that his father was alcoholic. He said it in an ambulance that was rushing his father to a hospital. He had never before used the word alcoholic, out of denial and loyalty to the "no self-expression" rule. His father never returned from the hospital. He died of cirrhosis of the liver.

The "no self-expression" rule is one reason why shaming parents are so negative and disapproving when they learn their adult children are in therapy. The rule is that they are expected to take family secrets to their graves. The greater the parental shame, the greater the need for absolute silence and secrecy. The family need for secrecy is illustrated in the following case example.

Nancy

Nancy, a thirty-six year old veterinary assistant, was referred by her employer after reporting thoughts about taking her life. She certainly was severely depressed, but her suicidal thoughts were more a reaction to intense underlying shame. Shame and depression often appear in tandem, especially when there is a failure to live up to expectations and an inability to express oneself. This appeared to be the case with Nancy and I wanted to affirm her right to self-expression. After assessing that her suicide risk was low, the session proceeded as follows:

Stan: If you had taken your life, and left a suicide note behind, what would you have said?

Nancy: I'd have said I'm a weakling and that this is the first time I've ever made a statement.

Stan: Okay, who do you want to make this statement to?

Nancy: (Long pause) To my parents, for expecting me to keep my mouth shut and eat shit.

Stan: In other words the statement is..."See what you did to me!"

Nancy: That's about it.

Stan: Your parents denied you your right to express yourself. Now it's too scary to break the rules and get mad at them directly, so you redirect the anger back at yourself...that's what cutting your wrists is about. What would happen if ou let them know how angry you are?"

Nancy: I'd be kicked out of the family.

Nancy was an only child in shame-based family. She was born innocent, but was set up for shame from the moment of conception. Conceived by accident as a result of a brief and casual relationship, her mother kept secret the circumstances of her birth. Not until age fourteen was she informed that "daddy" wasn't her biological father. She was shocked and felt deeply shamed and saddened by this disclosure. In addition, instead of finally setting the record straight, her mother continued to keep the family secret. In the place of the old lie, a new lie was told. Nancy was led to believe that she was the daughter of her mother's first husband. The truth was, mother had no first husband. When Nancy asked his name, her mother actually claimed to have forgotten! The message was, "Don't ask questions, you have no right to know!" Her mother's secrecy and outright lying convinced Nancy that there was something that must be kept hidden about the circumstances of her birth, something that must be awful. She began to see herself as a mistake, unwanted by her unknown birth father, and a source of embarrassment to her mother. Whatever the truth was, it was too shameful to be discussed openly.

There was still another family secret. Nancy's parents were closet alcoholics who hid their drinking habits from others while presenting themselves as pillars of the community. Family life became organized around the binge drinking that went on after work and on weekends. Nancy was not allowed to talk about the drinking issue which was handled neatly by denying it was a problem. She was discouraged from talking to anyone outside the family about any issue. Since she had no brothers or sisters, she felt completely isolated. She was expected to make the family look good by singing in the church choir and being an honors student. Nancy learned how to look good on the outside while she was dying on the inside. She wore the same mask her parents did.

Upon entering adolescence, Nancy discovered it was easier to hide or stuff her feelings if she was also stuffing herself with food. She developed a weight problem, a symptom of the real problems and a way of expressing herself indirectly. Her parents disapproved. It didn't look good. It implied there was a problem in the family. They tried unsuccessfully to control her eating behavior but, just as they drank secretly, she ate secretly. She had stumbled on an indirect way of breaking the "no self-expression" rule without doing so obviously. Becoming obese was a way of saying, "Screw you!" to parents who denied her right to express herself. She unconsciously wanted to get fat to spite them, but it was a masochistic, self-defeating triumph. It reinforced Nancy's shame, proof that she had no will power and was, in fact, the weakling she believed herself to be. As an adult, she hated herself for being obese but even more for not asserting herself in relationships. Suicide was a possible way out. It was a way to turn off constant feelings of shame and, at the same time, a way of expressing rage at her parents for transmitting the "Don't express yourself" rule. In therapy, she agreed to a no-suicide contract and made a commitment to work through her problems. The problem was that she was following a rule that protected her as a child but perpetuated her shamed sense of self as an adult. In learning to break this dehumanizing rule and affirm her right to express herself, Nancy worked through her depression and gained immeasurably in self-esteem.

Aftereffects of the "Don't Express Yourself" Rule

When a child is denied the right to talk about what he sees, hears, and feels, he suffers a developmental void that results in a distorted way of relating to the world. If he cannot check out his perceptions with an understanding adult, he is forced to interpret the events of his life on his own (Kritsberg, 1985, p.15). Without the sensible input of a mature adult, there is no way to make sense of what is happening around him and to him. He finds himself in a world that has no order. The result is poor reality testing, that is, an inability to make objective evaluations and good judgments about himself and others. Poor contact with reality is carried into adulthood, and he holds on to coping strategies such as avoiding confrontation that allowed him to survive his shame-based family. However, the same strategies that worked in childhood are obstacles to successful relationships in adulthood.

The "no self-expression" rule does not allow for the development of effective communication skills. Nor does it foster a relationship style that favors confronting and resolving conflicts. The adult who follows the rule is so cut off from his own feelings that he cannot communicate in a way that others can understand and support. It makes sense to avoid communicating if it always seems to lead to unresolved conflict. This avoidance of conflict is motivated by shame anxiety, the fear that exposing the self will result in being shamed. Coping, the ability to realistically face-up to stressful situations, leads to favorable evaluations of the self (Bednar, Wells, and Peterson, 1989, p.14). The opposite of coping is avoidance, a form of denial that is characterized by a fear of taking risks and a disavowal of personal responsibility. Avoidance is one of the "quintessential qualities of abnormality" and leads to negative self-evaluations (p.73). In other words, the inability to express one's self results in avoidance and perpetuates low levels of self-esteem.

Adults who grew up with no self-expression lose contact with their true selves and relate to others from a false self position. Just as the "no need" parent cannot tolerate extreme dependency, the "no self-expression" parent cannot tolerate the natural expressiveness of the child's true self. Hence, the child's true self is sent into protective hiding. The false self arises as the child discovers that the true self is unacceptable to his or her parents. In its place, the child presents a collection of acceptable behaviors. This false self is a defense adopted to ensure emotional survival. It is erected to protect the vulnerable and hidden true self from shame-inducing parents. The false self is based on core beliefs that the true self is unacceptably bad, thus it is experienced as a shamed sense of self.

A common false self adaptation is the "nice person" syndrome. Although this pattern is not exclusive to women, it is more prevalent among women because they are taught not to express thoughts or feelings that are considered negative. Even when she has every right to be angry, the "nice lady" stays silent, feels hurt, becomes self-critical, or cries (Lerner, 1985, p.5). Being nice, even in situations that call for assertiveness, becomes a way of hiding the part of her that is furious for not being allowed to be who she really is. It is also a way of hiding how inferior and unlovable she feels. Her unconscious belief is that if she can hide her faults, no one will see how defective she is.

The "nice person" image is designed to get approval and avoid confrontation. It is a social mask worn to avoid criticism, anger, or any response that might activate feelings of shame. Such "niceness" is motivated by a desire to protect the true self from further shame attacks. The "nice person" fears that she would be humiliated or abandoned if she expressed her true self, so she keeps it safely hidden away and hopes for a relationship where it can be rediscovered and affirmed. In the meantime, she is loyal to the "no self-expression" rule. The price she pays is never knowing if she is loved for the person she truly is or for the person she pretends to be.

Children learn to block self-expression to please their parents, so it is not surprising that many grow up overinvested in pleasing others. Again, this is more characteristic of women because of the way young girls are socialized. One way to please is to assume responsibility for everyone around her—especially her spouse, parents, and children. Her way of relating is based on the unconscious belief that caretaking and overfunctioning will win the esteem of others, and compensate for her low self-esteem. She wishes to make herself indispensable by being helpful and needed. She assumes, mistakenly, that others will never abandon her if they feel dependent and indebted. This is a woman who spends so much time weeding everyone else's garden, she gets weeds in her own. She sacrifices herself, and ends up with little or no self to esteem.

To make matters worse, she projects her sensitivity to shame onto others, expecting them to be as sensitive as she is. She remains loyal to the "no self-expression" rule by vowing never to hurt anyone's feelings. She adopts an overly cautious attitude and "walks on eggshells" in important relationships. When people hurt her, she is bewildered because she naively expects her code of unselfish goodness to be reciprocated. Unfortunately, others (especially men who like to be with women they can control) equate her non-expressiveness with weakness, and take advantage of her. Still, she will not assert herself because she is afraid she will be abandoned if she displeases.

Is there anything wrong with always being nice to or trying to please others? Yes! It may be healthy from a true self position, but as a manifestation of the false self it is merely "impression management," i.e., saying and doing whatever we believe will gain the approval of others. In reality, the only way to never hurt anyone is to manage the impressions of others by pretending to be what we are not. In order to be authentic, the right to express one's self must be affirmed and exercised. The authentic person will be open, direct, and honest, thus the feelings of others will occasionally be hurt. This does not mean it's okay to say whatever comes to mind or to humiliate others; it means that being true to one's self will sometimes result in hurting another's feelings. Being honest is a risk that goes along with being intimate.

It follows that the "nice person" or people pleaser has to bottle up a lot of feelings. Often their bodies keep score. The pattern of saying nothing when expression is called for is costly because suppressed feelings find expression through the language of the body. Harry Stack Sullivan, who formulated the principles of interpersonal psychiatry in the 1920's, was the first to identify psychosomatic problems as a defense against shame and low self-esteem (Sullivan, 1953). According to Sullivan, it is easier to accept that there is something defective about the body than to accept there is something defective about the self. The person with psychosomatic symptoms is used to being shamed for expressing the need for attention, sympathy, and support—the emotional supplies that were typically withheld by neglectful, rejecting or abandoning parents. Their physical suffering allows them to escape the parental bind by getting their much needed supplies without further loss of self-esteem.

A psychosomatic complaint is an acceptable way to express emotional neediness and distress in many families that deny the right to express oneself in a more direct way. This is not to say that psychosomatic symptoms are consciously feigned or that they are imagined. They are unconscious expressions that can be best understood as nonverbal communications. For example, the person with a chronically sore neck really does have pain, but the symptom may be an unconscious and indirect way of saying, "You're a pain in the neck!" to a parent with whom they cannot express themselves directly. Also, the physical suffering becomes a way of atoning for one's badness since it is shameful for the "nice person" or people pleaser to feel hostile, i.e., the pain or suffering is deserved.

Whereas the pattern of hiding feelings and then developing psychosomatic symptoms is more common in women (DSM-III-R, 1987, p.265), the pattern of hiding feelings and then exploding into violence is more common in men (p.322). Such violence can be physical or emotional, just as the injuries to the victim can be physical and/or emotional. Screaming an obscenity at a vulnerable child is no less violent than a slap on the face. Men who behave in this way seem to accumulate emotional energy as they bottle up feelings, and then at some point, when they can contain no more, they explode. I think of this containing/exploding phenomenon as a Mt. St. Helens. In the event that one of my clients doesn't know what I mean, I have a marvelous photograph of Mt. St. Helens taken moments after erupting.

Whereas "nice" women suppress feelings and develop physical problems that hurt themselves, explosive men typically hurt others with their aggressive outbursts. Feelings that are pushed out of consciousness and left unexpressed generate tension, and like the pressure cooker with no safety valve, these men proceed to "blow their tops!" This is more likely to happen under the influence of alcohol or other drugs, and often, the explosive male will drink to lower his inhibitions and then erupt. Later, after the damage is inflicted, he has an immature and ready-made excuse ("I was drunk"). He will often feel guilty, but his guilt is manipulative in that it is expressed to make his behavior more acceptable. If he beats up on himself, he unconsciously believes he has made a sufficient guilt payment to the victim and should be let off the hook. The guilt usually is for a loss of control that resulted in a battering of his wife and/or child.

Explosive men are unstable and depend on their wives and children to keep them emotionally intact. When they become aware of this dependency, most often at times when the marital relationship feels too distant, they are flooded with shame and erupt into violence (Lansky, 1984, p.28). Violence is controlling, and through intimidation he transfers his shameful feelings of vulnerability and dependency to the fearful others. The eruption into violence hides the tendency to fall apart emotionally and the need for others to hold him together, both sources of shame (p.35). If he had learned how to express his feelings appropriately in childhood, he would have no need for his explosive behavior.

It should be apparent that the "Don't express yourself" rule virtually eliminates emotional closeness and sharing between family members. In such families the child's need for intimacy is not satisfied; thus, the child learns to distrust his own feelings, fears emotional expression by others, and finds he has no guidelines for giving and receiving affection (Harper and Hoopes, 1990, p.28). When such children reach adulthood, they will inevitably fail in relationships that call for close emotional bonds. Lacking the tools and the confidence to express themselves, they cannot get their feelings validated. They feel misunderstood, isolated, and alone. They further alienate themselves because they do not know how to validate the feelings of others. Intolerant of differences, they discourage those who would be intimate from risking vulnerability. No vulnerability, no intimacy. Since open and direct communication makes them feel exposed and/or anxious about being shamed, they defend themselves by trying to talk others out of their feelings. They want their partners or children to follow the "no self-expression" rule by "keeping the lid on." Thus, neither the self nor the other is able to use feelings constructively to change or improve the relationship. Nor can they "clear their emotional registers," which results in the accumulation of unfinished business that almost guarantees they will never become intimate.

Rule Five: Don't Separate

The "Don't separate" rule is invoked by parents who need to hold on to their children. Here, the child functions as either a supplier of worth and/or a container for projected shame to the parent with low self-esteem. A shame-based family system needs all its parts, and the child plays an indispensable part to psychologically incomplete parents. For this reason, they deny the child's right to separate. Efforts to separate violate the rule and elicit shaming messages from clinging parents. Such messages command the child to give up any behaviors that move in the direction of separation.

This rule operates in most shame-inducing families but is most obvious when the child is not allowed to form a boundary that would separate her from the parent. The child is forced to stay psychologically merged with and meet the needs of the parent instead of developing a differentiated, or separate self. This merger is maintained by discouraging any expression of difference since being different connotes separateness.

I observed a demonstration of this intolerance for difference in a store that featured many flavors of ice cream. A little girl, about four years old, was ahead of me and was having a hard time choosing her flavor. Her mother, close at hand, was trying to talk her daughter into vanilla. The little girl ordered chocolate chip mint. Obviously displeased by her daughter's independence, she canceled the order and announced "You don't want chocolate chip mint—give her vanilla!" The little girl immediately became gloomy and withdrawn and did not appear to enjoy her ice cream cone. If this scenario was representative, she will have to learn to cope with a parent who invalidates her decisions and discourages her separateness.

Another consequence of this lack of boundaries between parent and child is the parents' exploitation of their children as containers for their own shame. Unable to tolerate the pain of their own shame, they defend themselves by projecting it into their children. The child must not only give up the quest for individuality, but also provide a place for the parents to dump whatever it is that makes them feel unworthy. The father who is feeling inadequate will belittle his child. The mother who is feeling shame about sexual impulses will brainwash her child into feeling sinful. This transfers the shame to the child who becomes the container or receptacle for the parents' unwanted parts, feelings, impulses, etc. Children are willing to perform this function because they are psychologically naive and don't know better. The child is easily induced to accept the shame and will even behave shamefully if it is helpful to the parent. By containing the shame, the child stabilizes the family in general, and the parent in particular. This function becomes indispensable to the parents' emotional stability, thus they exert intense pressure on the child not to separate (Wood, 1987, p.42).

Children are born with a strong need to form an attachment bond with their parents. Those who internalize shame-inducing messages fail to form a secure attachment. Lacking a secure attachment, they become "excessively vulnerable to even the slightest lack of support" and stay stuck in their families (Nichols, 1984, p.186). Even when subjected to severe mistreatment, children will cling to the most slender thread of attachment. To the child mind, letting go would be to face the world alone and experience overwhelming fear. It would be to risk not surviving.

Children first need the bond with their parents in order to survive and later to complete developmental tasks. Eventually, the most important of these tasks is to separate from the parents and develop a true sense of individuality. This process of separation is undermined by parents who rely on the child for validation of worth. Unlike the parent who affirms the child's basic rights, they deny the right to separate and use the child as a source of fulfillment. Children are considered extensions of themselves and are expected to make them feel whole. It is as if a job description was stapled to the child's birth certificate and that job is to complete the parent. Lacking self-esteem because of their own shame experiences in childhood, they see their children as suppliers of worth who are to make up for their losses. Their unconscious attitude is, "I'm running on empty with no feelings of worth. Fill me up."

The child tries to fulfill the empty parent in order to preserve the illusion of having an intact parent. This is an impossible task and reinforces the child's emerging feelings of inadequacy and failure. Nonetheless, "Fill me up" parents become overly invested in keeping their child available to provide for them. It is their low self-esteem and neediness that necessitates the "no separation" rule.

The Family Romance

Another way of communicating the "no separation" rule is by sabotaging the child's efforts to connect with the opposite sex. Parents who do this, play on their child's unresolved Oedipal fantasies of possessing the opposite sex parent as their own. This process of sabotage begins during early adolescence when the family romance between mothers and sons, and fathers and daughters, should come to an end. The "Fill me up" parents, needing their child to stay merged and available, hold on to the romanticized aspect of the relationship. They see their child's opposite sex interests as threats to the special relationship they have enjoyed, and exploited. A clinging mother may object to her son's dating, and a possessive father may object to his daughter's short skirts and makeup, but the underlying command is, "You don't need anyone else. Please don't leave me. Ever." They do not so much have children as take hostages (Middelton-Moz and Dwinell, 1986, p.49). Such parents, coming from a position of deprivation, low self-esteem, and unhealthy entitlement, sabotage any attempts at separation while making the child feel like the needy one.

Allan

Allan came to therapy because he had difficulty maintaining intimate relationships with women. Not surprisingly, mother was the primary issue parent. We focused on his distrust of women, alternating fears of abandonment with engulfment, and working through shame and grief related to numerous failed relationships. Near the end of long-term therapy he confided, "There's one thing I'm not ready to forgive mom for. In seventh grade, there was a party everyone wanted to go to. I was going steady and my girlfriend and I were invited. I was shy, and too scared to ever kiss my girlfriend, and I saw this as my big chance. Everyone would be making out so I figured I could do it too. Anyway, mom knew the party was really important to me, and an hour before I was ready to go, she had what I guess you call a nervous breakdown. I had to stay home and take care of her and I missed the party completely. The next day at school everyone was buzzing about the party. You know, who felt up who, that kind of stuff. I was so disappointed. I know...I mean I now know mom did that to keep me from going, and I hate her for that!"

In discussing this incident, I learned that Allan's mother had told him to go ahead and go to the party. Like many parents invoking the "Don't separate" rule, she had given him a mixed message. She knows the right thing to say that would affirm his right to separate, and says it, but does so in a confusing and self-serving way. If he obeys her verbal message to leave, he will feel shame for being a selfish, bad son. If he obeys the nonverbal message not to leave, he loses an opportunity to learn how to be sexual with girls, perpetuating his shame over fearing them. He sacrifices his own needs and emotional growth to avoid being shamed. He must handicap himself in order to fulfill his mother's expectations, and eventually ends up ashamed over his handicap. Allan was able to forgive his mother for reversing roles and expecting him to parent her, even for being physically abusive, but couldn't forgive her for sabotaging his efforts to leave her.

The Supposedly Emancipated Adult

Adolescents don't know when parents are giving "Don't leave me" commands because they are unaware of the family romance. This variation of the "Don't separate" rule becomes more obvious when supposedly emancipated adult children decide to marry. They anxiously present engagement plans to clinging parents because to marry would mean to break the rule and separate. Shame-based parents react in a variety of controlling ways to their sons' or daughters' intentions to marry. McArthur (1988, p.17-18), in her discussion of "impinged-upon" adults, lists four parental responses to an announced engagement:

1. Support followed by sabotage
2. A pretense of support
3. Direct sabotage
4. The silent treatment

I have seen these manipulative responses in action. They follow from the rule not to separate. Some parents devalue the spouse-to-be with the indirect suggestion that a tragic mistake is about to be made. Others will be more direct and simply pressure their son or daughter to break it off. One client was told in no uncertain terms to choose between his spouse-to-be and continued contact with the family. Another client was told she would be written out of the will should she marry her fiancé. Emotional and financial cutoff are potent threats when separation from parents is incomplete.

A couple I saw in marital therapy considered taking a hyphenated last name for themselves and their children. The parents of the husband responded by threatening to disown him. Having not yet "left home" psychologically, his primary loyalty was with his family of origin and he kept the family name intact. His wife was understandably furious that his parents, especially his mother, still had such control over his decisions. He was following the rule and felt like a "wimp" for doing so. Following the "no separation" rule perpetuated his low self-esteem.

Sabotage works because unemancipated adults are still invested in getting parental approval. Any move in the direction of separation will still elicit shaming messages. Also, unemancipated adults are ambivalent about marriage under the best of circumstances. There is often a grain of truth to the parent's judgments since every prospective spouse is flawed. The clinging parent plays on the part of the "child" that questions whether the marriage is a good idea. The spouse-to-be may be too critical, unemployed, alcoholic, or from the "wrong" religion. Pointing out these flaws amplifies the ambivalence. Some unemancipated adults more or less allow their parents to hand-pick a spouse so as to avoid displeasing them. The parents choose partners who would be easily controlled, or those who would have little chance of really coupling with their "child." In this way, the compliant adult child stays loyal and avoids separating.

Some clients report marrying to get away from parents who will not allow separation. They marry to get away from their parents' control and take the "geographic cure" by moving far away. One client eloped knowing that not only would she not get parental blessings, but she would also be pressured out of her decision. Other clients "marry garlic" (a wonderful Jewish expression for marrying someone unacceptable to the family) in a feeble and doomed attempt at separation. Of course marriage in no way ensures the process of separation. One can marry, move to the newly discovered moons of Pluto, and still not leave home psychologically. There is no escape from the internal parent who induces shame, or from the rule not to separate.

Aftereffects of the "Don't Separate" Rule

Shame-inducing parents do not stop shaming just because a child reaches the age of emancipation and physically leaves home. The "no separation" rule remains in place and the adult child remains entangled in the family. She is still her parents' child and makes only feeble attempts to separate. When she does attempt to pull free, she is shamed and guilt-tripped. She remains dependent and submissive in a parent-child relationship. She has been induced to believe that her survival depends on continued parental support.

By way of comparison, the adolescent who successfully separates develops a mother-adult daughter or father-adult daughter relationship. Such a relationship is based on respect for her individuality and acknowledges that she is capable of being on her own.

The unseparated adult is willing to stay in the one-down child position because she knows she will be punished if she breaks the rule. Also, she longs for the emotional supplies she was deprived of as a child. She has not yet given up the hope of getting the parent she always wanted, namely one who would love her for who she really is and respect her as a separate and independent person. Having never fully separated, she does not experience herself as a grown-up woman. She is her parents' "little girl," and continues to depend on mom and dad for advice, reassurance, and support. Her "map of the world" is that she can't make it on her own. Her parents have denied her right to separate and she has never developed a sense of mastery or pride over being independent. The shame internalized in childhood is perpetuated in adulthood.

Separation from one's parents is the primary developmental task of adolescence. The adult who never completes this task is not capable of true intimacy. In the context of marriage, an intimate relationship is one where there is vulnerability and emotional closeness, commitment and mutual trust, and satisfying sexual activity. The unemancipated adult cannot achieve intimacy because he or she is still entangled with parents. A successful marriage requires that one's spouse replaces the parent as the most important attachment figure. When one's loyalty is with parents and the rule not to separate, the marriage is doomed because the marital bond will never be strong enough to withstand the stress of unfinished business from the family of origin.

Intimacy is further undermined by the process of creating relationship triangles with an overinvolved parent in the middle. The spouse who is least separated will usually be first to triangle in a parent. By forming a marital triangle, the adult child gratifies the incomplete parent who needs to hold on. The triangle reassures the parent by nonverbally communicating..."See, I haven't really left you. I am still your little boy (girl)!" The triangle also stabilizes the marital relationship by focusing attention, and thus anxiety, on an outside person. A shaky relationship feels safer with a third person in the middle (a three legged-stool is in less danger of toppling than a two-legged one). Triangles function to keep the relationship "distant and safe while at the same time, providing the glue for the relationship" (Middelton-Moz, 1990, p.86). In the classic case of the mother-in-law triangle, the conflict shifts outside the marriage and away from the real issue, namely that until separation is accomplished, one cannot adequately bond and be intimate with his or her spouse. Unseparated adults often divorce their spouses when they should be divorcing their parents.

Another problem in forming an intimate relationship is that marital partners who have not "left home" find it difficult if not impossible to create the right amount of closeness. They form relationships that are characterized by distance conflicts, that is, one either feels too close or too distant. Women most often feel too distant and become pursuers who want more. Men are more likely to feel too close and become distancers who need space. A vicious cycle ensues. His distancing increases her anxiety, so she pursues him all the more. Her pursuit increases his anxiety, so he distances all the more. And so on. Actually this equidistant dance protects them both. Her pursuit protects him from his fear of abandonment, and his distancing protects her from her fear of being controlled. She pursues frantically because she is afraid of being abandoned, and he distances frantically because he is afraid of being taken over and controlled. She serves as the container for his unwanted dependent part, and he serves as the container for the part of her that fears engulfment.

The equidistant dance re-enacts the family drama, a drama that never ends as long as the "no separation" rule is in effect. The resulting inability to form an intimate relationship with the right amount of closeness reinforces a shamed sense of self—that one is defective and unlovable.

Chapter Four

Shame-Inducing Family Roles

A man found an eagle's egg and put it in the nest of a backyard hen. The eaglet hatched with the brood of chicks and grew up with them.

All his life the eagle did what the backyard chickens did, thinking he was a backyard chicken. He scratched the earth for worms and insects. He clucked and cackled, and he thrashed his wings and flew a few feet into the air like the chickens. After all, that is how a chicken is supposed to fly, isn't it?

Years passed and the eagle grew very old. One day he saw a magnificent bird far above him in the cloudless sky. It floated in graceful majesty among the powerful wind currents, with scarcely a beat of its strong golden wings.

The old eagle looked up in awe. "Who's that?" he said to his neighbor.

"That's the eagle, the king of the birds," said his neighbor. "But don't give it another thought. You and I are different from him."

So the eagle never gave it another thought. He died thinking he was a backyard chicken.

This Anthony de Mello story, "The Golden Eagle" (in McConnell, 1986), is tragically similar to the life situation of adults who were assigned dysfunctional roles in their families of origin. I am referring to those who were induced to play a scripted part in the family drama, a part that was internalized in the place of a true personal identity. These are individuals who were thwarted in their childhood quest for identity and do not know who they really are. Like the eaglet that observed his role models and forever believed himself to be a backyard chicken, they have never learned to appreciate their true nature, never learned to actualize their deeper potentials, never learned to fly. Like the adult eagle, who was led to believe he was different from the king of the birds, they see themselves as inferior beings, never experiencing the feeling of healthy pride and positive self-esteem that is their birthright.

Functional and Dysfunctional Roles

A family role is a repetitive pattern of behavior by which members of a family system fulfill family functions (Epstein, Bishop, and Baldwin in Walsh, 1982, p.124). If a family system is to be optimal in dosing the right amount of shame to children, it must function in ways that affirm their basic rights. We have seen that these include the right to be, have needs, make mistakes, express one's self, and separate from the family. Just as parental rules affirm or deny these rights, so do family roles. An optimal family will recognize that its most important function is the emotional and social development of its children. Parents tend to assign family roles in a way that gives the child a sense of belonging, a feeling of need satisfaction, permission to make and learn from mistakes, encouragement to be self-expressive, and enough separateness to become his or her own person. The family that functions to provide these basics imparts to its children an identity based on self-esteem.

In such families, children are assigned roles that reflect the normal, natural, and expected activities of a child at a particular stage of development. These roles will then contribute to and enhance the process of emotional development. For example, a three-year-old girl is assigned the role of helper and expected to pick up her toys after playing with them. Or, a teenager is assigned the role of student and is expected to attend school and do his homework. These roles are considered functional because they accomplish certain goals, namely, teaching the young girl to be considerate and responsible, and supporting the teenage boy's educational progress. Furthermore, each role is functional in that it is commensurate with the child's developmental skills. By carrying out the assigned tasks, the child can acquire a sense of mastery, thus building self-esteem.

In a shame-based family, children are assigned roles that do not reflect the normal activities of a child their age. Whereas a role in an optimal family is an age-appropriate task that enhances emotional development, a role in a shaming family is more like a scripted part in an ongoing drama. By playing that part, the child indeed fulfills an important family function, but at the expense of his or her emotional development.

A shame-based family role may thus be functional for the family system, but dysfunctional for the child. For example, an eight-year-old boy may reverse roles with his depressed mother and become her confidante and comforter. This role may function to stabilize the family because the mother feels nurtured and supported, but it is dysfunctional for the son she abandons. It is dysfunctional because he is assigned a part that is not in his own best interest. Moreover, it is above and beyond his developmental level and causes him to become overly responsible and emotionally burdened. He should not be expected to have the psychological skills necessary to care for a parent, much less a depressed one, and he doesn't. That he keeps her intact is a dangerous illusion that reinforces his pseudo-adult role playing.

A Shame-Based Identity

A personal identity is formed as children carry out assigned family roles and take on aspects of the family identity. Our personal sense of identity is that which allows us to experience the self as something that is both continuous and the same, and to act according to such qualities (Erikson, 1950, p.42). It is in this way that we come to know ourselves, and answer the question, "Who am I?" When a child is assigned a dysfunctional role, he or she suffers a loss of self-esteem and a shame-based identity is formed.

Consider the example of a thirteen-year-old girl who is placed in the role of sexual partner to her father. A typical scenario would be that he previously depended upon his wife to fulfill this function, but that she has withdrawn from him for any one of a number of reasons. Now he turns to his daughter, who he considers to be under his direction. She becomes the stand-in or substitute for the estranged wife. This role may fulfill the family function of providing adult sexual gratification, but it is clearly dysfunctional. It has nothing to do with actualizing the daughter's true nature and is devastating to her emotional and social development. Such a role results in "traumatic sexualization," that is, a process wherein her sexual feelings and attitudes are formed in a developmentally inappropriate way as a result of sexual abuse (Finkelhor and Browne, 1985, p.534). As she carries out her assigned and scripted part, she forms a shame-based identity. In response to the "Who am I?" question, she thinks "I'm damaged goods," reflecting her lowered self-esteem. It is important to note that she is not asked to play this part in the family drama—it is assigned and imposed by her father. He has the power to write the script and cast the characters. She is a victim of his psychopathology, and a powerless one at that. She cannot help but feel conflicted over her role in the family.

Role conflict occurs in the following situations: (1) when a child is unclear as to the role he is assigned to play (e.g., "Does mom really want me to be the man of the family?"); (2) when parents assign conflicting roles (e.g., one parent wants the child to be sickly and the other wants him to be invulnerable); or (3) when the role is incompatible with the child's true sense of identity (e.g., a constitutionally shy child is expected to act silly and entertain the family). These role conflicts intensify over time because one part of the child wants to please the parent and another part instinctively resists playing any role that lowers his or her self-esteem.

Family role conflicts lead to identity crises. Using the previous example, the daughter who is expected to play the role of sexual partner to her father experiences a role conflict and identity crisis of epic proportion. Part of her may want to be compliant because of what will happen if she refuses to follow her father's script. Another part of her, a natural and healthy part, may consciously or unconsciously want to castrate him. This leads to an identity crisis because her new role causes her to lose the sense of historical continuity and personal sameness she had before. That her father assigns this particular change in roles at a time when she is feeling a sudden increase in her sexual drive (she is in puberty) only amplifies her crisis. She cannot accept the role her incestuous father expects her to play, nor does she have the personal authority at age thirteen to refuse him. The role constitutes a profound violation of who she really is—an innocent human being and vulnerable daughter. A dysfunctional family role interrupts the process of identity formation when it leads to any violation of a child's boundaries. The experience of role conflict further undermines the child's quest for a secure and cohesive identity.

Children form a sense of identity not only by carrying out role assignments, but by taking on important aspects of their family identity. As they assume the family identity, they are once again induced to play roles that may be dysfunctional. Family identity refers to the way that family members have come to see the family as distinct from other families. It is a product of shared beliefs about rules and roles, and is subjective in that it is the family's view of itself that counts (Steinglass, 1987, pp.58-61).

Nancy's parents (in Chapter Three) kept secret the (objective) reality that they were alcoholic, and (subjectively) saw themselves as "pillars of the community." The family identity, based on denial that defended them against shame, was that they were puritanical and morally righteous. Nancy was expected to hide the family secret and take on the family identity of "pious churchgoer." She came to see her personal identity as based on dishonesty. She recalled a scene where their minister was coming to dinner and her parents hid all the alcohol in the house. "Even though I didn't do it, I lost respect for myself. I felt like a total hypocrite!" It is obvious that there was a merger between her own identity and the family identity. She cannot help but take on aspects of the family with which she identifies, in this case the pretense of moral righteousness. This identification causes her to see herself as someone who pretends to be what she is not, someone who is less than she pretends to be, thus contributing to her shame-based identity.

Vicarious and Contagious Shame

Shame can apparently be transmitted from parents to children vicariously through the family identity. Vicarious shame is that which is contained and suffered by one family member in the place of another. For example, Nancy felt vicarious shame whenever she played the role of "pious churchgoer," a crucial aspect of the family identity. That shame belonged to her parents, not because they were alcoholics or hypocrites, but because it was their shame. It was shame that was carried into the family as unfinished business from their families of origin. To some degree, the shame that they failed to work through got passed on to Nancy, their only child. Denial allows them to avoid their shame, as does their alcoholism and hypocrisy for that matter. When reality becomes too painful, they simply blot it out or distort it. This leads to a kind of unacknowledged or free-floating shame—shame that is present in the absence of an acknowledged reason. It floats around in the family system and ends up in Nancy's container as she takes on this aspect of the family identity. She identifies with her parents; that is, she incorporates images of them within herself, and then feels whatever they are disowning. As she takes them in, she takes possession of their emotions and experiences vicarious shame, thus, she feels shame in the place of her parents. They export their shame and she simmers in it for them. This unconscious process reinforces her shame-based identity. In response to the "Who am I?" question, she thinks, "I am a hypocrite...a phony!"

The idea that shame can be experienced vicariously is similar to the idea that it has a contagious quality. The contagion of shame has been described in autobiographical terms by Jane Middelton-Moz in her excellent book Shame and Guilt (1990). "I recalled memories of times when my father had experienced shame when I was with him. No words were spoken between us, but I remember feeling shame with him when we were with educated people. His shame eventually became my own. I then realized that shame could be contagious" (p.19).

Contagious shame is that which spreads from one family member to another. As is the case in Jane's example, the contact need not be direct to spread the contagion of shame. Her father was not communicating a shaming message, verbally or nonverbally, nor was he imposing a shame-inducing rule, yet shame passed from father to daughter. It was not completely transferred because he continued to feel his shame. Whereas vicarious shame is experienced in the place of another, contagious shame is suffered along with another. Both are transmitted through the unconscious process of identification, and are related to the family identity, but there is a difference. The child who takes on vicarious shame relieves the parent of the painful emotion and suffers instead of the parent. The child who catches shame because it is contagious suffers in addition to the parent, although each suffers alone.

The Adoption of Dysfunctional Roles

In her pioneer description of the alcoholic family system, Sharon Wegscheider (now Cruse) observed that family members invariably played one or more of five basic roles—the "Enabler" (motivated by anger), the "Hero" (motivated by inadequacy or guilt), the "Scapegoat" (motivated by hurt), the "Lost Child" (motivated by loneliness), and the "Mascot" (motivated by fear) (1981, p.86). While it is true that many shame-based families are not alcoholic, all alcoholic families are shame-based, therefore it may be assumed that variations of these roles show up in alcoholic and non-alcoholic families that are based on shame. I have repackaged these family roles and added several to the list to highlight shame dynamics. In the shame-based family, all roles are motivated by shame and instill an identity based on shame.

We have already seen how such families assign roles that are essentially scripted parts in the ongoing and unhealthy family drama. These roles may fulfill important family functions, but are dysfunctional for the child because they retard emotional and social development. As the child adopts one or more of the dysfunctional roles, he or she forms a sense of identity that is based on shame. This personal identity is further contaminated as shameful aspects of the family identity are taken on, and as the child experiences vicarious and contagious shame. The eight characteristic roles in the shame-based family are:

1. The "Impostor"
2. The "Bad Seed"
3. The "Loner"
4. The "Comedian/Comedienne"
5. The "Saint/Angel"
6. The "Little Prince/Little Princess"
7. The "Sick Child"
8. The "Chameleon"

The "Impostor"

The "Impostor" is typically either the first born child or the most resilient child. Unlike the true-to-life impostor, he does not deliberately deceive or cheat others. In fact, he is the one who is cheated in that he is deprived of his true personal identity by the parents who assigned this dysfunctional role. He presents himself as competent and secure, but deep down he feels that he is pretending to be something he is not. That is his family role, to pretend that everything is okay, to demonstrate that the family is normal. How does he normalize the family image? By appearing unharmed by the family dysfunction and making his parents proud.

Impostors learn to look good from the outside, and appear to be invulnerable to trauma. However, many of the so-called "Invulnerable children" are merely playing the "impostor" role and fooling the social scientists who study them.

It is true that there are active and competent children who are resilient in that they can recover more quickly from adversity (Murphy and Moriarty, 1976). Some of these "invulnerables" appear steeled or hardened by the shaming messages, rules, and roles with which they must cope. But these children are coping in spite of their family roles, not because of them. It may be that such children have a substitute attachment figure who provides the nurturance and support they lack at home, i.e., a "cookie person" (Middelton-Moz and Dwinell, 1986, p.55). There are no invulnerable children, precisely because they are children.

The "Impostor" often comes from a family where love is conditional and based on parental expectations of superior achievement. He strives for perfection and becomes an over-achiever to escape the criticism that would shame him. He expends tremendous energy trying to live up to the image his parents have of him and, in so doing, he fulfills a family function by making his parents proud. Like the "Hero" in the alcoholic family, he is expected to enhance the family identity through his accomplishments. In school, he becomes a star athlete or exceptional student and then goes on to complete medical school. He is fiercely competitive and feels driven to succeed because his role is to provide a feeling of worth to parents who feel like failures. He is sensitive to such feelings because their shame is contagious. His heroics represent an attempt to cure the family of the shame sickness. He may succeed in fulfilling the function of bringing pride to the family, but at a cost of forfeiting his true identity. And, he cannot really enjoy his accomplishments because he feels like an impostor—a fraud who is actually not worthy of esteem.

Girls who play the role of "Impostor" are typically oldest daughters or only children. They are encouraged to be "good little girls" who please, placate, and peacemake. Such behaviors function to stabilize the family by bringing the system into balance. If mom and dad are fighting, her role is to patch things between them. Although she is a child, she is expected to act maturely, a feat which functions to balance her parents' immature and irrational behavior. Of course, she is not mature, but gets reinforced for pretending to be. She turns into a pseudo-adult and loses her childhood in the process. In family therapy, she would be considered a "parentified" child. She pretends to be a substitute parent to her siblings and relieves her parents of many responsibilities. She babysits, cleans house, and cooks dinner. She may even reverse roles and become a caretaker to her needy parents. She will provide emotional support when her father is out of work and encourage her mother when she is feeling discouraged or inadequate. Her unconscious fantasy is that these heroic efforts will stabilize the family and restore her parents to health. Then, they would stop shaming her and she would have good enough parents to provide the nurturing she desperately needs. Then, she would be relieved of this heavy burden of responsibility. Then, she could stop playing this scripted part and form a self and an identity based on who she really is.

Outside the family, she is an overachiever and is likely to make a successful career for herself. This provides a source of pride to her "Fill me up" parents, but she cannot enjoy it because of survivor guilt. She feels ashamed for leaving her struggling siblings behind and often handicaps herself so she will not become too successful. After all, it would be disloyal to make more money than her unsuccessful father, or to be happier than her miserable mother. Playing the role of a responsible adult during her formative years eventually catches up with her. When she realizes that her part in the family drama left her feeling frustrated and deprived, she will feel taken advantage of. What success she does achieve is always tainted by her feeling of being an impostor who will someday be exposed as a fake.

Lois, an outwardly successful attorney, said it well, "I made it through law school with flying colors and joined a prestigious law firm. I guess I fooled everyone!" As a youngster, she had been the "perfect" child. She got straight "A's" in school and excelled in gymnastics. Her parents were immensely proud of her accomplishments. They were both high achievers who defended against shame by being perfectionists, and working sixty to seventy hour weeks in the family-owned business. Lois sensed that there was something wrong with them ("They seemed so depressed") and accepted the "impostor" role in an attempt to heal their wounds. Since this was an impossible task, it is not surprising that Lois felt inadequate, even when she looked in control to those around her. What brought her into therapy was a crisis involving her career that affected her achievement self. She had been fired from the law firm for drastically underbilling her clients. She simply didn't think she was worth the fees she was expected to charge.

The "Bad Seed"

The "Bad Seed" is as helpful to the family as the "Impostor" but in an opposite way. These are often second born in families that already have a child whose role it is to make the family proud. Whereas the former is into conforming and looking good, the "Bad Seed" is into rebelling and looking bad. His role is to act-out his parents' and his siblings disowned parts, especially their shame and anger. He is used as a container for parental shame, then experiences it in their place (vicarious shame). As a youngster he throws tantrums, talks back, tests limits, breaks rules, sets fires, lies, and steals. As he gets older he escalates by getting into fights, running away, skipping school, failing classes, breaking laws, and abusing alcohol and drugs. All of this acting-out behavior fulfills a family function by diverting attention from the real problems, e.g., parental rejection, battering, terrorizing, or any of the other shame-inducing parental patterns. By playing his assigned part as a troublemaker, he detours his parents from another dysfunctional part of the system: their unsuccessful marriage.

Like the "Scapegoat" in the alcoholic family, the "Bad Seed" takes the blame for all the family problems. There is something for everyone in his playing this self-sacrificing role. He allows dad to transfer shame and rage into his container. He sets himself up so mom can align herself with dad and forget their differences. He gets his siblings off the hook by taking the blame for anything that goes wrong. He plays his scripted part, indirectly asks for help, and says, "Screw you!" at the same time.

If the family should seek therapy, they will want him to go alone. He is the "identified patient," or the one with the problem. They attribute his acting-out behavior to some unknown but inborn flaw in his character, and so transfer even more blame to the sacrificial child. This adds psychological insult to psychological injury. He is simply a bad seed. Otherwise, they would have to take responsibility for their failure to adequately parent him, or acknowledge that they unconsciously want him to provide a diversion from issues they would prefer to avoid. Thus, they all either say or believe, "If only Jesse would stop doing drugs, everything would be okay." Actually, if Jesse should begin the recovery process and stop doing drugs, they would likely sabotage his recovery because the family needs him to play his part. If he stops playing his role, the family system becomes unstable. The emotional cost to Jesse is a shame-based identity—he comes to see himself as bad and unfit for healthy relationships. In the best interest of the family, he forfeits his chance to form his own unique identity.

Although it is more likely for boys to be assigned the role of "Bad Seed," girls too can play the part. Carla was the youngest of two girls. Her mother resented their alcoholic father, not so much because of his drinking, but because he refused to have much to do with raising Carla. "You're the one that wanted a second child, you take care of her!" was one of his favorite sayings. Needless to say, Carla felt burdensome and unwanted. The older sister, Joanne, played the "impostor" role and had always been an overachiever. She had a reputation as the family "brain" and earned a scholarship at a prestigious college. Carla felt belittled by offensive comparisons to her sister and was jealous of the attention she got for her academic accomplishments. Carla found a way she could get attention, even though it was negative. By the time she was thirteen, she began drinking heavily and using drugs. As is often the case, her substance abuse went hand in hand with promiscuous sexual behavior, and she would have sex with any boy that would pay attention to her. Sometimes she would sneak out at night and get picked up by grown men who would victimize her sexually. It wasn't sex that Carla craved, it was the attention and the feeling of being wanted, even if it was for her body. Nonetheless, Carla had formed a shame-based identity—that she was, in her own words, a "slut."

Following an argument with her father, Carla ran away and returned only because the police brought her home for curfew violation. She had been gone over a week. When her mother called for an appointment, I insisted that the whole family attend. Her mother was genuinely concerned but, allying herself with her alcoholic husband, blamed Carla for her acting-out behavior. It was immediately clear that Carla was the "Bad Seed," and that she was helping out the family by distracting attention from her father's drinking and her parents' failing marriage. Any attempt on my part to discuss family problems other than Carla's substance abuse or sexual behavior was resisted by her parents. They needed her to be the troublemaker who fulfilled the function of detouring the family from the real issues. My attempts to reframe her symptoms as manifestations of a family problem fell on deaf ears (except Carla's). Her father spoke for the rest of the family, "It's Carla's fault and she's got to get her act together. We never had any of this trouble with Joanne." After four sessions, the father fired me and hired a therapist who agreed to see Carla individually. I later learned he fired that therapist too.

The "Loner"

Unlike the "Impostor" and "Bad Seed," the "Loner" stays out of the limelight and seldom calls attention to herself. As noted by Friel and Friel (1988), she takes care of the family's need for separateness and independence by keeping her distance (p.55). Another function she fulfills has to do with managing family size. In effect, the family feels no larger with her in it because she is essentially a missing person. She is assigned a role intended to relieve a family system that is already overloaded, and she plays her part by making no demands on her beleaguered parents.

The "Loner's" family is in a state of perpetual chaos and seems to live from crisis to crisis. There may be too many kids (loners are typically younger children), not enough money, or a failed marriage characterized by bitterness and emotional fatigue. Her parents are likely to feel crushed by the burden of their responsibilities. Many loners come from single-parent families where the custodial parent, typically a young working mother, is simply overwhelmed. In any event, the child adopts the role of a loner who is expected to stay out of the way. Parental messages to "get lost" are taken both figuratively and literally. She follows the script by hiding out in her room, staying late after school, or spending time at friends' homes. She decides never to ask questions, express feelings, break rules, or rock the boat. In short, she does a disappearing act in the service of a family system that is already stressed to the maximum. She tries to make things better by not making things worse.

Like the "Lost Child" in the alcoholic family, the "Loner" must erect a false self and squelch her inborn and ongoing neediness. She becomes fiercely counter-dependent and "licks her own wounds" because there is no one available to comfort her. She is like the character in the soap opera who is written out of the script, like the lone wolf who is expelled from the wolfpack because there is not enough food to go around.

"Loners" are unwanted and forgotten children and, sadly, they know it. Perhaps their parents didn't want more children, or wanted a boy instead of a girl, or made a mistake thinking that another child would save their stormy marriage. When a child adopts the role of a loner, her parents can forget about her without appearing neglectful because her shy and withdrawn behavior looks like a manifestation of her true nature. While it is true that some children are constitutionally shy, the "Loner" is allowed and even encouraged to disappear. The naturally shy child with more optimal parents is encouraged to join in and participate. She is convinced she belongs.

It is true that adopting the role of "Loner" protects the child from the family dysfunction, but it is dysfunctional in itself because it aborts the development of a true identity. The "Loner" is an assigned role that has little or nothing to do with who she uniquely is. No child would ever willingly choose to play this particular role in the family drama. It means being isolated and giving up the sense of belonging that a child desperately needs. It goes against her basic needs to relate and be comforted, and results in shameful feelings of being unimportant and unwanted.

Rejected in the real world, the "Loner" withdraws into a world of fantasy. This is an attempt to detach from the chaos around her while imagining or pretending she is getting her needs met. By withdrawing from contact, she protects the deprived and hidden true self from further shame.

I met Phyllis in the hospital where she was being treated for compulsive overeating and substance abuse. Talk about a shame-based identity—she described herself as a "drug addict and a pig!" She entered treatment morbidly obese and addicted to prescription drugs, primarily narcotic analgesics like codeine. She was being considered for a stomach stapling procedure which was supposed to cure her obesity, and I was called in to give an opinion as to whether this was a good idea. It wasn't, and I convinced her physician that psychotherapy was a better idea.

Phyllis came from an alcoholic family and was the youngest of four girls. She was born six years after the sister who came before her and assumed she was a "mistake baby." She described herself as a quiet and unobtrusive child who received little or no attention from her parents. Her sister resented sharing the small bedroom she had previously had to herself, so Phyllis tried not to take up space. "I learned to be invisible," she explained, "and I got good at it." It was clear that Phyllis had been assigned the role of "Loner," and felt deprived and lonely as a result. The combination of an eating disorder and an addiction is a typical symptom picture for an adult who played this role in childhood. Just as she had escaped into fantasy as a little girl, she had avoided a painful reality as an adult. Food and drugs were her means of escape, her way to numb pain and fill the emptiness inside her. As is so often the case, shame brings on more shame. Until dysfunctional roles are fully acknowledged and understood, the destructive patterns that once served the family (and may still) cannot be changed.

The "Comedian/Comedienne"

The "Comedian" (or female "Comedienne") is handed a script that defends the family from what would otherwise be intolerable levels of shame. This role is usually assigned to the youngest child who then serves as a receptacle for unresolved family conflicts. In playing this part, he functions like a lightning rod to divert tension from the structure of the family.

Like the "Mascot" in the alcoholic family, he learns very early that showing off or acting cute can release pent-up energy in stressful family situations, and at the same time get him some positive attention (Wegscheider, p.140). As he grows up, he becomes more and more adept at using humor to reduce tension created by parental dysfunction. Like the court jester in medieval times, his role as comedian is to keep things light. This provides the family "a sense of fun or playfulness, of silliness and a distorted type of joy" (Friel and Friel, 1988, p.55). In fulfilling this function, he allows himself and other family members to maintain a "smiling depression." The family can be disintegrating before its own eyes and yet act as if everything is okay.

The "Comedian" is exploited by the family to play a role that suppresses conflict and hides emotional pain. Shame and other painful feelings, especially grief and fear, are hidden behind his mask of laughter. This mask is proof that he has forfeited his true self, but in the service of his family. If everyone is laughing, then everything is normal. He takes center stage to help maintain family denial, keeping dreaded feelings out of everyone's awareness. It is also a way to defend himself against parental ridicule. Humor becomes a means of controlling the scene, getting others to laugh instead of getting laughed at (Kaufman, 1989, p.103).

I remember when the immensely talented TV comic Freddie Prinze committed suicide. He was the star of a series called "Chico and the Man." I was in my doctoral program at the time and heard about his death while en route to my Gestalt therapy training group. I wondered aloud why someone so funny, so gifted, and so successful could take his own life. Our group trainer, Jan Rainwater (author of "You're in Charge!"), shared that she had treated several comedians. She explained that behind the mask of laughter, they were usually hiding pain, particularly shame and grief. My belief is that this defense was learned in childhood as a role that first served the family, then later became self-protective. It may allow the comic to bypass shame and cover over painful feelings, but at a cost of forfeiting a true identity.

Humor is considered a mature defense, but the "Comedian" goes too far because for him being funny becomes a way of life. Sometimes the role becomes so consuming that he shifts into a mood that is abnormally elevated. This is called a "manic triumph" over the shame and depression that threaten to overwhelm him. He stays "on" and "up" to protect the dejected and demoralized true self from sinking into a morass of shame and grief. While he is in this elevated but disturbed mood, he typically shows an enthusiasm for interactions that are ultimately self-destructive, e.g., sexual indiscretions, buying a round of drinks with the rent money, calling sleeping friends in the early morning hours. At such times, he is likely to get ego inflated to the point of marked grandiosity. If he feels himself crashing, he may use drugs to stay "up," particularly stimulants such as cocaine.

Chip

Chip, a group therapy client whom I affectionately called the "prince of pun," had everyone in the group laughing at his quick wit and outrageous antics. The laughter stopped when he tried to convince us he was funnier than Robin Williams and was ready for the Johnny Carson show. That he had no professional experience made no difference, and he deflected our collective concerns. It was only after "rapid cycling" (shifting from up to down, to up to down) that Chip consented to a psychiatric evaluation for medication management. He was diagnosed as suffering a mixed bipolar disorder (once referred to as manic-depressive illness). Never missing a cue, Chip called it "easy glum, easy glow!" He was put on lithium carbonate, which helped greatly. There is controversy as to whether such a mood disturbance is caused by genetic factors or family dysfunction, or both. It is a "chicken or egg" question. Does a biochemical imbalance cause the mood disturbance, or does the mood disturbance cause a biochemical imbalance? I believe that both heredity and environment are at work here.

Regardless of his body biochemistry, it was clear that Chip had been the family "Comedian" practically from the day he was born. His father was a petty tyrant who terrorized his wife and six children (Chip was fourth in the birth order). It was his job to clown in order to defuse potentially explosive situations that would otherwise result in shameful and frightening scenes. He did it so well that he was not allowed to separate from the family. They needed him to continue playing his scripted part, and at age twenty-four he was still living at home. With the support of the group and his individual therapist, Chip moved out and began the process of emotionally separating. Predictably, his family, including all five siblings, did everything conceivable to pull him back into the family dysfunction, e.g., escalating violence, tearful pleading, blatant guilt-tripping, threatened cutoff. Chip was well coached to expect such moves and held his ground. He began the difficult process of quitting the family role and actualizing his true personal identity—one that included a good sense of humor but allowed for a serious side too.

The "Saint/Angel"

The "Saint" (or female "Angel") role is assigned to the child who is expected to uphold the family image of goodness and virtue. Just as the "Impostor" is supposed to bring home a feeling of pride, the "Saint/Angel" is expected to bring home a feeling of moral excellence and chastity. This fulfills the function of maintaining a family identity—that the family is righteous and beyond reproach. This role defends the family against shame, especially shame that results from family secrets involving sexuality, e.g., masturbation conflicts, premarital sex, extramarital affairs, incest, urges to act-out sexually, etc.

The defensive aspect of this family role is called reaction formation, that is, the role substitutes a socially acceptable behavioral pattern for one that is not. The family preaches sexual restraint that diametrically opposes impulses to act sexually unrestrained. The child is programmed to adopt the parents' beliefs and values and is molded into a little "Saint" or "Angel." The role prohibits sexual expression (especially for girls) so the dreaded shame over sexuality is warded off. As would be expected, this shame-inducing family role is typically assigned in brainwashing families where religious beliefs are converted into a dogma, and where sex is considered bad and immoral.

The "Saint/Angel" is expected to demonstrate the family's religious virtue to extended family members and the community. In order to carry out this role, he or she may be expected to sing in the church choir or attend Sunday School every week. When parents have more of an investment in having a saintly or angelic child, they may program them to become a minister, priest, or nun (Friel and Friel, 1988, p.56). These expectations may be spoken and/or unspoken. Either way, the child takes the cue and begins to play the scripted part. The part goes hand in hand with a feeling "that he or she will only have worth if they act out the spirituality for the family" (p.56). The child completely buys into the parents' view that "our moral worth depends on you enhancing the family image of spirituality." The child functions to reinforce an image of morality to parents who would unconsciously like to behave immorally.

An optimal family may support a child's wish to devote his or her life to religious matters, but it is the child's wish, and it is not the determinant of the child's worth in the family. Furthermore, it is not a role that is programmed; it is a desire that emanates from within the child. There is no pressure to become what the parent ideally would like the child to be, and if he or she becomes interested in something less spiritual, it's fine.

In the shame-based family, the parents assign a spiritual role regardless of the child's desire. It is dysfunctional because it has nothing to do with the child's unique identity. It is a reflection of the parent, not the child. It has to do with the parents' fantasy of what their ideal child would be and do, and the projection of that ideal onto the impressionable child. The child is used. He or she spends a lifetime trying to actualize an ideal image rather than actualize a true self. The true identity is sacrificed for the family identity.

Peter

Peter was raised in a dogmatic Catholic family; that is, Catholicism was presented as the only true and indisputable religion. He began as an altar boy who would help the priest during Mass. It was clear that his role was to make the family proud by becoming a "man of the cloth," and he was encouraged to do so in some not-so-subtle ways. His parents would tell relatives, and anyone else who would listen, that Peter was studying to become a priest. This began shortly after the time he learned to read! Upon completing high school he entered the seminary, but dropped out when he realized that what he really wanted was to marry and start a family. He realized it had never been his desire to enter the priesthood.

His parents were disapproving when Peter decided to pursue a career outside the church. They really needed him to save the family by becoming a priest, and made it obvious they had a lot on the line. His mother cried for weeks and his father threatened to disown him. Peter felt deeply rejected, and it was at this point he entered therapy complaining of guilt and low self-esteem. In our first session, I asked him to complete some sentences with the first thoughts that came to mind.

Stan: My father expected me to...

Peter: Become a priest.

Stan: My mother expected me to...

Peter: Become a priest

Stan: And I always wanted to...

Peter: I have no idea!

Stan: Sex is...

Peter: Sinful unless you're married.

Peter, in adopting the role of the "Saint," had forfeited his true identity for a shamed one that required a false self. In accepting his family role, he overdeveloped the feminine at the expense of the masculine side of his personality (the opposite of most men in our culture). His avoidance of anger and sexuality was boyish and in conflict with his true self. Behind his facade of saintliness, Peter was struggling with rage at his parents, and sexuality that had been repressed. He felt ashamed because these impulses clashed with his force-fed self-image of being saintly. They were simply unacceptable given his moral code. The resulting conflict left him tied in knots. He was unable to masturbate without enormous shame and guilt, and worried that he might be homosexual. The therapy was geared toward owning and integrating these disowned parts of his self, those parts we referred to playfully as "the rebel" and "the sinner." Until Peter could embrace these perfectly human characteristics, he could not actualize his unique personal identity—one that was based on acceptance of his true self, and based on self-esteem rather than shame.

The "Little Prince/Little Princess"

In order to fully understand this shame-inducing family role, we must examine the incestuous triangle known as the Oedipus complex. In Greek mythology, Oedipus was born to the King and Queen of Thebes. An oracle informed the king that Oedipus was fated to kill him, so the king gave his infant son to a shepherd who was instructed to leave the boy on a mountain to die. However, the shepherd felt compassion for little Oedipus and gave him to the King and Queen of Corinth who had no children. When Oedipus reached puberty, he was informed by an oracle that he was fated to kill his father and marry his mother. Horrified, he chose to leave Corinth to spare the man he believed to be his father. On his way to Thebes he came in contact with his real father. They quarreled, and not knowing who he was, Oedipus killed him in a fit of rage. Entering Thebes, Oedipus was confronted by the Sphinx, a winged monster with the body of a lion and the head and breasts of a woman. Unless Oedipus could solve the riddle presented by the Sphinx, it would strangle him. Oedipus solved the riddle and the appreciative Thebans presented him with a wife, who turned out to be his real mother. Later, when they discovered they were mother and son and guilty of an incestuous crime, Oedipus blinded himself and his mother suicided.

In classic psychoanalysis, the Oedipal complex refers to the intense love relationship between children and their opposite sex parents. According to Freud, little boys and little girls wish to sexually possess their opposite sex parent. The young child (three to five-years-old) feels rivalrous with the same sex parent and wants to get rid of him/her so he or she can have the other parent exclusively. The complex is resolved as the child represses sexual impulses toward the opposite sex parent and hostility toward the same sex parent. Instead the child identifies with, or wants to be like, the same sex parent. In the process of identifying, a beginning conscience is taken in which serves as a strong reminder of the incest taboo. As the child passes through puberty and into adolescence, there is a resurgence of oedipal feelings for the opposite sex parent. Again, the romanticized and sexualized aspect of the relationship is given up. This time the instinctual and incestuous love is reinvested in new and more appropriate relationships, namely girlfriends and boyfriends, and eventually potential wives and husbands.

That there is a sexual component to parent-child relationships may shock or elicit disbelief in some readers (especially those whose parents botched the oedipal phase, or those who are botching it with their own children). We want to deny such feelings because of our dread of any thoughts or impulses that smack of incest. It is important to realize that the sensual and sexual aspect of parent-child affection is "totally normal, natural, and healthy" (Halpern, 1976, p.131). However, the parent who acts from the position of his or her own inner child and imposes those drives or needs on the child does "great psychological damage" (p.132-133).

In an optimal family, the Oedipal situation is resolved in a way that benefits the child's emotional and sexual development. Take for example a family where a four-year-old daughter is feeling oedipal love for her father and competition with her mother. The father makes it clear to his daughter that he is married to the child's mother, without rejecting the child's love or shaming her sexuality. When the little girl says, "I'm going to marry daddy when I grow up," he smiles and responds, "No, mommy and I are a married couple. You will find your own husband someday, if you decide to get married. Meanwhile, we love you." This reassures the child that, as a result of her fantasies, she will not lose her mother's love, nor will she lose the parental couple as a stable and supportive family subsystem.

The understanding parent encourages the child to put limitations on her sexuality. In his book, Incest and Human Love, Jungian analyst Robert Stein explains this process by stating, "Restriction is not repression" (p.75). The child is restricted from sexual contact with the opposite sex parent (it is the adult's responsibility to make sure there is no acting-out), but is not so shamed that sexuality must be repressed.

In families where the "Little Prince/Princess" role is assigned, the child is confronted with a seductive parent who is emotionally needy. Such a parent encourages and capitalizes on the child's oedipal strivings. The child is not asked to put limits on his or her instinctual, but innocent, sexuality. He or she is, in effect, allowed to win the Oedipal struggle and defeat the same sex parent. An inappropriate bond is formed with the opposite sex parent, one that has strong overtones of a romantic and sexual nature. He or she is given the role of "Little Prince" or "Little Princess" and takes the place of the same sex parent.

Parents who assign this role are acting-out their own unresolved oedipal conflicts. They choose their favorite opposite sex child for the part and then give that child admiration for providing emotional supplies. Children need to be admired, but not for adopting pseudo-adult roles and responsibilities. The "special" mother-son or father-daughter relationship that ensues is unconsciously incestuous and represents a breakdown of family boundaries.

In the optimal family, there is clear boundary between generations such that everyone knows who is the parent and who is the child (Beavers in Walsh, 1982, p.48). Children are not "parentified," and parents are not "childified." There is no possibility for the kinds of role conflicts and role reversals that impinge upon the "Little Prince" or "Princess." Whereas the shame-based parent exploits the child, the optimal parent claims and exercises power in a wise and careful way. Parental rules affirm the basic rights of the children. Family roles are assigned in accordance with the child's age, personality, and level of competence. They are functional in that they enhance emotional development and instill an identity that reflects the child's unique individuality. Such roles are age-appropriate tasks that serve the child, rather than scripted parts that serve the family or the parent at the expense of the child. The combination of a clear generational boundary and the judicious use of parental power invites emotional closeness and sharing between family members (pp.48-49).

Families with "Little Princes" and "Little Princesses" have unclear boundaries. The boundary that should separate the family system into a parental subsystem on top and a subsystem of children below is either missing or blurred. Children are pulled across this faulty generational boundary and become cross-bonded with an opposite sex parent. Not only is it unclear who is parent and who is child, it is also unclear who is the most important couple. Instead of the parents really coupling and forming a strong marital bond with one another, they encourage an inappropriate bond with their child.

The child is assigned a family role that inflames oedipal passions and retards emotional and sexual development. Young boys become mommy's "Little Prince," and young girls become daddy's "Little Princess." John Bradshaw considers this role relationship a type of sexual abuse because the parent-child bond becomes romanticized and sexualized (1988, p.49). He quotes Pia Mellody, who states that when "one parent has a relationship with the child that is more important than the relationship they have with their spouse, there is emotional sexual abuse (p.50)." The combination of unclear boundaries and abuse of power creates insecurity and instills a fear of intimacy in the child. More correctly, he or she fears what can happen when they form a close bond with another person, e.g., exploitation, abandonment, sexual abuse, domination, etc.

The "Little Prince/Little Princess" role fulfills the family function of providing emotional gratification and companionship to the needy parent. This role is typical for "gifted children" (Miller, 1981) who reverse roles and adapt to the needs of their parents. Here, the child becomes a "little spouse" who loses the sense of being a child, and is "seduced into the role by a parent who is too afraid and too dysfunctional to get his needs met by another adult (Friel and Friel, p.56)." This pattern is especially prevalent in families where one parent is emotionally or physically absent. This may be due to a workaholic spouse, an untimely death, a failed marriage where the couple is emotionally divorced, or circumstances that require one spouse to be away from home for long periods of time.

In such families, the parent who is left to deal with the children feels cut off, lonely, and starved for companionship. He of she may expect the "Little Prince" or "Little Princess" to replace the missing spouse and function as a grown-up. The child gets reinforced for playing the part of spouse and holds a position of importance in the family. He or she feels admired, and will do whatever is necessary to continue being admired. If the child steps out of role, this admiration changes to harsh disapproval, and the severed parent-child bond activates shame.

This arrangement obviously changes the quality of the parent-child bond and fuels the family romance. The attachment now feels more like a marital bond and the child feels shame over his or her unconscious and incestuous marriage to the opposite sex parent. The child is hopelessly confused and trapped in an Oedipal conflict that cannot be resolved.

The most likely scenario to produce a "Little Prince" or "Little Princess" is a shame-based family where the parents have actually separated or divorced. Regardless of how bad the marriage might have been, such parents usually experience a sense of loss, and then turn to their children to ease their grief.

In their discussion of the "dilemmas and pitfalls" of single-parent families, Morawetz and Walker (1984) include: (1) "when a child is seen as the embodiment of the absent parent," and (2) "when a parent marries his child..." (pp.13-14). The child, who may look, speak, or act similar to the absent spouse, may serve as a reminder of "unacknowledged passionate feelings," and be forced "into a stabilizing role which is almost always to his detriment" (p.14). They go on to state that it is common for separated or divorced parents to move closer to their children to obtain companionship and comfort. This is true for both custodial and noncustodial parents (p.14).

When single parents replace their partnership with a husband or wife with a partnership with a son or daughter, the "Little Prince" or "Little Princess" cannot help but feel as though they have won the oedipal struggle. At some level of consciousness they believe they have defeated the same sex parent and now possess the opposite sex parent sexually and exclusively. That this complex, or group of repressed impulses, is unconscious only makes it more difficult to resolve in adolescence or adulthood. In most cases, the resulting sexual abuse is emotional and disguised rather than physically acted-out, especially if we are talking about mommy's "Little Prince." Daddy's "Little Princess" is at greater risk to become a victim of overtly incestuous behavior. Either way, the role is severely dysfunctional, although the molested child internalizes more shame.

The former husband of a divorced client shared custody of their two daughters, twelve and seven. My client learned that when it was her former husband's turn to have the girls, he would allow the oldest daughter to sleep with him in his bed. There was apparently no overt incest. When confronted with the inappropriateness of this arrangement, he claimed his daughter was lonely (a projection of his own loneliness). My client was also disturbed by a letter she found, written by the daughter to her father, that had a jilted lover quality. My antenna up, I asked some questions about the family romance.

Throughout the marriage, it was clear that the ex-husband treated the relationship with his daughter as far more important than the marital relationship. From dinner until bedtime, he and his "Little Princess" would curl up together in front of the television and touch in various ways. It was clearly sexualized—she would sit on his lap, they would exchange back and foot massages, or they would hug and kiss. He would display none of this affection to his seven-year-old daughter, who incidentally felt quite rejected. Nor did he show any affection whatsoever to his wife during the marriage. They had sexual relations approximately once a year and then he was sexually dysfunctional. When my client would express feelings of jealousy, and that she would like some of his affection, he would fly into a rage and humiliate her in front of the children. These rage reactions represented a defense against the shame he felt over exploiting his daughter for his emotional and sexual gratification. By humiliating his wife, he transferred his shame to her. The intense hostility he carried toward his own rejecting mother was also transferred onto my client. In his eyes, she became the "domineering bitch" that his mother had been.

In an attempt to heal his own oedipal wounds, he cast his oldest daughter in the role of "Little Princess" so she could be the mother and partner he always wanted. This is an unconscious process and, as is usually the case, he intended no harm to his daughter. His acting-out is a reflection of the deprived child within himself, who is attempting to resolve his own oedipal complex by turning to his child for salvation and admiration. Nonetheless, the cost to his daughter, who is seduced into adopting a severely dysfunctional role, is enormous confusion about intimate relationships and sexuality. She comes to see herself in ways that reflect a shame-based identity, e.g., she experiences a vague but chronic sense of badness as a result of the unconscious incestual relationship with her father. She feels consciously guilty in regard to the competitive and outright hostile feelings towards her mother. Because her needs are being sacrificed as a result of the family function she fulfills, she is an easy target to be revictimized outside the family. Revictimization reinforces shame. Only by understanding and changing her family role can she heal the shame that is induced as a result of becoming daddy's "Little Princess."

The "Sick Child"

The "Sick Child" fulfills a function similar to the "Bad Seed" in that he or she detours attention from a dysfunctional part of the family system. The difference is that instead of being a rebellious troublemaker, the "Sick Child" is a compliant placater. To compare, the child who adopts the "Bad Seed" role acts-out to defend against anxiety and shame, discharging these painful feelings into the environment. His defensive behavior is directed against others. On the other hand, the "Sick Child" absorbs anxiety and shame like a sponge and contains them in his body until physical symptoms eventually emerge. He is loyal to the "no expression" rule and his body keeps score. His defensive behavior is directed against himself.

Parents assign the "Sick Child" role when they stumble onto the reality that focusing attention on one of their children avoids tension in the marital relationship. This detouring process is often a multi-generational legacy and they may have fulfilled a similar role in their own families of origin. Assigning such a role is not a conscious process, and such parents do not intend to harm their child. The process begins as one particular child is chosen for the part. The focused-on child is typically the "most sensitive to disturbances in the balance of the family relationship system and, at points of significant tension, is vulnerable to the development of mental, physical, or social problems" (Kerr in Gurman and Kniskern, 1981, p.245).

In terms of family roles, the focused-on child who develops social problems becomes a "Bad Seed." The focused-on child who develops physical problems becomes a "Sick Child." If the focused-on child develops a mental problem, he or she adopts a "Disturbed Child" role (a variation of the "Sick Child"). This does not imply that all children with mental, physical, and/or social problems are victims of parents who assign shame-inducing family roles, only those who are being unconsciously used to divert attention from other areas of family dysfunction. However, some experts state that because physical and emotional illnesses are related to impaired adaptiveness, they are "disorders of the family emotional system—present and past generations" (Kerr and Bowen, 1988, p.243). These authors consider illness to be an outcome of the family emotional process rather than a result of a biological or psychological defect (p.253). It is difficult to simply dismiss this viewpoint as radical because it comes from psychiatrist Murray Bowen, one of the founders of family therapy and the originator of family systems theory. Having trained to some extent with Dr. Kerr, I am certain he would not wish to imply that a child stricken with leukemia in the first year of life is a victim of present family dysfunction. However, he may wish to imply that such a child, as a part of nature, is subject to naturally occurring processes (including generations of family relationships) that culminate in disease (pp.252-253).

Whether illness is the result of constitutional defects or dysfunctional family role relationships, we know that certain children are asked to fulfill a family function that leads them into adopting the "Sick Child" role. How a child is induced to play the part of one who is ill and dependent is hard to accept because it is so insidious. As described earlier, the process begins when a parent chooses (unconsciously) the most emotionally sensitive and constitutionally vulnerable child. It is usually an over-involved and engulfing mother who makes this selection, but she does so with the blessings of an underinvolved and abandoning father. This sets is motion the "perverse triangle," consisting of a controlling mother, distant father, and troubled and symptomatic child. This mother-father-child triangle is driven by chronic anxiety and relationship shame that typically results from the parents' inability to achieve intimacy. By focusing attention on the symptomatic child, the parents can avoid the tension that permeates their relationship and the shame associated with a failed marriage.

The next step in the induction of a child into the sick role is the parental focus, especially the mother, on any indication of illness in the child. A runny nose, a sign of fatigue, or any vague physical symptom is quickly worried over. Out of a need to triangulate the child, this mother will relate to the child as if he or she were ill. Looking like an attentive and loving parent, she is in fact using her child to meet her own selfish needs. The chosen child, who is not resilient in the first place, is reinforced for producing and reporting bodily symptoms. He or she is molded into the desired image by the mother's overreaction and, seeking to gratify her, adopts the "Sick Child" role.

According to Frank Dauer, a clinical psychologist and consultant to many Pacific Northwest therapists, such children become ill by absorbing all the negative energy and dysfunction in the family. They do so in accordance with the unconscious fantasy that they are responsible for sparing other family members from suffering. The child may take this sacrificial attitude even further and entertain a fantasy, again unconscious, that by dying they can take the dysfunction with them—getting rid of it once and for all. Thus, they have an unconscious wish to die that may precipitate a life-threatening illness, suicide, or fatal accident.

Kerr (in Gurman and Kniskern, 1981) refers to this induction as the "family projection process." It is a process in which the child becomes defined by parental emotional reactions, "a definition that originally may have little to do with the realities of the child, but that eventually does become a reality in the child" (pp. 245-246). The induction process leads to a role assignment that fulfills a family function, but at the expense of the child's true personal identity. The focused-on "Sick Child" provides a detour that stabilizes a conflicted marriage, but comes to know himself or herself as a physical weakling or an emotional defect, i.e., the identity is based on and perpetuates shame. Just as the "Bad Seed" takes the heat off his or her siblings, the "Sick Child" protects other children in the family by reducing parental over-involvement and instability.

Jerry

Jerry, a thirty-year-old mental health professional, entered therapy complaining that he was converting stress and anxiety into bodily symptoms during counseling sessions with his clients. "By the end of the day, especially if I see difficult clients, I have trouble breathing. My clients feel better, and I feel worse!" A family of origin interview showed that he had played the "disturbed" and "sick child" roles in an alcoholic family system. His parents were quite unhappy with one another and he was expected to distract them from their marital problems.

Jerry described this detouring process in the autobiography he wrote as a part of treatment. "Both my parents would have sudden and dramatic mood swings. Their emotions were totally out of proportion to whatever stress brought them on. Like the dog would poop on the carpet and mom would go nuts, then dad would beat the dog. The way they acted was mostly determined by my mom's blood alcohol level. If she was bombed, it was what I called crisis time. If she was sober, things were relatively calm, but I knew it was the calm before the storm. Then, out of nowhere, lightning would strike, the clouds would burst, and I would witness terrifying arguments that would almost always lead to threats of divorce. I was subjected to drunken driving, drunken affection, drunken mealtimes, drunken holidays, and drunken friends of the family. I was a little kid trying to cope with crying spells, nervous breakdowns, suicidal gestures, and violent fights. I felt defenseless until one time, in the midst of a fight, I started having an asthma attack and the focus shifted to me. From then on, if I had an attack, or even pretended to have one, mom and dad would stop fighting. It was like magic. Even if mom was drunk, she would pull herself together. I learned that my illness was a way to short-circuit whatever was happening in the family, and get things back to normal, whatever that was."

By diverting attention from parental conflicts, Jerry was able to elicit more stable and functional behaviors from his alcoholic mother and codependent father. His role as "sick child," regardless of its personal cost, gave him some control in an out-of-control family. His symptoms called "time out" and fulfilled a family function by cooling the system until things were less intense. Two mechanisms help explain the payoff for adopting a role that necessitates physical illness. In the first mechanism, Jerry achieves a "primary gain" for his illness in that it pushes his fears of abandonment out of conscious awareness. In the second mechanism, he achieves a "secondary gain" in that he gets support from both parents that otherwise would be withheld. He came to know himself as weak and highly vulnerable to stress, yet went into the mental health field in an attempt to heal his unconscious shame wounds (a common phenomenon).

The recovery process necessitated separation from his parents, especially his engulfing and alcoholic mother, and a willingness to discharge (express) the emotional energy that he had learned to contain and convert into bodily symptoms. Defining a self apart from his family of origin meant quitting the familiar role. He replaced his "Sick Child" role with one that he called the "Separated Son." His newly discovered expressiveness represented a return to natural self-regulation and a rebirth of his true self. He forged a new and true identity in which he came to know himself as sensitive, but tough when he needed to be.

The "Chameleon"

The "Chameleon" is one of the least common, but most shaming, family roles. Like its namesake, the "Chameleon" can change roles at a moment's notice, adapting to the ever-changing family environment. The ability to take on different roles makes such children an indispensable part of the family and, at the same time, may protect the developing self. One day, the child plays the "Impostor" and brings home a good report card or hits a home run that makes his "fill me up" parents proud. The next day, the same child may switch roles and behave like a "Bad Seed," getting into trouble and detouring angry parents who are fighting. If family tensions are running high, the chameleonic child may turn into the "Comedian/Comedienne" and defuse that tension by clowning around and making everyone laugh. When one parent feels isolated and starved for companionship, the child will slip into the "Little Prince" or "Little Princess" role and accept the role of surrogate spouse. The "Chameleon" is not so much an assigned role as a way of characterizing the child who is always switching roles.

Most often the "Chameleon" is an only child, although some children adopt this role regardless of family size. There are no disadvantages to being an only child in a family with good parenting, but in a shame-based family it often means playing different roles at different times. Here, the only child is asked to fulfill several family functions and becomes hopelessly confused as a result of continual role conflict. She is treated like an interchangeable part in the family drama. The cost of playing so many roles is a diffuse identity—she comes to know and experience herself as scattered and unintegrated. The normal process of identity formation is interrupted and the child simply has no idea who she truly is. She becomes an actress, playing one part after another in an unconscious attempt to provide what the family needs. These parts are scripted in the family, but she is unable to leave her role-playing at home. Having forfeited her true self and true identity, all relationships lack stability and authenticity.

A sequence from a family therapy session illustrates this process of aborted identity formation. A concerned father confronted his chameleonic teenage daughter about whether she had sex with a boy she had dated the previous weekend. The daughter, an only child we will call Marilyn, acknowledged that he tried to seduce her but said she told him, "I can't because I'm really into Mother Theresa right now. Too bad, last week I was into Madonna (the rock star)." It was true. The previous week I had been aware of Marilyn playing the "Bad Seed" role and serving as a container for family shame. She had come to the session dressed provocatively in black leather and wearing makeup that resembled war paint. Her mother, who had recently been caught having an extramarital affair, accused Marilyn of looking like a "tramp." This was precisely the reaction Marilyn wanted, and one that fulfilled the family function of taking the heat off her mother.

Now Marilyn had switched into the "Angel" role, and was upholding the family identity of being morally righteous. Her dress, her manner, her makeup, everything about her was reserved and sexually conservative. On other occasions, I saw her play the "Comedienne" and the "Loner," always adapting to what was happening in the family triangle. When her father asked for a separation as a result of his wife's infidelity, Marilyn developed a mysterious neurological disorder that baffled several physicians because there were no objective signs of illness. She had slipped into the "Sick Child" role in an attempt to cement her parents' marriage by giving them a reason to stay together. None of these roles had much if anything to do with Marilyn's true personal identity, and all were based on family shame dynamics.

The phenomenon of multiple personality disorder (MPD) may be related to the family role of "Chameleon." MPD is far more common than was once believed, and is an adaptive response to overwhelmingly shaming trauma, primarily the combination of molestation, battering, and terrorizing. In various studies of psychiatric patients, MPD is three to nine times more prevalent in females than in males (DSM-III-R, 1987, p.271). The essential feature of the disorder is the coexistence of two or more distinct personalities that sometimes take over and assume full control of the person's behavior (pp.269-270). A developmental model of MPD would suggest that everyone is born with the potential for multiple personalities, but that during the process of development most children are more or less successful in forming an integrated self (Putnam, 1989, p.51). In other words, most of us are able to combine different behavioral patterns (roles) into a single and whole self. The multiple, faced with extreme and repetitive childhood trauma, dissociates or spaces out in order to escape the scene, numb the physical and emotional pain, repress the memory, and detach the self (e.g., the rape is happening to someone else) (p.53).

Most children who adopt the "Chameleon" role are in no danger of developing MPD. Those who do are especially vulnerable to the family trance. They prove to be exceptionally good hypnotic subjects, prone to using dissociation as a defense, and are subjected to shame-based parents who act like human monsters. Such children become chameleonic to adapt to their extremely traumatic family environments. Each time these vulnerable and dissociative "Chameleons" switch into a certain family role, additional scenes are internalized and a personal history accumulates for that role. The failure to consolidate these roles into an integrated self leads to the existence of distinct alter personalities. An alter personality is an entity with a persistent sense of self and a characteristic way of thinking, feeling, and behaving (Kluft, 1985).

These alter personalities respond to internal and external cues by periodically taking over and controlling the multiple's behavior. Some alters know about other alters, some don't. Those that are aware of the others may form coalitions, viewing one alter as an ally and another as an adversary. The behavior of an alter personality resembles the behavior that is consistent with a specific family role. For example, the multiple often switches into an impostor-like alter that appears competent and successful and is expected to handle the stress of work and career. There is typically a bad seed-like alter who is promiscuous and abuses alcohol or drugs. Because sexual abuse is almost always a predisposing factor in the development of MPD, other alters often feel contemptuous toward this acting-out personality. The chief adversary is an angel-like alter that is religious and feels repulsed by sexuality and substance abuse. Such alter personalities almost always have proper names. In one client, a seductive alter was appropriately named "Jezebel" (after the shameless woman who married Ahab in the Bible), and the angelic and anti-sexual alter went by "Victoria" (for her prudish Victorian morals).

Continuing with the parallels between family roles and typical alter personalities (doing individual therapy with a multiple is similar to doing family therapy), a loner-like alter isolates herself from others to provide space and autonomy. She is generally unaware of other alters, rarely calls attention to herself, and frequently feels suicidal. She is offset by a more outgoing comedienne-like alter who is brought out to mask depression and defuse tension in social situations. The little princess-like alter is a Pollyanna who comes out to minimize family dysfunction. She idealizes and clings to the abusive parent because she will otherwise feel completely abandoned and overcome by the fear that she cannot survive without her parents (fear of annihilation).

Although multiples are at risk to suffer a psychotic breakdown, they are not crazy. Rather, their symptoms represent a brilliant adaptive reaction to a crazy environment. For example, a sick child-like alter may emerge to get some much needed attention and care from otherwise cruel and neglectful parents. At the same time, this alter punishes the multiple for acting-out, for "losing time," for having hallucinations, or for finding clothes in her closet and not knowing how they got there, e.g., by producing physical symptoms such as painful headaches.

Finally, there is even a chameleon-like alter that psychiatrist and MPD expert Frank Putnam calls an "imitator." This alter mimics other alters and can look and sound just like the personality they are imitating (1989, p.113). If a bad seed-like alter propositions a man and then disappears, the "imitator" might be brought out to help a sexually inhibited alter who finds herself in an unexpected predicament, i.e., by mimicking the missing "bad seed" who knows how to handle sexual situations. It may be the "Chameleon's" early experience of changing roles quickly that makes possible the multiple's ability to switch between alters in times of stress.

To summarize, given overwhelming trauma and defensive dissociation in a child who has already adopted the role of "Chameleon," the different parts she plays for the family may take on lives of their own and develop into distinct personalities (MPD). What originated as a role that served family function, crystallizes into an alter personality that protects the vulnerable child from recurrent trauma. Regardless of whether the "Chameleon" role results in ordinary role conflict or full-blown multiplicity, the child who adopts this role has no chance to form an integrated self and cohesive identity. The sexual, interpersonal, intrapsychic, achievement, and spiritual parts of the self never consolidate into a unified and whole self. The chameleonic child forms a diffuse identity that doesn't hold together—it feels different and defective. It lacks continuity and sameness. Such an identity has little to do with who he or she truly is and is based on shame rather than self-esteem.

Commonalities and Consequences of Shame-Inducing Roles

We have examined eight distinct and characteristic roles that children take on in shame-based families. Although the roles appear quite different, they share common features and function in nearly identical ways. The first point of commonality is that while they are relatively stable over time, children occasionally switch from one role to another. In other words, these roles are flexible. It is not often that a child fits perfectly into one role and stays put. He or she is likely to change roles in accordance with changes in the family. Role changes may be responses to a crisis caused by internal or external stressors. An example of an internal stress would be a parental fight that pulls the child into a role that provides distraction, e.g., the "Comedian" who defuses tension. An example of an external stress would be a situation where father loses his job, mother returns to work, and daughter changes into the "Little Princess" role as daddy's surrogate spouse.

Other changes in the family may be reflections of different stages in the family life cycle, and these too may lead to switching roles. For example, an "Impostor" who has been a perfect child

leaves home at age eighteen, then begins to act-out his unacknowledged anger, now taking on the role of "Bad Seed." It is
not that this rebelliousness is a new character trait, it was merely
suppressed in order to play the part of "Impostor." Another
sibling, still at home, may take over the vacated "Impostor" role
that once belonged to his now wayward older brother. This
move returns the family to its previous state of balance and
maintains parental pride. Children sometimes play a version of
musical chairs with family roles, especially in larger families. As
one role opens up, it is filled, opening a new role for another
sibling. And, different roles overlap and blend so that one child
may play several parts at once, e.g., taking on an identity that is
part "Impostor" and part "Saint." We see that it is not just the
"Chameleon" who plays different parts at different times, although he or she does the most switching.

Second, the eight roles establish and maintain more consistent
and predictable patterns of behavior in an unstable family. Instability is the norm in many shame-based families. It is experienced
as a feeling of dread or chronic tension. This tension is generated
by the fear of what might happen and is usually related to shame
anxiety; that is, the fear that one could be shamed at any moment.
Shame anxiety motivates the self-protective wish to hide, and the
eight dysfunctional roles become hiding places. While the child
is pretending to be someone he or she is not, the authentic and
more vulnerable parts of the self are safely hidden away. Adopting a role means that you agree to repeat specified patterns of
behavior that fulfill family functions. This stabilizes the system
by bringing a semblance of order to a chaotic and unsafe environment.

Third, most of the roles call attention to the child's behavior
and away from shameful and shame-inducing parental behaviors.
This is especially true in families where the child becomes the
focus of attention, e.g., the troublemaking "Bad Seed," the entertaining "Comedian/Comedienne," or the focused-on "Sick Child."

I once treated a teenage girl with "globus hystericus," a lump-
in-the-throat feeling that made it difficult for her to swallow.
Under stress, she would also suffer choking spells where she
would practically turn blue. I saw her individually for several
sessions and we got nowhere. Then, I asked her to make a

statement that began with the words, "One thing I can't swallow is..." and she responded "...the way dad pushes mom around!" Her physical symptoms were an expression of an intense emotional conflict—one part of her enraged with a bullying father, another part terrified of expressing it. These symptoms were not consciously manufactured, but served to keep her inner conflict out of awareness (primary gain), as well as elicit support from her parents (secondary gain). Her choking episodes distracted her parents at times of imminent marital conflict and warded off further instances of wife battering. The "Sick Child" role fulfilled an important family function, but exacted a cost from this unfortunate girl.

Less obvious was the cost to the family, namely that detouring attention from the real issues maintained denial, thus preserving the status quo in a rigid and violent system. Family therapy was indicated and family members slowly came out of denial. The father was confronted over many sessions and, fearing the loss of his family, signed a written agreement to stop using any form of intimidation or violence. He learned to take time outs whenever he felt explosive and eventually order was restored. The girl's symptoms disappeared along with the family's need for her self-negating role.

The fourth feature the different roles share in common is that playing a role and fulfilling a family function gives the child a sense of purpose. This is critical in a family that fails to convince him or her that they truly belong. Although the role denies the child's basic rights and retards emotional development, it reduces the uncertainty about what is expected and secures his or her place in the family. This is especially true of the roles that contain the most socially desirable elements, namely the overachieving "Impostor," the charming "Comedian/Comedienne," and the "Saint/Angel" who represses the dark side of the personality and appears full of goodness and light. All these roles reinforce the child's belief (and later the adult's) that getting love is conditional upon performance and that feelings of worth must be earned and then earned again.

The fifth commonality is the most important and has to do with the issue of authentic selfhood. By playing an assigned and scripted part, the child is forced to give up the real life being that is uniquely them. This means that each role requires that the child hide away the true self, i.e., become codependent to ensure survival. This is a good news, bad news scenario. The bad news is that, in the guise of a family role, the child must erect a false self to buffer emotional wounds that shame the true self. The greater the ordeal, the deeper the wound, the greater the suppression of the true self and reliance upon the false self. The false self can be thought of as a collection of behaviors which coalesce into different and dysfunctional family roles. Each role begins as an assigned part in the family drama and becomes a way of being. This false self role may fulfill a family function, but at the expense of the child's emotional and social development. It may even teach and instill socially desirable qualities, e.g., being unselfish, but such qualities are never experienced as genuine and may impede healthy functioning. The same behaviors that allowed the child to survive a shaming environment often become obstacles to satisfying adult relationships.

The good news is that even though these family roles are self-negating and dysfunctional, they also serve a protective function. By presenting a false self disguised as a family role, the true self can be safely hidden away. This unconscious strategy allows the vulnerable and wounded true self to survive by minimizing further encounters with shame. The true self is preserved in a dormant state and can later by reborn in the context of an affirming and corrective relationship. This rebirthing process, perhaps the principal goal of psychotherapy, leads to the formation of a true personal identity that is characterized by positive self-esteem.

Part II

Rising Above Shame

If patients were in touch with what they really feel, if they were able to verbalize what they truly yearn for, they would confess what they want most desperately is a relationship in which they feel worthwhile. They want to be assured that they are valued.

Sheldon Cashdan, Object Relations Therapy

You need only claim the events of your life to make yourself yours. When you truly possess all you have been and done, which may take some time, you are fierce with reality.

Florida Scott Maxwell

Chapter Five

The Process of Healing

The process of healing shame always occurs in the context of a relationship. That relationship must be an affirming one that says positively and convincingly, "You are lovable and worthy of respect!" This process may begin in childhood when a playmate tells you your parent shouldn't have treated you that way, or when, as an adult, a close friend gives you a supportive hug during a crisis. There is no substitute for the affirmation that comes from relating to another human being who validates you and your experience.

It is true that you can make changes by reading self-help books and repeating positive affirmations, but this approach won't heal a shamed sense of self. It deals with symptoms and does not address the real source of the problem. Affirmations alone amount to skating over the surface of the personality when the hard work of healing is to be found at a deeper level. Until internalized shame is acknowledged and released, positive affirmations simply don't compute for the person with low self-esteem. For example, if you had a belittling parent and tend to be self-critical, parroting "I am a competent person" umpteen times a day will only clash with your core belief ("I am inadequate!"). Instead of bringing about a positive change, it may create more internal conflict. Affirmations that are disbelieved have the potential to backfire. They are deflected by the shaming parent who now resides inside the self. This internal parent steps up the attack in response to positive affirmations. The inability to self-heal is then experienced as one more failure, one more example of how the person is inadequate.

With the exception of those individuals who took in optimal amounts of shame, a deeper and more intensive approach is required if shame is to be healed. For those who internalized too much shame, the hard work of healing must be done "closer to the bone." In order to release internalized shame and replace it with a positive sense of self-esteem, you are going to need help. Trying to do the work on your own, given the necessity for remembering and re-experiencing painful shame scenes, would be like trying to surgically remove your own ruptured appendix. This is not to imply that getting help will enable you to avoid the pain, because it won't. However, a therapist who understands shame dynamics and has worked through most of his or her own shame, can help you avoid dead ends and support you when the going gets rough. Furthermore, a therapist who consistently affirms your worth is instrumental in providing new scenes to be taken in—positive scenes to replace the ones that resulted in shame.

I make an assumption that every client is capable of resolving shame given an affirming relationship with their therapist, a commitment to heal, and sufficient time. An affirming relationship is corrective in that it repairs the damage to the self and re-parents the shamed child within. A commitment to heal is your promise to that internal child to complete the therapy process. This means not quitting if things get worse before they get better. This is often the case because therapy "stirs up the pot." It means facing your shame and tolerating the pain when it would be easier and more familiar to go back to booze, drugs, food or whatever. Committing to therapy means you begin to take the shamed child within seriously, validate his or her experiences and feelings, and vow to do a better job re-parenting than your parents did the first time around.

Healing shame takes time and there are no short cuts. This is a source of frustration to those who are suffering most and those who feel impatient about the process. This is understandable because we long to love ourselves and desperately want to be free of emotional pain. Nevertheless, "don't push the river" is a reminder some clients need in order to slow down and stay with the issue at hand.

Some clients want to plunge into highly charged shame issues before they are ready. I have been asked many times to hypnotize clients in order to facilitate the recovery of suspected childhood molestation scenes. While this could conceivably be appropriate and good therapy, it is more likely to be disrespectful of the person's defenses and could precipitate a decompensation, i.e., a breakdown in the person's defense mechanisms that leaves her feeling overwhelmed. There is a reason, and a good one, that certain scenes are repressed from conscious awareness. When the time is right, they will emerge to be processed and worked through. Stripping a person of her defenses in order to speed up the process always has the opposite effect. It accesses traumatic memories and either interrupts or stops the process altogether by destroying trust in the therapist.

Every client presents different resources and works at a different pace. How much time you will need in therapy is a function of several factors:

1. Your unique combination of internalized shame-inducing messages,rules, and roles, i.e., the severity of parental mistreatment.

2. Your self-esteem as a reflection of how positively or negatively you evaluate the five different parts of the self, i.e., how much shame you have around the issues of body-image or sexuality, relationships, identity, achievement, and/or spirituality.

3. Your current life circumstances as a reflection of a shamed sense of self. This includes the ways in which self-inflicted shame, e.g., self-blame, and shame-based relationships re-enact childhood scenes, e.g., marrying a wife batterer who repeats the pattern of being battered by your father.

4. Your inborn or constitutional tendency toward emotional vulnerability versus resiliency, and the adaptiveness or maladaptiveness of your learned defensive style.

5. Your support system consisting of family, friends, church, support groups, and perhaps most importantly, the extent to which the relationship between you and your therapist is affirming.

6. Your financial resources. Therapy can be expensive even if you have insurance coverage and your therapist believes in a sliding scale fee (pay in accordance with income). If your resources are limited, you may need to see your therapist less often than is ideal, or plan periodic recesses from therapy. Such

arrangements stretch out the process. Group therapy is a less
expensive but workable alternative to individual therapy. There
are many self-help groups (usually without professional leaders
and modeled after the twelve-step program of Alcoholics Anonymous) that are free.

The alternative to getting help and healing your shame is to be
bound by it, to allow it to control your life. Until shame is
acknowledged and worked through, we are compelled to re-
enact scenes from our childhoods—either by shaming others,
shaming ourselves, or setting ourselves up to be shamed by
someone else. The compulsion to repeat the past is at some level
of awareness an attempt to find a good ending to a bad aspect of
childhood, but it only results in more pain and shame. We will
be haunted by a feeling of being inferior, inadequate, or defective
as a person. We will suffer symptoms such as low self-esteem,
depression, relationship problems, and all kinds of addictive
behaviors. The self-affirming choice is thus to commit to the
process of healing, and I believe the treatment of choice is
individual psychotherapy.

It is my experience that this process involves the following six
steps:

1. Acknowledging your shame
2. Developing an affirming relationship
3. Releasing your shame
4. Countering messages, breaking rules, and quitting roles
5. Confronting your shame-inducing parents
6. Forgiving and letting go

Each of these steps is actually a process within a process and
this is not a "cookbook" approach. These steps overlap in that
the psychotherapy client is always working on several steps at
once, even if the focus is on one particular step. We will examine
each step, one at a time. They are of crucial importance. Completing these steps serves as a launching pad for rising above
shame.

Step One: Acknowledging Your Shame

We were approaching the end of our first session and I asked Trudy for any dreams she'd had the night before. She said she had a "weird" dream in the middle of the night and that it was embarrassing, but she was willing to disclose it. I asked her to close her eyes and get the dream back in full detail. I encouraged her to allow herself to feel what was happening in the dream, and to tell it to me in present tense, as if it were happening right now. She took a deep breath and started slowly, as if she was opening Pandora's box. "It was more of a nightmare. I'm lying in bed in the house I grew up in...in my bedroom. My closet door is opening and a skeleton walks over to my bed. I'm really scared and I run from the room into another room I don't recognize. Then I realize I'm naked and I'm trying to cover myself up because there's a man in the room with me. Then I woke up."

Trudy's unconscious was being most helpful in sending her this dream message on the eve of beginning psychotherapy. The dream informs her that she has a "skeleton in the closet," symbolizing a dark secret that is leading her into therapy (I later learned that it had to do with incest). Running from the skeleton, refusing to acknowledge her past, is what she had always done and, as a result, she has unhealed shame. The room she doesn't recognize is surely my office and I am surely the man in the room. Her nakedness is both a reference to feeling exposed and a desire to be less secretive, less defensive. Trying to cover up is an expression of her conflict, namely the wish to be "seen" and the fear of being shamed—hence she hides herself.

I thanked Trudy for being so open and willing to take the risk in her first session. I explained that therapy activates feelings of shame in everyone because the therapist focuses attention on the client as he self-discloses private details of his life. I reassured Trudy that I would respect her privacy and that I would not pressure her to reveal herself. I told her that the first step toward healing is acknowledging the painful emotions that necessitate treatment. Then, I quoted Oscar Wilde: "If you have skeletons in the closet, take them out and dance with them!" We laughed together and she seemed less self-conscious.

When a client's primary complaints indicate internalized shame, coming out of denial and acknowledging parental mistreatment is the first step in the healing process. Preparation for this first step is often the encouragement of a friend, teacher, physician, minister, or family member to get help. In Trudy's case, this encouragement had come from her sister, who was also molested as an adolescent. Both had been victimized by a father who gave "sex education" lectures that included masturbating in their presence. For Trudy, acknowledging her shame meant admitting that her father was not teaching her about sex, and that masturbating in front of her took advantage of her powerlessness. It also meant acknowledging that being molested by the most important man in her life damaged her self-esteem and ability to trust others. Her entire life, Trudy coped with the trauma of sexual abuse and betrayal without support. In order to "make it not be true," she relied on the defense mechanism of denial and either pretended the abuse never occurred or, when she remembered it, pretended that it wasn't abuse.

Denial is a defense that avoids the awareness of shame by not acknowledging that one was subjected to the messages, rules, or roles that induce shame. It is a strategy where the child, and later the adult, refuses to acknowledge the painful reality of her family life. As an adult, she typically perceives her childhood experiences from one of four positions:

1. "I was not shamed." This is what therapists refer to as massive denial. The adult shamed as a child simply denies that she was abandoned, molested, terrorized, or whatever. She refuses to admit that she was expected to live according to dehumanizing rules or adopt a self-negating family role. Massive denial is employed when an acknowledgment would threaten to flood one's awareness with shame, e.g., "My father had sex with me!"

2. "I was shamed, but it was my fault." Here, the shame-based person attempts to deny a painful awareness by blaming herself. There is an acknowledgment that there was rejection, or a "no mistakes" rule, or a "bad seed" role, or whatever, but it is effectively denied by an assumption of responsibility for the shame that was induced. During an initial interview, a male client with a sexual addiction told me he was raised in a "wonderful, loving family" (I knew I was in for some hard work). I later asked him how he was disciplined and he answered, "I was spanked with a belt." I told him, "That's called a whipping," and he

quickly added, "But it only happened when I deserved it!" By denying his early trauma through self-blame, he avoided the shame associated with being battered and feeling unlovable. Taking the blame also allowed him to protect his abusive father from the retaliatory rage he experienced at a deeper level. His sexual compulsiveness was in the service of maintaining denial. It not only allowed him to stay away from unacceptable feelings of shame, grief, and rage, but each sexual conquest proved to the child within that he was lovable.

3. "I was shamed, but it wasn't that big a deal." By denying that things are really that bad, the minimizer avoids the feeling of being overwhelmed by shame. Those who take this position convince themselves they do not need to deal with unfinished business because whatever harmed them "wasn't that bad" to begin with (Simon and Simon, 1990, p.88). The wound is simply disavowed. This strategy usually comes straight from the internalized voice of the shaming parent who minimizes the damage they inflict, e.g., "Don't tell me your butt hurts, I barely laid a hand on you." This was Trudy's position. She tried to convince herself that it wasn't that big a deal because her father never actually touched her. A variation of this position is the client who makes invalidating comparisons in order to minimize her wounds, e.g., "God, you read about these children who were raped by their fathers. All my dad did was fondle my breasts a couple of times." A broken toe doesn't hurt any less because someone else has a broken leg.

4. "I was shamed, but I've forgiven the shamer." This denial strategy is what I call "premature forgiveness." It acknowledges the wound, but makes believe that the wound is already healed. By taking this stance, the person not only avoids the pain and shame associated with the wound, but escapes from the hard work of healing. Marsha, a young mother, entered therapy because she could not let her five-year-old daughter out of her sight. The daughter was having separation anxiety and difficulties adjusting to kindergarten. I asked, "What are your fantasies about what would happen if you weren't always there to protect her?" "Sexual abuse," she replied. I asked if she had been a victim of sexual abuse as a child. Her head bowed, her shoulders slumped, and she looked like she wanted to disappear. In a little girl voice she said, "My father molested me, but I've gotten over it." "How?" I inquired. She looked up, and still wearing her little

girl voice told me, "I forgave him when I became a born-again Christian." Marsha hadn't really forgiven her father because she never allowed herself to acknowledge the intense feelings associated with being molested and betrayed. There is neither healing nor forgiveness without full acknowledgment and understanding.

Marsha was defending herself against shame and rage and tried to take a shortcut to wellness. What's so bad about that? Nothing, if she were still a child. But as an adult who is denying the impact of incest on her life, she perpetuates her shame and passes on her own unfinished business to her already troubled daughter. True forgiveness for the shamer is almost always the last step in the process of healing, and isn't necessary to heal shame. More on that later.

Denial is foremost among many defenses used to protect the self against intolerable feelings. The same messages, rules, and roles that induce shame also threaten to overwhelm the child with other powerful emotions. To fully acknowledge the effects of shame, we must also develop an awareness of the secondary emotions that accompany it, primarily grief and rage. The child who internalizes too much shame always suffers irretrievable losses that result in painful grief, e.g., loss of family and self-esteem. It hurts, and it hurts bad, to be shamed by someone you depend upon, and parental shame attacks activate primitive impulses to get even. To ward off secondary grief, retaliatory rage, and other negative feelings that accompany shame (fear, loneliness, disgust) the child develops a protective shield of defenses.

These defense mechanisms are relatively unconscious and involuntary mental strategies develop to withstand the assault on the different parts of the self. Their purpose is to hide from awareness any feeling or impulse that might be overwhelming if experienced, and shamed if expressed. Emotions that become bound by shame, that is, those that automatically activate shame once they are experienced, are too painful to experience in awareness. For example, being battered activates shame, but it also generates fear—which automatically activates even more shame, because the victim has been taught that it is shameful to be afraid. Hence, the battered child is caught in a vicious circle of unwanted feelings. The blend of shame and fear (not to mention rage) is too much to experience in awareness. Shame, as well as feelings that are bound by shame, however valid and authentic, are excluded from awareness. They are either avoided altogether or replaced by feelings more acceptable to the parents. In this way, the child's defenses become involved in erecting a false self to do business with a shaming parent.

Children typically use a variety of defense mechanisms to avoid awareness of shame and its accompanying emotions. Such defenses also protect the hidden and vulnerable true self from the threat presented by the shaming parent. They arise in response to the perception of danger to the integrity of the self, then seek to hide certain feelings or conflicts from awareness. A particular defense, or combination of defenses, is used depending on the particular combination of shaming messages, rules, and roles. The child draws conclusions about how he or she has to be in order to live with the shame-inducing parent, and their defenses help them to be that way.

In childhood, our defenses were our salvation, but in adulthood they resist the process of healing. What was once adaptive becomes maladaptive, and prevents acknowledgment of shame. Thus, part of the healing process involves the breakdown of defenses. I believe it was Freud who said, "In order to make an omelette, you have to break the eggs." If we are to put aside defenses, it is important that we understand the functions they have served. Then we can work through our previously hidden feelings, and develop more mature ways of taking care of ourselves. The most common defenses are (in alphabetical order with an emphasis on shame issues):

Acting-Out

You are acting-out when your behavior unconsciously expresses a forbidden feeling or impulse that is really intended for your parent. This is an action strategy that seeks to discharge repressed emotional energy and relieve inner tensions by acting impulsively. It is designed to resolve conflicts with shaming parents to "even the score" for being rejected, molested, battered, or whatever. The person acting-out doesn't think and doesn't consider the consequences. I've had several clients who as adolescents acted-out by making unsuccessful attempts to kill their abusive parents. One put ground glass in her incestuous father's food, and another put rat poison in her sadistic father's coffee. These are extreme examples, but feelings of rage and fantasies of revenge are normal reactions to parental humiliation. More typical ways of children acting-out to get even are wetting the bed (being pissed off), lying (defeating the all-knowing parent), stealing (getting something for nothing to balance the books), or fighting (displacing rage from the parent to a safer target). Adults are acting-out when they compulsively overeat to spite a controlling parent, engage in promiscuous sexual behavior to defy a religious parent, or practice a self-destructive addiction to show a parent how damaged they are.

Denial

As explained earlier, you are in denial when you pretend that something didn't happen or that, if it happened, it had no impact on you. It is a mechanism where one simply refuses to acknowledge a painful aspect of reality. Because denial must refuse incoming data, it leads to the development of distorted perceptions of reality, i.e., poor reality testing. For example, one client who denied the impact of being molested by her grandfather, reported that in college she saw a counselor because she was convinced of being pregnant, even though she had never engaged in sexual intercourse. Another client, overwhelmed by grief, insisted that it was not his mother that was lowered into the grave, it was "someone else." Several days later, he "came to his senses."

Dissociation

You are dissociating when you "space out" in order to disconnect from an emotional experience that is traumatic. It involves a temporary disruption of normal consciousness during which overwhelming thoughts or feelings are split off and not experienced. A dissociative reaction results in a change in one's sense of self and in one's ability to remember what happened while he or she was dissociating. The child may feel like she is dreaming or that her feelings belong to another person. Children subjected to the betrayal and humiliation of incest invariably use dissociation as a primary defense. It is as if they say, "Do what you want to my body, I'm not in it!"

Intellectualization

You are using intellectualization when your energy is invested in thinking as a way of avoiding the experience of intense and disturbing feelings. The child who broods over abstract matters or insignificant details is staying "above his feelings" and "in his head." By staying "out of his body" (the feeling center), he spares himself the agony of shame, grief or any other painful emotion. This defense is especially prevalent in families where the "Don't express yourself" rule makes the world of emotion an unsafe place.

Passive Aggression

You are being passive-aggressive when you are expressing anger or rage indirectly. This strategy allows children to covertly express feelings that would be unsafe to express overtly. The child, or adult, passively resists the parents' demands by procrastinating, dawdling, forgetting, stubbornness, or intentional inefficiency (DSM-III-R, 1987, p.394). One client, who had been terrorized by her father, gleefully related how at age sixteen she baked him meat loaf made with dog food, "And the dumb shit ate it!" She dished out the same disrespect that he showed her, and did it in a way she could get away with, thus sparing herself more humiliation.

Projection

You are projecting when you ascribe to others your own unacknowledged and unwanted thoughts, feelings, or impulses. It is the unconscious process of throwing painful emotions out of the self and onto another. An angry child who tells his parent, "You hate me!," may be projecting the anxiety-provoking feeling "I hate you!" The projective defense is necessitated by the parent's inability to accept the child's rage without counter-attacking. If the hateful feeling is allowed in awareness and expressed, the child is likely to elicit more shame, e.g., getting battered. It makes sense to defend the self by projecting, which may even elicit a nurturing response from the parent, e.g., "Mommy doesn't hate you. She loves you!" Projection may involve an accurate perception, but it is still a way of getting rid of an undesirable personal experience. For instance, a client recently accused me of being stubborn. I replied, "It's true. I'm stubborn as hell, but I'd like you to check that out as a projection." She did and was able to own her stubbornness, which led to an awareness of how it was holding her back in therapy.

Projective Identification

This defense is similar to projection in that one person puts something into another person that really belongs in his or her own container. It is a remnant of the preverbal wish to be understood without having to use words, and is thus a primitive form of communication. For example, a wife may behave in a way that makes her husband feel crazy, which is precisely how she feels. Her behavior not only induces him to feel a certain way, it induces him to act a certain way. He becomes the container for her craziness, and then acts it out for her, e.g., exploding into a fit of rage. Thus, she rids herself of an unwanted part, then proceeds to attack him for being like she is (she identifies with him). She is essentially having a relationship with a disowned and enraged part of her self. The other side of projective identification is to put good parts of the self into another for safekeeping. This strategy protects the good parts from the bad, especially the internalized bad parent. A client repeatedly told me, "It's a good thing you care about me, or I'd really go to pot!" By depositing the self-caring (good) part of himself in me, whom he saw as protective and dependable, he kept it safe from his self-destructive (bad) parts. When he became more stable and dependable, I explained this defense to him and he re-owned this integral part of himself. Back in possession of this good part, he could take care of himself in my absence.

Repression

As a child, you relied on this strategy to force powerful and painful feelings out of awareness, especially during traumatic experiences. It is different from suppression, which is a defense where you intentionally avoid thinking about some shameful or anxiety-provoking scene. An example of repression would be the boy who feels enraged in response to being humiliated by his father, but unconsciously pushes the rage out of awareness in accordance with the parental "no expression" rule. This defense would be considered adaptive in that it protects the boy from feeling overwhelmed and from the consequences of breaking the rule. If his repressed rage is highly charged, it may reappear in consciousness but in a disguised form, e.g., the boy dreams of killing a monster (symbolizing father) or displaces his hostility somewhere less threatening ("I hate the cops!"). If you were administered overdoses of shame in childhood, you may be unable to remember much of your childhood as a result of repression. Scenes that induced shame have often been ejected from conscious awareness, and are not allowed to return. During the course of therapy, after a safe and secure environment is established, much of what has been pushed into the unconscious returns to awareness to be healed.

In childhood, these defenses, and others, are emotional life-savers that serve to buffer the child from traumatic experiences that would otherwise be overwhelming. They are to be honored. Such defenses are far less needed in an environment where parents function as an emotional buffer, standing "between the child and the trauma" as is their responsibility (Middelton-Moz and Dwinell, 1986, p.7). In a shame-based family, where the parents are the source of trauma, such defenses are essential for emotional survival, but a price is paid. However adaptive, these self-protective strategies siphon off a great deal of energy that should be going into emotional and social development.

In addition, defense mechanisms cannot prevent the internalization of shame. And, once shame has been taken into the self, these defenses block acknowledgment of shame and thus resist the process of healing. This means that the same defenses that were once lifesaving must be set aside to allow shame scenes into conscious awareness where they can be worked through. It does not mean being at the mercy of others, because everyone needs to defend themselves. The idea is not to leave the client defenseless, but to gain access to and work through feelings so that childhood defenses become less necessary. Then clients can learn to cope rather than merely defend themselves.

To acknowledge shame implies that you recognize and accept (not approve of) the shaming messages, rules, and roles in your family of origin. It is a process of becoming aware of the ways in which you were induced to feel inferior, inadequate, or defective as a person. This is difficult enough, but becomes even more so because you are likely to feel shame about feeling ashamed.

Setting aside your defenses in a safe environment allows you to remember, look at, and feel what was previously excluded from awareness. To acknowledge fully requires that we re-experience our past, rather than merely talk about it.

The process of putting aside defenses and fully acknowledging shame was apparent in Trudy's case. When she reported the molestation scene in which she was forced to watch her father masturbate, she told her story with no emotion whatsoever. After examining (and honoring) her defenses, she decided to stop minimizing what happened to her. This time she chose to allow her previously unaccepted feelings to surface. She felt disgust at the memory of him ejaculating, and came close to vomiting in my wastebasket. She allowed herself to regress and re-experience the feeling she had as a teenage girl when the molestation scene occurred. For the first time, she really understood how she had taken the bad qualities of her father into herself and formed a core belief that said, "I am dirty!" She accepted a painful reality, one that had led to an identity as a helpless victim and nothing more. In therapy, she came to know herself as a survivor, someone who made it through a traumatic childhood to blossom as an adult.

To fully acknowledge a painful reality brings about a new way of "being-in-the-world," one that enhances self-honesty and the potential for change (Greenberg and Safran, 1987, p.194). Accepting a feeling in awareness informs us of what we want; that is, feelings are information that motivate a person to act in a way that fulfills desire (pp.193-194). Since each feeling has a corresponding action, I asked Trudy questions like, "What is your disgust telling you to say or do?", and "How do you want your relationship with your father to change?" These questions were designed to encourage her to express her long-discarded true self and thus break the parental rule of silence. Permission to express herself led to the release of shame, rage, and disgust that she had carried since adolescence. Given that her father continued to insist that his "sex education" lectures were harmless, she chose to end their relationship. And, given that he was a schoolteacher who had access to children, she sent a letter to the school board in his home town documenting his history of sexual offending. These actions were taken because she wanted to do the right thing and get well, not because she wanted to get even—hence she had my full support.

Acknowledging her shame and the memories of being molested was a first step in Trudy's process of healing. The next step involved developing an affirming relationship with me, one where she felt openly valued. By telling her story to someone who validated what happened, and validated her feelings about it, Trudy was eventually able to rebirth her true self and form an identity that was based on self-esteem. She was well along in the process of healing her shame.

Step Two: Developing an Affirming Relationship

If you have never been in therapy, or even if you have, you are not expected to know what to look for or how to find a therapist. Ask friends if they can recommend a good therapist, or if they know someone who can. Attend Adult Children Anonymous (ACA) groups and chat with others who are familiar with therapists in your area. Then make some phone calls and ask a few questions.

Keep in mind that you are considering hiring someone who would fulfill an important and demanding position, so think in terms of interviewing more than one person. Such an interview is ideally done in person, but if this is not practical, then a telephone interview is the next best idea. Most therapists are more than happy to give you some time to ask questions over the phone. Some will even consent to a brief face-to-face interview at no charge, but beware of anyone who feels too invested in having you become their client.

You may wonder whether you would work best with a male or female therapist. Some clients prefer to see a therapist who is the opposite sex of the parent who inflicted the deepest shame wounds. While this is understandable, it isn't necessarily the best decision because it eliminates the possibility of a corrective relationship with a therapist who is the same sex as the shaming parent. I certainly don't believe men should see only male therapists or women should see only female therapists. Clients should see therapists who are competent and affirming, and they come in both sexes. Trust your intuition.

It is also a good idea to "take your new therapist for a test drive" before committing to the process. Think of the first couple of sessions as time to decide whether you can work well as a team, whether you have a good feeling about your therapist. Therapy can be expensive, so in the long run, it's cost effective to get with the right person from the outset. Be sure to ask about fees. Don't make the mistake of contracting for what needs to be two years of therapy if you have one year's worth of fees. Remember, if you hire a therapist, he or she works for you. You have the right to be a discriminating consumer.

Don't be afraid (if you are, do it anyway) to ask your therapist about his or her experience working with your particular issues or the type of family you come from, especially if it is incestuous. Ask about his or her theoretical orientation and approach to doing therapy. Be cautious about contracting with someone whose orientation is psychoanalytic because they offer (hide behind?) a neutral relationship. My bias is that such a relationship is nonaffirming. Kaufman states, "Therapist distance and neutrality, the so-called blank screen, damages client self-esteem by reproducing shame" (Kaufman, 1989, p.169). The traditional psychoanalytic stance is to take a "one up" position in relation to the client, thus re-enacting many of the shame-inducing elements of the family.

In order to be affirming, the therapist-client relationship must be human, authentic, and equal. The most affirming relationship is, to use Martin Buber's term, an "I-Thou" relationship that requires both therapist and client to be fully human. Listen to Joseph Melnick writing in the Gestalt Journal (1978, p.80): "I can best be a model to you by doing and being—not by telling you what to do and how to be. So what do I model? I try to model being human: showing my flaws, sharing my uncertainty, making mistakes. If I cannot do these things in front of you so that you experience a fellow human struggling and wrestling with life, then how can I expect you to openly share your struggle with me?" My former trainer at the Gestalt Therapy Institute of Los Angeles, the late Harold Oaklander, had an amusing way of reminding us to be "I-Thou"—present and authentic. He said, "Therapy works better when there are two people in the room."

This next point is important! Ask your prospective therapist if he or she has had their own personal therapy and roughly how long it took. Remember, a healing relationship is a two-way street. Your therapist will be asking you intrusive questions, so give yourself the same right. He or she can put up a stop sign if a question seems inappropriate or too intrusive, just as you can. If the therapist is unwilling to answer these questions, find someone else. I can't imagine a therapist doing good, solid work without having had at least two years of weekly individual or group therapy. Without having spent some time in the more vulnerable client position, a therapist will not be able to understand and pace your feelings of exposure as you reveal yourself. The therapist who hasn't done his or her own work ends up trying to heal their own unconscious wounds. They will project their issues onto you and try to fix them. If they're in denial, then they will try to strip you of yours. If they haven't separated from a parent, they will push you to do so. If they are shame-based, you just might come out of therapy feeling worse about yourself. If he or she admits to not having had personal therapy, and a disturbing number haven't, run (don't walk) to another therapist.

The initial appointment between you and your therapist sets the stage for the therapy and marks the beginning of what needs to be an affirming relationship. Regardless of the presenting problem that led you to seek help, shame anxiety (the fear of being exposed) is likely to be activated. It will be apparent in your facial expressions and body language, references to self that reflect core beliefs, and behavior toward the therapist. It is important that the therapist is sensitive to the potential for feelings of exposure, and not just yours, in this first face to face contact. If internalized shame is an underlying issue, it is crucial that the therapist makes the establishment of an affirming relationship the number one priority. You will know you are being affirmed to the extent that you feel respected, valued, encouraged to tell your story, listened to, believed, and understood. If you are already in therapy, and your therapist does not meet these criteria, bring it up as an issue that must be resolved.

It cannot be overemphasized that the process of healing shame always takes place in the context of a relationship. The process is one of "healing through meeting" (Friedman, 1989, p.1). An affirming relationship is thus one that fulfills the recurring need to be recognized, admired, and openly valued as a unique self (Kaufman, 1989, p.79). Such a relationship allows the client to form a secure attachment bond in place of the one that either failed to form or was repeatedly severed by the shame-inducing parent.

In other words, the client must be affirmed for the first time or re-affirmed if there was faulty (insufficient or inconsistent) parental affirmation. This new affirmation, in essence, re-parents the child within. It is the relationship, what happens between therapist and client, that fills the developmental voids that resulted from too much shame. By encouraging the rebirth of the hidden true self, an affirming relationship leads to the formation of new core beliefs and heals the shamed sense of self. As the affirming therapist is gradually internalized, the capacity to be self-affirming is gradually realized.

The affirming therapist consciously and unconsciously, directly and indirectly, values his or her client. This is done by relating in ways that facilitate the acknowledgment and release of old shame experiences, making room for the internalization of new corrective experiences. This process is in accordance with the Zen parable, "before you can fill the cup, you must empty the cup." To be more specific, shame scenes involving parents are replaced by scenes involving the therapist that build self-esteem. The therapeutic relationship "restores the interpersonal bridge" by enhancing security and inviting the client to identify with an affirming human being (Kaufman, pp.164-165). Whereas acknowledging shame reconnects a client with his self, an affirming relationship reconnects him with another human being.

Psychotherapy is a corrective experience because it repairs the damage done to the client's self. According to Harper and Hoopes (1990, p.22), children form a "shame-prone identity" when parents are not accountable for their behavior, when they deny emotional needs, and when they withhold emotional closeness and sharing. A corrective relationship with a therapist must provide, to the extent it is possible, what was missing in the parent-child relationship. The therapist positively affirms the client by being dependable and gratifying, and by providing appropriate emotional closeness. These corrections are made in a safe and secure environment. They lead to the formation of a new identity based on who the client uniquely is, not on who he or she had to become in order to accommodate shaming parents.

I have never had a client enter therapy and announce they want to heal shame induced by faulty parenting. More likely, a new client will complain of symptoms that reflect the presence of a shame damaged self: low self-esteem, chronic depression, sexual and relationship problems, eating disorders, and addictions of all kinds. To begin to establish an affirming relationship, the therapist must offer the client undivided, but undemanding, attention. The task at hand is to provide a safe space that will encourage the client to believe—"Here is someone with whom I can be me and feel valued." Again, it is what takes place between therapist and client that stimulates the work of healing shame. What gives the client hope is the conscious or unconscious feeling of having developed a relationship that will provide positive affirmation.

In my office policy, (handed out to clients prior to the initial interview), there is a description of my approach to psychotherapy. I do this, not only because of the need for informed consent to begin treatment, but because I want to lay the foundation for a "healing through meeting." It reads: "(1) The relationship between the therapist and the client is the most powerful element in the process of change, (2) that relationship must be characterized by trust, support, and validation of the client's emotional experience, (3) the therapist's responsibility is to facilitate self-awareness and the working through of painful emotions, and (4) we will focus on the here and now problems that led you to seek help and on your personal history as it affects these problems."

Of course an office policy cannot give clients good feelings about a therapist who is at this point a stranger, but I want my clients to associate my office with safety, and this begins in the waiting room prior to our first meeting. In time, I want them to feel that, upon entering my office, they have passed into a secure vault, a place where they can "speak the unspeakable!" It must be sensitive enough to accept their most intimate self-disclosures, yet strong enough to withstand their most intense emotional explosions. Unless a safe space is created, the shamed adult will not allow access to the shamed child within, and the remedial need for affirmation goes unmet. Only a client who feels safe can experiment with being who he or she really is, and without fear of being shamed by still another significant person. A safe space is one where the client's defenses are honored before being carefully put aside. A safe space thus provides emotional warmth and contact in an atmosphere of safety and security.

This does not mean that the therapist allows the client to trivialize the therapy by avoiding emotionally charged issues. If the topic for discussion is "whether the rain will hurt the rhubarb," the therapy is not going to bring about an affirming relationship.

Nor does a safe space mean the client is allowed to act-out in self-destructive ways without being confronted. Quite the opposite! If my client reports driving a car while intoxicated over the weekend, I am not going to pretend to approve. I would probably express anger. I will let him know I am concerned for his safety and ask what precipitated the drinking episode, but I will be clear that such acting-out has to stop.

Fritz Perls, the founder of Gestalt therapy, described the ideal therapeutic environment as a "safe emergency." It must be safe enough that the client is willing to risk exposure, and emergent enough that real, emotionally charged issues are being dealt with. Exposing a self that feels inferior, inadequate, or defective creates an emergency, but it is a safe one in that it ultimately leads to an affirmation of the client's inherent worth.

The therapist creates safety by giving the client the support to acknowledge feelings of shame while feeling "held" by the therapist. Feeling "held" does not mean that the client will always feel comfortable. If my clients aren't "sweating bullets" a good part of the time, I don't feel like I'm doing my job. It means that the therapist provides a "holding environment"—one that contains the client's emerging feelings and, at the same time, allows the therapist to face his or her own feelings that are stirred up during the course of treatment (Scharff and Scharff, 1987, p.156). The "holding environment" contains any client shame that emerges in the relationship to the therapist, as well as the therapist shame that emerges in relation to the client, e.g., feeling incompetent. The therapist "holds" the client's feelings of shame so they can be looked at, acknowledged, understood, released, and healed. It is the feeling of being "held" that allows the client to speak the unspeakable and, ultimately, rise above shame.

In a safe space, the client identifies with the therapist who points out and gently confronts the false self while affirming the previously hidden true self. This frees up the child within to do what is unfamiliar and try on more authentic behaviors, such as breaking the parental "no expression" rule. For example, the client may become angry with the therapist when he or she makes a mistake, or when the client transfers feelings that belong on his parents onto the therapist. Validating the client's anger is a corrective emotional experience. The therapist who is secure enough to take the anger without becoming too defensive, or counterattacking, affirms the client's true self.

The following case example illustrates this process. Sarah, an adult battered as a child, characteristically tried to disown her feelings of rage. During a time when we were having difficulty relating to one another, she called an hour before her session and asked if she could skip therapy and go to the beach. I told her it was her decision, but that I would charge her for my time whether she came in or not, and that I much preferred that she come in. At the start of the session, I asked her if wanting to go to the beach could be connected to wanting to avoid something in therapy. She denied it, but at the end of the hour handed me a letter and insisted that I not read it until she had time to get to her car. "Are you lobbing a grenade on your way out?," I joked, but she was already well on her way to the parking lot. I waited as she requested, then read the letter in which she informed me that she "hated me with all her heart and soul!"

Before our next session, Sarah phoned and asked if I still wanted her to come in. "Most definitely," I replied, "we need to talk about the progress your letter is indicating." At the beginning of our next session, I thanked her for being so straightforward and indicated that such self-expressiveness was a sign that trust was developing between us. She relaxed and said she felt like it was the first time she had ever been able to show anger without suffering some dire consequence. She firmly expected me to attack or abandon her the way her parents had. Having someone accept and validate her feelings of rage allowed Sarah to integrate a part of herself she was forced to deny in childhood. She then apologized, realizing her rage was really directed at her abusive and shaming parents. By re-owning a disowned part, a part she called "the monster inside," she made herself more whole and became more of who she truly is. When "bad" parts are split off and disowned, they can take over and become the personality, i.e., Sarah would occasionally act in a way she considered monstrous. Once integrated, the "monster" blends in with all her other parts and makes available some aggressive energy that can be used to protect the self against further abuse. It is self-affirming to integrate a previously unacceptable part while maintaining a position of positive self-esteem.

In a sense, the affirming therapist functions as a midwife who assists the rebirth of the true self. The late Jim Simkin, often referred to as the co-founder of Gestalt Therapy, made this point in what he called his "mini-lectures" to trainees. "I see myself as a midwife who is present at the births of new attitudes, feelings, and discoveries about the self" (personal communication, 1977). What is reborn is a unique and true self that feels valued and therefore affirmed. This rebirthing process is difficult and the therapist-midwife may be seen as the one who is dragging the client into and through the pain.

Being a therapist who facilitates the re-experiencing of a painful past does not win you any popularity contests, a lesson I learned in graduate school. I was working in an out-patient clinic and doing therapy with a number of hard-core substance abusers. At one point, I told my supervisor, "None of my clients like me. Not one." He immediately replied, "No wonder you're doing such good work!" As I look back on that time and the difficulty in working with addicts, I realize that I was very firm about setting limits on their use of alcohol and drugs. I communicated the idea that we were a team, and that they could get "straight" (off drugs) only by being honest with me, as I would be with them. I impressed upon each client that being in an honest relationship was the most important part of their recovery. By forming an alliance with their healthiest and most mature parts, I was, without knowing it, creating a safe space and affirming each client as worthwhile. As we worked through the feelings that fueled their addictions, their need to self-medicate diminished. Without alcohol and drugs to numb their senses, many found it difficult to tolerate the shame and grief that they had learned to avoid. Those who successfully stayed "clean and sober" were the ones who invested themselves in the therapeutic relationship and stayed with the process. They were the ones who felt affirmed and gradually became more able to affirm themselves.

Ron

Ten years after my experiences at the drug abuse clinic, I began working with a substance abuser named Ron. Coming right to the point, Ron started the initial session by saying he was

"hopelessly addicted to alcohol, marijuana, cocaine, and ciga-
rettes," but that the real problem was loneliness. His next
comment suggested that he was afraid of exposing himself and
being seen as a bad person (shame anxiety). He said, "You must
think I'm scum," a projection that told me what he thought of
himself. I wanted to begin creating a safe space so I decided to
make a self-disclosure that I would ordinarily reserve for later on
in the process. I told Ron that I "drank like a fish" and "did all
kinds of drugs" in the late sixties. Ron looked relieved but didn't
say anything. I explained that I no longer drank or did drugs, and
that if he wanted, I would help him quit. I told him he could
become stronger than any habit, but that it would take time.

Some therapists would question such an early self-disclosure
and promise of help (some question any self-disclosure or promise of help), but I believe a therapist must be willing to risk being
an authentic person if the therapeutic relationship is to be corrective. Also, I wanted Ron to know that I wasn't going to play
the "I'm the healthy doctor and you're the sick patient" game—a
game based on unacknowledged therapist's shame that is unconsciously transferred to the client, who is seen as "lowly."

I asked Ron why he came for help now rather than last month,
or last year, and learned that he was suffering from chest pain and
heart palpitations. His physician had done a number of tests and
decided these were symptoms of a panic disorder, hence the
referral to me. Ron was not convinced and, fearing the worst,
expected to die a premature death from years of self-abuse. More
reason to create a safe space, and I reassured him that his bodily
symptoms were merely an exaggeration of the normal reaction
to stress. I quickly added that I understood how frightened and
out of control he must feel, but that the prognosis is much better
for a psychological problem than for cardiac disease. After taking
a family history, and collecting a number of clues about the origin
of Ron's shamed sense of self, I contracted with him for an
estimated two years of once-weekly therapy.

Ron's habit of self-medicating with various substances was
most definitely a problem, but not "the" problem. It was a
symptom of, and attempted solution to, the real problem—intolerable feelings of shame. His addictions served him by maintaining denial and anesthetizing the emotional pain left over from a
difficult childhood. They also made him feel less shy and self-con-

scious in social situations. He was not "hopelessly addicted" because his body was racked by disease, but because he had a shamed sense of self—he felt unwanted, disgusting, and absolutely defective as a person.

Ron's predominant symptoms, apart from low self-esteem and substance abuse, were loneliness and depression. He was attracted to women, but terrified at the thought of approaching them. At age thirty-five, he had never had sexual intercourse, despite longing to be in a relationship and wanting to be sexually active. I asked about dreams and he reported a recent one where he was afflicted with leprosy and confined to a solitary existence on a distant island. When I asked him to "be the leper" he said, "I'm a social outcast. No one wants to be near me because I'm repulsive." This was Ron's core belief.

Ron's self-esteem was so low and his loneliness was so painful that I was concerned he might take his life. As it was, he was committing suicide on the installment plan—his lifestyle was severely self-destructive. His fantasy solution to all his problems was an intimate relationship, but he was so terrified of women that he felt defeated before ever getting started. I convinced him that when (not if) we improved his self-esteem he would feel differently about approaching and connecting with women. Not that he would feel self-confident and comfortable doing so, but that he would be able to do it in spite of his discomfort. I also convinced him that all men, including myself, are at one time or another afraid of women. We either get over it or hide it with a "macho" front. This helped him feel less "different," less of a leper, and more optimistic about his future.

There were several factors that accounted for Ron's intense and lifelong fear of women. First, his parents divorced when he was five-years-old and his father abandoned him. His mother never remarried and Ron was assigned the shame-inducing role of mommy's "Little Prince"—companion to the lonely and engulfing woman whom he idealized. At some level of consciousness, Ron felt that he had won the oedipal struggle and vanquished his missing father. This made him feel guilty, as if he were responsible for his parent's divorce. In addition, he felt ashamed about the unconscious incestuous relationship with his mother, with whom he still lived. To make matters worse, he felt sexually inadequate due to his inability to maintain an erection, even during masturbation fantasies involving imaginary lovers.

Second, Ron's fear of women was magnified because he saw them as sources of humiliation. He recalled a childhood scene when at age seven he wet his bed after years of being dry. His mother, wanting to punish him, hung his urine stained sheets out his bedroom window for all to see. Ron was mercilessly ridiculed by his peers. He felt mortified and began the slow process of withdrawing inside himself. He continued to wet the bed and his mother continued to scorn him. This went on until the family physician determined that he had a bladder infection and could not control himself.

Another shame scene, which took place in the back seat of a car, reinforced Ron's worst fears about the opposite sex. It also confirmed his suspicions that he was sexually defective (sexual shame). He had picked up a "girl with a bad reputation" at a high school dance and "parked" in the hope of having his first sexual experience. Both had been drinking and Ron, filled with shame anxiety, was unable to perform. Unfortunately, the girl questioned his manhood and accused him of being homosexual. Again he felt mortally shamed. Seventeen years had passed, but Ron hadn't attempted intercourse since.

I chose to present Ron as a case example because it seemed so clear that his healing was a result of an affirming relationship. I saw him as someone who desperately needed to be admired and affirmed, and proceeded accordingly. It was what happened between the two of us that brought about a new sense of self and a host of lifestyle changes. He internalized the caring person in me and began taking care of himself. By the end of the first year of therapy, he had stopped all use of substances. He developed a support group of friends who were committed to sobriety. He emotionally separated from his mother and moved out on his own. He met a woman who worked in a bookstore and asked her out on a date (they married six months after he terminated therapy). As he struggled with his fear of women, fear of abandonment, fear of engulfment, and fear of sexuality, I grew very close to Ron. I often had the distinct feeling that I was re-parenting him. I felt like the father he never had, someone who initiated him into manhood and taught him how to make his way in the world. I also felt like an affirming mother, teaching him to embrace the child within and helping him rediscover his true self. I openly admired him for his courage in acknowledging his feelings and risking new behaviors. I felt parental but knew that ours was a professional relationship that needed clear boundaries, e.g., I declined invitations to play golf with Ron or attend his wedding (much as I would have liked to).

On one occasion, Ron accused me of caring about him only because it was my job and because it was what I was paid to do. I understood and validated his distrust of me and my motives. After all, why should I care and be trustworthy when his own father would have nothing to do with him. Then I explained that the fee I charge is for my time and expertise—not my caring, which is mine to freely give or not give. Ron eventually learned to trust me because I was emotionally available, authentic, and accountable to him for my behavior. I took responsibility for my feelings. By sharing myself and my story, when it was appropriate to the issue at hand, I served as a role model for the process of healing. Our relationship made Ron feel good about himself. When he felt convinced that I valued him as a person, and not just as an interesting case or source of income, he looked at and then countered his lifelong belief that he was a disgusting social outcast who would never find love.

Sometimes, especially at the conclusion of an emotionally intense session, I would offer Ron a supportive hug. This was not a reward for doing the work, it was part of the work. It was one more way I could affirm Ron as a likeable person and someone I cared for. At the beginning of the next session we would discuss what the hug meant to each of us and whether it created any conflicts. Ron liked it. He had been quite deprived of touch as a child and it helped him feel connected to me and less alone in the world.

Clients from shame-based families are typically not touched and held in ways that satisfy their basic needs. When touch is a natural outgrowth of a therapeutic relationship that re-parents the client, and is done with the client's consent from a position of respect, it is tremendously affirming. Touch that is therapeutic satisfies all the requirements of Harper and Hoopes' (1990, p.21) "affirmation triangle"—it fulfills the need for intimacy, affirms the need for dependency, and is done with accountability. However appropriate, this kind of physical intimacy creates a conflict for clients who have learned to associate touch with shame. For example, many clients equate touch and sexuality, and sexuality with exploitation and betrayal.

Your therapist should avoid initiating touch without your permission, e.g., "Would you like me to hold your hand?" A therapist should never touch you in any way other than the way he or she would if another person was present. Remember, all forms of touching, however innocent, must be in the interest of gratifying your needs, not the therapist's. Otherwise, touching may become an anti-therapeutic reenactment of your family of origin—you being exploited, or you taking care of the needy parent. Finally, the experience of touching should always be discussed and understood, e.g., "What did the hug mean to you?"

Although I have used the concept of re-parenting to describe the process of affirming or re-affirming the child within, it should be noted that no relationship can completely make up for what a child endured or lost in their early years. To make the point, there is a crucial period for forming secure attachments and developing basic trust, and it is in infancy. I can affirm a client's worth and restore trust, and I can help a client learn to discriminate between who is and isn't trustworthy, but I cannot orchestrate the kinds of affirming scenes that I (in partnership with my wife) can provide my own daughter. This is because I am not capable of feeling the kind of unconditional love for my clients that I do for my child, and because I meet clients at a less crucial stage of development. It is also important to note that therapists who are too parental unwittingly encourage clients to stay stuck in and relate from a dependent child position at the expense of learning self-parenting skills, e.g., self-support, self-soothing, problem solving.

It is part of the healing process that a client give up trying to get unconditional love from me, or their parents, or their spouse, or anyone else. Clients must grieve their losses and move on. There are parallels between parenting and doing therapy, but parents are obligated to assume responsibility for the helpless beings they bring into the world. Therapists, on the other hand, are not responsible for their clients (except in rare instances) and provide a professional service with the expectation of being paid for it. This does not mean we don't care, but we are foster parents at best, and only then at times when it is therapeutic for our clients.

Step Three: Releasing your Shame

Having come out of denial and acknowledged shame in the context of an affirming relationship, it is time to begin the process of releasing your shame. To be released from shame implies that we are being let loose of or set free from a feeling that binds us, or holds us down. In a moment of courageous soul searching, John Bradshaw reveals, "I discovered that I had been bound by shame all my life. It ruled me like an addiction. I acted it out; I covered it up in subtle and not so subtle ways; I transferred it to my family, my clients and the people I taught" (1988, p.vii).

We can see how shame ties us in psychological knots and exerts a dominant control over how we think, feel, and relate. We find ourselves automatically feeling ashamed for having certain feelings or needs. For example, if our parents were uncomfortable with and shamed us for expressing anger or sexuality, then we cannot express those feelings as adults without feeling ashamed. Our natural way of being is bound by shame. In order to get back control of ourselves and our lives we need to be released from shame.

Shame can be released in any relationship that affirms and enhances self-esteem. In the safety of a therapeutic relationship, this means that the shame-damaged client tells his story to a therapist who validates what happened, validates his shame and related feelings, and affirms his worth. This is consistent with the theory that resolving a trauma depends on validation of the traumatic event, validation of the feelings associated with the event, the support of another adult, and time (Middelton-Moz and Dwinell, 1986). As the story is told, the therapist is sensitive to symptoms of shame in the areas of cognition (e.g., low self-esteem, shame-based core beliefs), affect (e.g., embarrassment, humiliation), and behavior (e.g., avoiding eye contact, perfectionism, powerless rage). Helping the client acknowledge these symptoms in awareness is crucial if shame is to be released.

The warmth and respect of the affirming therapist creates a safe space that allows the client to open up and risk being vulnerable. Without a feeling of trust the client is unable to get past the fears of exposure and judgment, i.e., of feeling even more ashamed. The therapist must be careful not to re-enact any aspect of the family system that originally induced shame. This is easier said than done because clients, who are still in the family trance, are quite able to induce their therapist into acting as their parents once did.

I once transferred a client to another therapist because I could no longer tolerate her attacks on me. My only excuse for this therapeutic error was inexperience. I had incompetency buttons the size of Texas and this client pushed them. In so doing, she re-enacted scenes from her childhood but recast herself in the role of the belittling parent and me in the role of the inadequate child. I failed to understand that she was doing to me what her alcoholic mother had done to her. She protected her vulnerable child self through the defense mechanism of projective identification—by putting her anger into me and inducing me to act like her rejecting parent. Had I understood she was unconsciously showing me how it felt to be her as a child, frightened and ashamed, we could have put aside her defenses and gained access to the child within. Had I understood that by going for my emotional jugular, she was transferring shame, I could have helped her re-own her shame and heal it. Instead, I succumbed to the family trance and rejected her just as her mother had, unwittingly re-enacting her family of origin dynamics. It was a masochistic triumph for her. She defeated me but, in the process, defeated herself.

Obviously, a client will not release shame in a therapeutic relationship that fails to provide safety and affirmation. This doesn't mean the client should pull out of therapy in response to any and every therapist error, because therapists are human and humans make mistakes. However, if a therapist fails to establish a safe and secure environment, due to inexperience, poor impulse control, or their own unfinished business, a wise client will look elsewhere for help.

Actually, an occasional therapist error provides good "grist for the mill" and affords excellent opportunities for new learning and behavior. As previously explained, it gives the client a chance to try out being angry at a significant person without having to face a counterattack, or in some way being shamed. The errant therapist needs to say "I made a mistake. My mistake elicited your response of...," and "I'm sorry for hurting you." The therapist models humility, the acceptability of making mistakes, and a willingness to take responsibility and make amends. He or she apologizes because they mean it, not because it is a valuable technique or a way to shut off the client's healthy anger.

Clients from shaming families are not used to someone taking responsibility for their mistakes. Being in a relationship with someone who does so releases shame that is bound by the need to be perfect. The therapist not only gives permission to make mistakes, but validates the client's anger over being hurt by someone who is supposed to be protective. This is certainly not how the shaming parent handled his or her mistakes. The therapist models accountability to self and other, whereas the shaming parent did not.

According to the British theorist, D.W. Winnicott, the therapist who struggles to discover what the client really needed at the time the error was made, helps that client to understand early and similar parental failures, thus producing a sense of release and a "new sense of self" (Wood, 1987, p.91). The well-handled therapeutic error leads to a new sense of self because in the process of repairing the severed therapist-client bond, the client is openly valued. New scenes involving reparation and respect are internalized and replace the old scenes that involve blame and shame. The errant therapist relates in a way that says, "You are worthy of respect and deserve to be treated fairly."

The therapist affirms the client's basic rights, including the "right to protect the self against a well-intentioned therapist" (Wood, p.130). This statement applies to a common mistake made by therapists, that of shaming their clients by directly or indirectly asking them to do something they are not developmentally ready to do. Their intentions may be good, just as were the client's parents, but nonetheless shame is induced. They have unintentionally re-enacted the family drama. For example, women clients in emotionally or physically abusive relationships are subtly (or not so subtly) pressured by both male and female therapists to get out of their relationships. While this implies that they deserve better, it only makes them feel more ashamed for tolerating the abuse. Rather than trying to control or change them, the affirming therapist empathizes with their feelings of desperation and entrapment, and their fear of independence. He or she understands their sense of worthlessness, thus validating the shame while respecting their defenses and current level of functioning. It is helpful to confront such clients for the purpose of bringing to their awareness how abusive relationships maintain shame and to get them to consider a self-affirming response, e.g., "Since you find it so humiliating to be slapped around, why do you not set limits on your husband's behavior?" The idea is to demonstrate to clients that it is self-defeating to stay stuck in relationships that have painful consequences, and that there are alternatives.

Confrontation may challenge a client to look at some behavior they would rather hide, but it must not be done in a way that communicates disrespect. If clients are treated disrespectfully, they will leave the therapy hour in worse shape than when they came in, feeling paralyzed by shame.

I made this mistake in working with a woman who was being repeatedly raped by her alcoholic and sexually deviant husband. Frustrated by my inability to get her to stop his abuse, I told her she was "being a wimp." Realizing my mistake, I apologized and shared how powerless and frustrated I felt (which of course was exactly how she felt). I explained how I was expecting too much, too soon, and how this re-enacted her parents' expectation that she should act like an adult when she was still a child. I got back on track by being more understanding and by providing support for resisting his abusiveness. I asked if a part of her thought she was "being a wimp" and if that part could help her take better care of herself. When I stopped playing her strong part for her, she reowned it, and within a month initiated a divorce.

As clients develop a secure bond with their therapist, they become more willing to break parental rules such as "Don't need" or "Don't express yourself." Feeling the therapist's support, clients risk being disloyal to their families of origin. The therapeutic relationship invites clients to tell their stories, break secrecy, and speak the unspeakable. It is the telling of the story that is healing, but it is more than that. It is what happens between the client and therapist as the story is told that potentiates the release of shame. The therapist must not only believe, understand, respect, and value the client, but must also communicate all this in a convincing way. The client must actually feel believed, understood, respected, and valued in order to release shame.

Shame is released as it is acknowledged in awareness and as the client re-experiences the original scenes where shame was taken in. According to Kaufman, the process of healing shame involves a developmental reversal: "internalized shame must be returned to its interpersonal origins, its governing scenes" (1989, pp.177-178). In other words, the therapist helps the client identify and acknowledge parental behaviors and childhood scenes that induced shame, e.g., "Of course you feel inadequate and incompetent. If your own father repeatedly belittled you, how could you grow up feeling good about yourself?"

The client works at remembering the internalized scenes that resulted in a shamed sense of self, e.g., "Dad would never play catch with me, even if I begged him. I wondered what was wrong with me." These scenes contain the spoken or unspoken parental messages that induced too much shame, e.g., "You are worthless!" These shame scenes are charged with emotion that is released as the client relives the childhood experience—not just by talking about being humiliated, or frightened, or enraged, or sad, but actually experiencing these painful feelings. In order to do this, it is crucial that the client is "clean and sober." If the client is using alcohol or other drugs, he or she will have difficulty accessing deep feelings. That's the unconscious goal of self-medicating—it allows a person to suppress and avoid painful scenes and feelings (but at a cost). I don't tell my clients they must quit using, but I do tell them that psychotherapy and addiction are in competition with one another. A feeling cannot be released if it cannot be felt, and mood-altering substances numb the mind and body. Thus, there is no healing without sobriety, and no sobriety without healing.

It is the trust in the therapist and the atmosphere of safety that allows the client to tolerate the intense emotionality contained in childhood scenes. In this way, the hidden true self reappears and is given the validation that was missing in the original scene. The memory of the scene is not erased, but the painful feelings, including shame, are released. New scenes, based on the relationship with the affirming therapist, replace the old scenes based on the relationship with the shaming parent. If an addictive state has been present, the client eventually gives it up for their newly discovered ability to self-parent.

David Calof (1989), speaking about the issue of how shame is transferred from parent to child, asks the question, "Whose shame is it anyway?" He uses as an example the incestuous father who, in effect, rids himself of shame by putting it in his daughter. The daughter becomes the "container" of shame that rightfully belongs to him. He is the one who has committed the shameful act of molestation. However, he disowns this unwanted part of himself and his disowned shame takes up residence in his victimized daughter. She carries it for him (vicarious shame) until such time as it is given back. Calof then puts forth an important principle of healing: "When you own what is yours, what is not yours goes away." This means that as the molestation scenes are re-experienced, the daughter will not only express her shame, but her rage, terror, grief, etc. In the process of owning and re-experiencing the feelings that are hers, the shame that is not hers is given back to the molester. She comes to understand that she really was a powerless victim. She has released her shame.

Nancy

The following case demonstrates the process of releasing shame, and how shame scenes can be replaced by self-affirming ones. It also shows how shame can transfer containers. Nancy referred herself to therapy because of repeated relationship problems, guilt over her sexual behavior, and insomnia. A family of origin history revealed that she had been an only child subjected to multiple shame-inducing messages, in particular brainwashing, terrorizing, and belittlement. The cardinal rule in her family was "Don't express yourself," but she was also expected to squelch any sign of neediness. She was assigned the role of "Angel" in accordance with her parents' need to project an image of being good Christians.

Nancy's father showed an inordinate need to control and often exploded in situations where he felt powerless. At his worst, he battered his wife while Nancy would helplessly watch in a state of terror. Her mother also had a violent streak, and at times it was directed at Nancy. Then, she would lose all control of her aggressive impulses and turn into "another person, as if she was possessed" (to use Nancy's description). For unknown reasons, her mother was tormented by sexual shame and taught Nancy that sex was not only immoral, but painful. "It is something men do to you," she informed her daughter, and to convince her she made noises during intercourse that let Nancy know she was in a great deal of pain.

At first, Nancy remembered little of her childhood other than being frightened when church members would "speak in tongues." She was even more frightened when they would accuse others of being possessed by Satan. Nancy's family attended a fundamentalist church that stressed inspiration by the Holy Spirit. There and at home, she was systematically programmed to uncritically accept her parents' dogmatic religious beliefs. She had been brainwashed into believing, at the core of herself, that she was bad and sinful. And, she had taken into herself the bad qualities of her parents—leaving her self-critical and ashamed of her sexuality. As an adult, she tried to be the "perfect Christian" and when she failed, by having sex, or taking a drink, or even thinking a "bad" thought, she would become guilt-ridden and filled with shame (due to the harsh and judgmental internalized parent voice).

Nancy was afraid to fall asleep at night because of recurrent nightmares about the Devil, who symbolized her unacceptable sexual drives and the dark and disowned parts of herself. A breakthrough occurred when she wrote and mailed me a letter between sessions. It read, "I'm sorry I didn't tell you this earlier, but I'm afraid I am lying and that this is merely the product of a lonely person with too active an imagination. Also, I just want to be all better. Anyway, in the past few months an old fear has come back to me and I'm laying awake half the night. If I sleep on my left side, I can feel the presence of someone—about ready to touch me on my right shoulder. It's the Devil! As I write this, I feel absolutely terrified and have a bad pain in my stomach—I feel like I'm going to throw up!"

Upon receiving this letter, I phoned Nancy and asked her to come in later that day. She gladly accepted. I explained that her fear of sleeping on her left side was probably the result of a childhood trauma that was repressed from memory. I asked her if she felt safe enough with me to try to recover the scene in question. She consented and I asked her to lie on the couch, on her left side, the side she was afraid to sleep on. After several minutes, I touched her right shoulder, enacting her worst fear (Wilson Van Dusen calls this experiential technique "invoking the actual"). A shudder ran through her body and she began to cry, a little girl cry.

"How old are you?" I asked.

"Three," she answered.

"Tell me what's happening?" I continued.

"I'm in my bedroom and someone else is in the room with me, a boy. I'm turning away from him and pretending he isn't there. He is touching me...he put something in my vagina—a pencil I think. Bad!"

"Who's bad?" I asked.

"I'm bad," she answered.

"Who is it that's touching you?"

"I don't know."

For the next hour I helped Nancy release her fear and shame. I urged her to stay with it, stay with her feelings, stay with herself, stay with the three-year-old within. She did a lot of crying. I told her (the traumatized child) that I had a daughter about her age and that I'd like to talk with her. In as supportive and forgiving a parental voice I could muster, I explained: "It's not your fault this happened. You didn't ask the boy to touch you and you didn't have any way to stop him. Just look at how little you are. It's true that something bad happened, but the badness belongs to the boy who made it happen. You're a good girl, Nancy." I asked if she wanted me to hold her. She said yes. Again I spoke to the frightened little girl inside her to provide comfort and reassurance. I said the same things that I would have said were I in session with a three-year-old girl who had just been raped. Before sending her home, I made sure that she was back in her adult ego state and made an appointment to follow up on this session. I also urged her to use her journal to process any leftover feelings and to phone me if she needed to talk.

She didn't call but before the next session another letter arrived. In part it read, "When you asked if I wanted to be held—I didn't really think you'd do it. I felt like I was so untouchable, so unworthy, so wrecked, so contaminated—that you would touch me and say, Yuk, forget it! Also, I was really scared, but you apparently knew that and said it's okay, I won't hurt you — and then it was wonderful. I've never felt so safe and protected."

I was pleased that Nancy allowed me to hold her and that she got something she needed. I knew it was a risk at the time and had been cautious given that she was so vulnerable, and knowing that she associated touch with sexual abuse and shame. I was quite sure that she wanted to be held, and positive that my motive was to meet her need for comfort, not mine to give it. As such, my offer to hold her was a natural outgrowth of the affirming relationship. It said that I was emotionally available and did so in a way that strengthened her ability to trust others. It was a corrective emotional experience because it communicated that touch can be other than sexual—it could be supportive and protective. There are times when words are not enough. This was one.

Nancy felt frustrated that she could remember the emotional memory but did not have access to the complete cognitive memory of this childhood scene. She had lingering doubts that it really happened (this is typical for molested children), and if it did, she wanted to know who molested her. I told her I believed it really happened, that I trusted her emotional memory, and that the full memory would become available in awareness when she was ready to receive it. To help her recover more of the scene, I had Nancy draw the little girl in bed with the unknown boy touching her right shoulder. Next we used a hypnotherapeutic technique to help her regress to age three and recover the full memory. The remnants of her self-protective denial and dissociation gradually gave way and she was able to let more and more of the memory surface.

In time, Nancy remembered the original scene in detail. It was not her imagination, nor was it the Devil in her bedroom—this was the defensive strategy of a traumatized little girl who could not face an overwhelming reality in awareness. She dissociated so as not to be present during the molestation, then she attributed the "badness" to the Devil—just as her parents had taught her to do. She could not go to them for protection or support because she was not securely bonded—she would have likely been disbelieved, or worse, accused of being bad or sinful. The unknown boy turned out to be a troubled teenage cousin who sometimes stayed with Nancy's family when he was in trouble at home. With this revelation, she was able to get in touch with her disgust and rage, which were discharged by putting him in an "empty chair" and letting him have it with words and fists. Nancy indicated she occasionally saw this cousin at family reunions. She said that he "undresses me with his eyes and ... touches me inappropriately." Later on in therapy, the work shifted to getting her power back by confronting him and setting limits.

The next session we again walked through the molestation scene, replaying it from start to finish. Nancy was much less emotionally reactive, indicating she had released a great deal of emotional energy. Then we did some re-parenting imagery where I had the grown-up (survivor) Nancy go back and comfort the little girl (victim) Nancy. This time I had Nancy imagine bursting into the scene and rescuing the child Nancy. The shame was given back to the molester, where it rightfully belonged all along. I instructed her to hold herself (I gave her a teddy bear to hold), and have a healing dialogue with the child within. She had released much of the shame, terror, disgust, and rage, and was left with a feeling of compassion for the victimized little girl she had been. Even though it is absurd to think that the little girl had done anything wrong, she needed to be forgiven—because she believed she had done something wrong. So Nancy forgave little Nancy for being little and unable to prevent what happened. She reassured her of her goodness as I had done weeks before. She held her in her arms and heart and pledged her unconditional love.

Nancy was now free of the shame that was contained in the previously unconscious molestation scene. There was more work to be done, but she had taken a giant step toward healing her shame in general, and her sexual shame in particular. The process had been one of acknowledging shame in the context of an affirming relationship, then bringing the original scene into awareness where it could be re-experienced and worked through. She literally released her shame as she told her story. The shame scene was not forgotten, but it was replaced by the scenes of me and the grown-up Nancy affirming the child within. Her core belief changed from "I am bad and dirty!" to "I am good, I am a survivor!" The developmental process that led to internalized shame had been reversed. Her self-esteem was restored. She slept like a baby.

Step Four: Countering Messages, Breaking Rules, and Quitting Roles

Countering Shame-Inducing Messages

The release of shame and other negative feelings creates a new way of "being-in-the-world," but it also creates a psychological void. As the saying goes, "Nature abhors a void," and clients are often at a loss as to how to fill that void. The combination of greater self-awareness and freer emotional expression creates a new experience of self, making change possible. The change that fills the void in the best possible way is the one that fills it with a new set of core beliefs. Believing "I am good and lovable" places the client at their "growing edge," ready to complete the process of letting the true self be reborn.

Understanding how shame was induced and releasing the emotions embedded in childhood shame scenes allows the client to make actual changes. The cup has been emptied and must now be refilled. As we have learned from psychoanalysis, bringing emotions into consciousness and then purging them is not enough—the client who wishes to rise above shame must fill the void with new and different ways of relating to themselves and others. According to Potter-Efron and Potter-Efron (1989), "Shame must be replaced rather than just removed" (p.205). The healing process continues as the empty cup is filled with a new set of core beliefs—ones that lead to a self-affirming rather than shame-based identity.

Bevery Engel (1989) says it well, "You are not your parents. You do not have to act like them, and you do not have to treat yourself the way they treated you" (p.157). The key to doing a better job than they did, and affirming the child within, is to counter the messages they conveyed that resulted in too much shame. It doesn't matter that they shamed you unintentionally or that "they did the best they could." What matters is that they behaved in ways that suggested there was something wrong with you. You were suggestible, and as you took in negative messages you became convinced you were somehow bad and unlovable. You took the bad qualities of the shaming parent inside the self, and now you shame yourself with their voices. Only by learning to catch yourself inflicting self-shaming messages, and then countering them, will you form new and affirming core beliefs about the self.

The psychotherapy process is, here, one of helping the client identify internalized messages and core beliefs that first induced and now perpetuate shame and low self-esteem. The therapist always helps the client understand how the core belief was formed and how it elicits shame. For example, a therapist might say, "When your parents criticized, blamed, and belittled you, you took in a message that you were inadequate, and you believed it. You still do, only now you have the bad parent voice inside your head and you put yourself down. If you're going to have the self-esteem you deserve, you're going to have to start treating yourself better than they did." The therapist clarifies the client's problem by calling attention to the connection between parental messages, core beliefs, and chronic low self-esteem. At the same time, the client is motivated to change, and affirmed as deserving of esteem.

The healthy part of the client wants to change for the better, and it is with that part that the therapist allies himself or herself. The motive to change is driven by the wish to release shame and feel good about oneself. Since the primary function of the self is to strive for and maintain self-esteem, most clients are eager to make such changes and heal their shame.

The therapist facilitates change by supporting a shift from a shame-inducing core belief to a self-affirming one. This shift is accomplished through the cognitive restructuring technique of countering. The theory is simple: by changing a core belief about the self, the emotion induced by the belief will also change. Shifting from a negative to a positive core belief results in a shift from shame to self-esteem. The structure of the damaged self is repaired as negative core beliefs are countered and replaced with positive ones.

Countering is, for our purposes, the technique of using a self-affirming thought to contradict a self-shaming thought. Counters work because "when a client argues against an irrational thought, and does so repeatedly, the irrational thought becomes progressively weaker" (McMullin, 1986, p.3). All shame-based core beliefs are irrational because they are the result of a child mind trying to make sense of parental behavior that makes no sense. For example, a rational thought in response to a mother who has just battered you would be, "Mom must have hit me because she was enraged and lost control. I wonder what her problem is?"

Of course this is not the way children think. They personalize the parent's message and blame themselves, as if in a state of trance. Using the above example, the child would think, "Mom hit me because I'm bad. I got what I deserved." Personalizing maintains an illusion of control and security, but at the cost of lowered self-esteem. The bad quality of the parent is now on the inside and experienced as a part of the self. This irrational thinking process paves the way for a core belief about the self, and the battered child concludes, "I'm unlovable." This belief is what cognitive therapists call a logical fallacy. It is a judgment about the self that is accepted as a proven fact, despite being based upon the implied message of a parent who is behaving at his or her worst. The adult client needs to understand that the message was not about them, even though in childhood it was taken personally. They need to believe "It is not that I am unlovable, but that mom was abusive."

This brings us to self-affirmations, one way to counter the shame-inducing messages we internalized and believed. Affirmations are "positive, powerful statements concerning the ways in which we desire to think, feel and behave" (Lerner, 1985). They are messages we can learn to communicate to ourselves to bring about changes in our sense of self. Self-affirmation is a way of saying "yes!" to the process of change, and saying it emphatically. It enables us to mobilize our inner resources and transform "what was and is" (negative self-esteem) into "what will be" (positive self-esteem).

Self-affirmation "makes firm" some desirable thought, feeling, or image by countering some undesirable thought, feeling or image. To illustrate, the adult client molested as a child desires to change the core belief that she is dirty. If she finds herself thinking that way, she gets the "shame siren" going (Terry Kellogg's suggestion) and forcefully counters her core belief by saying something like, "I am not dirty and never was. He was! I will not carry his dirtiness for him." Or, suppose she experiences bodily sensations that she associates with shame, causing her to feel disgusted about her sexuality. Such signals are countered with, "I was made to feel dirty about my sexual feelings through no fault of my own. I am free of guilt and shame and feel good about my body. Here and now, I can allow my natural and healthy sexuality to come through." Mental images that reflect sexual shame should be red flagged as they appear in awareness. This alerts the client to counter the images by saying something like, "I was a victim and he spoiled something that was meant to be good and pleasurable. Now I am a survivor, and I reclaim what is rightfully mine. I visualize healthy images of me enjoying sex!" In these ways, thoughts, feelings, and images that reflect shame-based core beliefs are relentlessly countered.

Self-affirmations only work when the client has already acknowledged and released shame, creating the psychological void that can be filled with new core beliefs. The cup must be emptied before it can be refilled. Pouring fresh, clean water into a container of stale, dirty water will freshen it, but it will still be dirty. Similarly, old, shame-based core beliefs must be released before new, self-affirming core beliefs are added. In this way, the new belief system is uncontaminated by the one constructed by a naive and suggestible child mind subjected to too much shame.

By re-experiencing scenes and discharging the emotions embedded in them, the client is motivated to dispute shame-based core beliefs. He wants to set the record straight and countering gives him the power to do so. If shame has not been released, the client is merely trying to think positively. Countering is different than "the power of positive thinking," where a client tries to convince himself or herself that a long held core belief is untrue. Mere positive thinking invalidates the child within. It is as if the positive thinker is trying to talk the little boy or girl out of what they know about themselves. This might work if these beliefs were logical, but they are not—they are psychological! They make perfect sense given the child's experience and immature ways of thinking.

Countering is "the power of mature thinking," and demands that clients understand how shame-based core beliefs were formed by an immature and suggestible child mind. The self-affirmation approach validates the child within and acknowledges his belief system. Self-affirmation is a means of re-parenting the shamed child self. For example, an abandoned child within believes that there is no one emotionally available and that they are unwanted. The client acknowledges this child part, but refuses to merge with it. When the child and grown-up part merge, the child always takes over and becomes the personality. By separating into two parts, the grown-up part can enter into a relationship with the child within. This way the grown-up part can talk and act like an ideal parent who is emotionally available, e.g., the grown-up sticks up for the child when he or she is frightened. The self-affirming counter is the grown-up part "making firm" a new core belief, and coping in situations or relationships where shame has been activated in the past.

The client is instructed to use the countering technique each and every time they find themselves thinking, feeling, or relating according to one or more of the twelve shame-based core beliefs. As these beliefs are forcefully and consistently countered by an appropriate self-affirmation, each shame-inducing message is replaced by a self-affirming one. Again, this technique will not be effective unless internalized shame has been acknowledged and released. The attempt to use affirmations alone, or before reaching step four of the healing process, will barely scratch the surface of the problem. However, when the groundwork has been done, self-affirmations extricate clients from the painful past and bring them home to the experience of the rediscovered true self. This process of self-affirmation takes place at the same time the client is being affirmed by the therapist. Healing is done from the inside-out and outside-in. The holes in the self-structure are plugged and the self can, perhaps for the first time, fill up with good feelings.

Some self-affirming counters to each shame-based core belief are presented below:

Core belief of the adult belittled as a child—"I am inadequate!" Self-affirming counters—"I am adequate, competent, good enough! I accept my mistakes and learn from them. I can do it! I believe in myself!"

Core belief of the adult rejected as a child—"I am worthless!" Self-affirming counters—"I am worthwhile, valued, special! I have every right to exist. There is room in the world for me. I belong!"

Core belief of the adult scorned as a child—"I am disgusting!" Self-affirming counters—"I am okay just the way I am! I am a human being! I have dignity and honor! I am worthy of love and respect! I belong, too!"

Core belief of the adult abandoned as a child—"I am un-wanted!" Self-affirming counters—"I am a desirable person! I deserve to be in fulfilling relationships! I take myself seriously! I stick up for myself!"

Core belief of the adult neglected as a child—"I am unimport-ant!" Self-affirming counters—"I am an important person! I de-serve to be taken into account. My needs count. I count! I take good care of myself!"

Core belief of the adult engulfed as a child—"I am nothing!" Self-affirming counters—"I am somebody. I am unique. I am not an extension of my parents, I am myself! I am a separate person, an individual. I am my own person! I am self-determining!"

Core belief of the adult molested as a child—"I am dirty!" Self-affirming counters—"I am innocent! I am a survivor! I de-serve and demand respect. I am proud of myself. I accept my body and my sexuality as good!"

Core belief of the adult battered as a child—"I am unlovable!" Self-affirming counters—"I am lovable! I deserve love! I want to be touched lovingly. I have rights! I am entitled to be treated with respect!"

Core belief of the adult terrorized as a child—"I am powerless!" Self-affirming counters—"I am powerful! I face my fears head on. I can protect myself by taking charge when I need to. I have choices! I can cope! I have rights and I'm not afraid to assert them!"

Core belief of the adult brainwashed as a child—"I am sinful!" Self-affirming counters—"I am a good person! I affirm my God given sexuality and natural expressiveness. I am different from my parents. I choose my own moral values and religious beliefs."

Core belief of the adult corrupted as a child—"I am deviant." Self-affirming counters—"I am basically good! I can stay on track by making responsible choices. I choose to go by the rules. I choose to be honest. I take my place in society. I can fit in fine!"

Core belief of the adult confused as a child—"I am crazy!" Self-affirming counters—"I understand now. I know what hap-pened. I am clear! I am detached from my parents. I know what's what!"

Most, if not all clients tap into some healthy anger when they realize how they took in too much shame in response to negative parental messages. This anger can be used constructively by attacking shame-based core beliefs with their appropriate counters. The feeling of indignation over having been mistreated as a dependent child gives life and meaning to the countering technique. McMullin states, "The expression of emotion virtually eliminates the repetitious, mechanical parroting which so often renders counters ineffectual" (p.21). He espouses a "Melted Wax Theory" to explain why emotion is important to changing beliefs. Adapting his theory for our purposes, it goes like this. Consider that a core belief is like a wax impression in your mind. It is often formed when we experience an intense emotion like too much shame. When the heat of intense emotion dissipates, the core belief solidifies. To change a core belief, a person can do one of two things. He or she can chip away at the wax impression, which takes forever, or reheat the wax, so the belief can be molded into a new shape. If a person gets angry with a core belief, and counterattacks it, it heats it up and liquefies it so it can be poured into a new mold (p.21).

Core beliefs that reflect and reinforce shame must be countered aggressively, but remember it is a belief that is being counterattacked, not yourself. A shame-based core belief is really nothing more than the voice of the internalized parent and has little or nothing to do with who you really are. On the other hand, the self-affirmation that counters it is a reflection of your true self. In order to form a new belief system, old beliefs must be countered as often as they are encountered. It takes time to change the way we think about ourselves and this makes repetition an essential aspect of the healing process. McMulling reminds us, "Just as clients can't learn to speak Spanish or to play the cello in a week, so they can't change their thinking instantaneously (p.57)." Clients who understand how they were shamed and who release the emotions embedded in shame scenes, can effectively counter shame-based core beliefs and literally form a new sense of self. This process is essentially one of awakening from the family trance, expelling the shaming parent, and replacing self-shaming messages with self-affirming ones.

Breaking Shame-Inducing Rules

Whereas shaming messages are countered by affirming self-worth, shame-inducing rules are broken by affirming basic rights. These are the rights to be, to need, to make mistakes, to express oneself, and to separate from the family. These rights were denied when shaming parents imposed and enforced a set of dehumanizing rules that controlled their child's behavior. Children become loyal to such rules and follow them faithfully because their emotional survival depends on it. Following the rules minimizes (but does not eliminate) the likelihood of further shame attacks, and protects the developing self from further harm.

When parents fail to affirm their child's rights, they sever the attachment bond and activate shame. These shame wounds are carried into adulthood and the adult whose rights were denied remains loyal to the rules, indicating they are still in the family trance. Each rule is associated with certain predictable aftereffects or consequences. "Don't be" leads to depression and emotional withdrawal; "Don't need" leads to caretaking, dependency issues, and/or addiction; "Don't make mistakes" leads to striving for perfection and control; "Don't express yourself" leads to the reliance on a false self, difficulties in intimate relationships, psychosomatic symptoms, the "nice person" syndrome, or explosive behavior; and "Don't separate" leads to prolonged emotional immaturity.

In order to break free of these unspoken rules, they must first be brought into awareness so they can be challenged and processed. Once acknowledged and understood, the adult can re-decide whether he or she wishes to live life according to parental rules.

As David Calof warns his clients, "Be careful about who you make your mental health experts!" In accordance with this sound advice, the client whose behavior reflects a shame-inducing rule is asked: "Do you want to live the rest of your life according to the rules your parents laid down when you were a child?" Of course no one in their right mind wants to, but who ever said that everyone comes to therapy in their right mind? In reality, people say they don't want to continue following rules that perpetuate shame and low self-esteem, however, they usually resist changing them. This is because the child within the client is afraid to break the rules. It is considered an act of disloyalty that leads to swift and severe punishment. For example, if you grew up knowing that you would get hit for expressing anger, it is not easy to unlearn the "no expression" rule and relearn a new one. If you were treated as an extension of one of your parents, and reinforced for meeting their needs, it is difficult to define a separate self and break the "no separation" rule.

Breaking free of the rules necessitates breaking the rules! It is inevitable that clients feel disloyal when they begin to affirm rights that were previously denied. I tell clients that feeling guilty for breaking the rules is a good sign—it means we're headed in the right direction. To illustrate, an incest victim may feel guilty for breaking secrecy because she is violating the "no expression" rule. Having reframed guilt as a positive indicator, she doesn't take it to mean she should have remained silent. Instead, it means she is affirming her right to self-expression, and in the process she regains her power and separates from the family.

I also prepare my clients for the inevitable "change back" responses from parents who feel anxious or angry because they can no longer control their child. A "change back" response is a countermove intended to get the client to change back to the old way of behaving that stabilizes the family system (Bowen, 1978, p.495). Such countermoves are manipulations designed to ensure loyalty to the parents' rules. When it is clear that the client has not only broken a rule, but intends to continue breaking it, the shaming parent or parents mount an opposition. The opposition is an attempt to get the disloyal "child" back in line by convincing him he is wrong to change, that he will be accepted back in the family if he "changes back," and that if he refuses to "change back," he will suffer such and such consequences (p.495).

If challenging parental rules is thought of as a "move," the most common "countermove" by a shame-inducing parent is the guilt-trip, e.g., "If you tell your mother I molested you, she'll leave me and my life will be ruined!" This manipulation is often followed by a threat, "If you tell anybody about this, I'll never speak to you again!" The parent may act desperate and "play all his cards," as he tries to re-establish the status quo. For example, I have had clients whose parents have threatened suicide, or threatened to write them out of the family will in order to give teeth to a "change back!" response. Clients who begin to break parental rules by affirming their rights need to be prepared for such opposition and to stand firm. Obviously this will not work if the little kid part gets hooked and feels intimidated by the parents' countermoves. Again, we need to separate the little kid part of the personality from the grown-up part who is capable of making changes and holding his or her ground. This is done by going inside and finding the part that is most mature and determined to live according to his or her own rules. From this position, the client carries out what is essentially an ongoing, lifetime commitment to affirm her right to be, have needs, make mistakes, express herself, and separate—regardless of what her parents think!

Dennis

The following case illustrates how rules learned in childhood perpetuate a shamed sense of self in adulthood. Dennis called me for an appointment on the recommendation of his physician who diagnosed a major depression. Dennis seemed unusually evasive and refused to give me any information about his situation over the phone. This was not unreasonable since we had never met, and we scheduled an initial consultation. I was curious about his evasiveness but eventually forgot about it. About six months into therapy I was explaining to Dennis how he was induced to feel bad about himself, and how he felt exposed when he got close to others. It was then he brought up the subject of his initial evasiveness. He told me of his fear that I wouldn't take him on as a client. His exact words were "If you knew what a mess I was, I was pretty sure you would refuse to see me." Dennis expected others to reject him for having flaws. After all, his own parents had.

Dennis was the oldest in a sibling complex of two and had two schoolteachers for parents. Like most shaming parents, they were basically good but wounded people who had not resolved their own shame issues. As a result, they unintentionally passed them on to Dennis and his sister. The cardinal rule in the family was "Don't make mistakes" and it was enforced at all times. Despite the fact that he was an excellent student and a "good boy," his every mistake was criticized and held over him as evidence of deficiency. Love was conditional and based on his parents' expectations of superior achievement. Dennis was expected to bring home a perfect report card to make his parents proud. He became a perfectionist to minimize the criticism that shamed him and to compensate for a self that felt inadequate and flawed. He had no difficulty remembering scene after scene where he endured parental criticism for making the slightest mistake, or for not living up to their ideal.

After these shame scenes were re-experienced and understood as the source of his depression and low self-esteem, I asked Dennis to do an experiment. For one week, I asked him to do everything according to the rule, to avoid making any mistakes whatsoever. When (not if) he made a mistake, he was to belittle himself just as his parents had when he was a child (of course he was already doing this anyway). When he came back in a week, I asked him what he learned from the experiment. He said, "I could only do it for two days. I felt like a robot. It's impossible not to make mistakes and I got tired of criticizing myself. But then I realized that I wasn't doing the experiment right, and that was a mistake too. I felt like I was tied in a knot. Also, I discovered that the things my parents said when I screwed up are the same things I've been saying to myself for years—like, 'How could you be so stupid?'"

Several sessions later, Dennis called to cancel a session. He was about to fly home from a business trip but had left his briefcase in his hotel room and had to return to get it. This caused him to miss his flight and he was being sadistically self-critical. He left a message on my answering machine that said he "felt like a heel" for canceling on such short notice, and that he "couldn't believe how stupid it was." His voice sounded very agitated and self-condemning.

Dennis began the next session by apologizing and again criticizing himself for making "such a stupid mistake." He was crying. I wondered if he was attacking himself to ward off an anticipated attack from me—sort of a "beat them to the punch" strategy, but it didn't have that quality. So I asked him, "Dennis, who is it that you have on your back right now? Who is it that is always criticizing you?" He drew a blank. I reminded him of our experiment and how he discovered it was the internal "shamer" that "went to town" on him. He then realized it was his father's voice that he heard criticizing him. He added, "Dad would never allow a mistake like forgetting something so important. It was unthinkable!"

I explained to Dennis that as a result of learning the "no mistakes" rule as a child, he had internalized a critical parent voice, but no forgiving parent voice. Therefore, when he made a mistake, which was inevitable, he could only become self-critical but never self-forgiving. Mistakes were unacceptable and he was unacceptable when he made one. Forgiveness just wasn't in the family vocabulary. I told him I didn't think any less of him for forgetting his briefcase, or missing his flight, or canceling our session on short notice. Not one iota! I told him that if anything, I felt closer to him knowing that he was fallible like I am, and that his fallibility was endearing to me. I let him know that there was an important lesson in this, and that he might as well get it now, because lessons tend to repeat themselves until we learn them. The lesson was, not that he should be more cautious about avoiding mistakes, but that he could be more forgiving once he made them. I suggested that he take me in, that my voice could go with him, and that the next time he screwed up, he could imagine what I would say to him instead of what his perfectionistic father would say. My hope was that the new affirming scene with me would kick in, taking the place of the old shame scene with his father.

About four sessions later, Dennis came in excited and radiating a sense of pride. He reported that he had left work in a hurry the day before, and that he had driven to the Post Office to mail some letters to clients. Then he said, "As I dropped them in the mailbox, I realized I had forgotten to stamp them. My first response was, You stupid son of a bitch! How could you be so dumb? I was really into the critical stuff, but when I drove off I remembered what you said about the forgiving voice. I pretended you were in the passenger seat and you said, Dennis, it's okay! You don't have to be perfect. You're entitled to make mistakes just like everybody else. So they'll send the letters back for stamps. It's no big deal. It's okay! And it worked! For the first time in my life I admitted I had made a mistake and it was okay. I'm okay!"

Affirming our basic rights is how we take over responsibility for how we act and interact with others. Taking responsibility implies that we shift the locus of control for our lives from an external source (parental rules) to an internal source (self-determined rules), and that we become the "agent of our own experience" (Greenberg and Safran, 1987, p.199). We break the rules that dehumanized and shamed us, making a choice to be loyal to ourselves rather than to our parents. This is an act of giving ourselves permission to exist, to have needs, to make mistakes, to express ourselves, and to separate. It frees us up to be who we really are.

Moving from a position of being passive and other-determined to one of being active and self-determined is an enormous step in the process of healing shame. It is not enough to be aware of the dysfunctional rules we were handed and how they induced shame. We must affirm our basic human rights, and change the rules so we can relate to ourselves and others in a way that enhances self-esteem. When we slip and find ourselves following the old, self-negating rules, we "right the ship" by remembering the self-affirming rule, and then taking the risk of behaving in accord with the new rule.

The new, self-affirming rules are as follows:

I Have The Right To Be!

I Have The Right To Have Needs!

I Have The Right To Make Mistakes!

I Have The Right To Express Myself!

I Have The Right To Separate!

When you catch yourself following the old rules and denying your rights, e.g., automatically criticizing yourself for some mistake, or squelching an important feeling rather than expressing it, remind yourself of the new rule by repeating it over and over. Exercise your rights and they will become a part of you!

Quitting Shame-Inducing Roles

Countering shame-inducing messages and breaking shame-inducing rules are new behaviors that promote self-esteem and maturity. To be consistent with this new way of relating to oneself and others, the client must also quit any and all assigned family roles that are dysfunctional. The reward for quitting is a heartfelt sense of independence and a chance to form a self-affirming identity based on who one really is.

Quitting an assigned family role means freeing oneself of expectations and obligations that perpetuate internalized shame. Such roles were scripted parts in the family drama that fulfilled a family function, but at a cost. The cost to the child is that he or she forfeits optimal emotional and social development. The cost to the adult, who is still stuck in a dysfunctional family role, is a shame-based identity. As long as we accept our parents' definition of ourselves, we are like the eagle who was led to believe he was a backyard chicken. The act of quitting a disabling family role is the act of spreading our wings and taking off. When we find out who we really are, we can fly!

Old family roles are hard to get out of because they are habitual patterns of relating and, as such, have become deeply ingrained in our sense of identity. We play a particular role because it was assigned by a powerful parent and because we were reinforced for doing so. It is how we came to know ourselves, a part of who we think we are. We actually believe we are supposed to make our parents proud, or detour them from marital problems, or provide companionship for a needy opposite sex parent.

When we quit a family role, a family function goes unmet, and we can count on getting pressure to "change back!" The togetherness forces in the family will include siblings as well as parents because if one member refuses to play his or her part, the entire family drama is thrown out of balance. Regardless of which one of the eight characteristic roles we adopted, to the extent we still play it, we are in a trance that must be broken. Part of healing shame is developing a self-affirming identity that is uniquely ours.

It is not possible to quit a family role without breaking the "no separation" rule. By affirming one's right to separate from parents and family, the client is differentiating a self. This is a confusing concept that simply means, "I can allow you to be you, letting you be different from my expectations of you. It also means I can allow me to be me, different from the expectations you have of me" (Valentine in Titelman, 1987, p.87). In a shame-based family, the expectation is that the client will forever continue to fulfill a particular role. To differentiate is to quit the role, striking a blow for one's true self and unique identity.

Betsy

The following case example shows how difficult it can be to quit a role that stabilizes a needy parent. Betsy was the only daughter and oldest in a sibling complex of three. Her parents divorced when she was twelve, and because her mother "ran off with another man," she and her two brothers lived with their father. She had always been "Daddy's Little Princess," but following the divorce she also became his surrogate wife. She was immediately parentified and expected to keep house, prepare meals, and take care of her younger brothers. Her needy father, depressed and lonely as a result of losing his real wife, turned to Betsy for emotional comfort. She was assigned the role of "little spouse" and reinforced for providing companionship and support.

On several occasions, Betsy's father asked her to wear some of her mother's clothes that had been left behind. She did so, not wanting to displease him, but felt "weird" about it ("I didn't like the way he looked at me"). Although there was no obvious sexual abuse, this inappropriate request made her feel self-conscious and ashamed. Betsy had been seduced into a "special" relationship with her father that felt unconsciously incestuous on an emotional level.

Betsy entered therapy with a specific problem. At age twenty-two, she was still living at home with her father, but wanted to move out. She was romantically involved and wanted more personal freedom. It was her wish to live on her own and prove to herself that she could be independent before considering marriage. She discussed this idea with her father but, predictably, he was adamantly opposed. At first, he said it was impractical and too expensive. Then, when it became apparent she wasn't going to give up on the idea, he tearfully told her he would feel "all alone" if she left him. He reminded her that her mother left him and that he had never been the same.

Betsy felt caught. She explained, "If I leave him it would mean I'm like my Mom, someone who 'flaked out' on her family." Betsy lived under the "Don't separate" rule and in accordance with an unconscious contract that bound her to her father—"I'll never leave you, if I can pretend you're the parent I always wanted." Her depressed and dependent father induced her to believe that he could not survive without her.

I had to resist the temptation to give Betsy advice. Part of me wanted to tell her to leave home because she was his grown daughter, not his wife—and even if she was, it wasn't her job to take care of him. But first, she had to acknowledge shame by fully understanding how she had been and still was being exploited. This was not immediately apparent to her. She considered herself selfish "for even thinking about leaving him when he needs me so much." We spent many sessions reviewing her family of origin history and bringing her out of denial. Betsy came to realize that she had taken in engulfing messages that made her feel like a nothing, that she had followed a rule that denied her right to separate, and that she had been assigned a family role that was emotionally incestuous. She was being used as a parent to her siblings and a surrogate spouse to her father.

In acknowledging that she had been shamed by these family processes, Betsy got in touch with some repressed anger. Now she had access to a part of her that wanted her own life and I didn't have to give any advice. If I gave her advice and it turned out to be wrong, she would be angry with me. If I was right, she might become dependent on me. It was a no-win situation unless she learned to trust her own feelings. That's what feelings are for—to provide information that tells her how to live her life. By acknowledging her angry feeling of being exploited and using it as a guide, Betsy made her own decision. She would tell her father that she was moving out because that was what she really wanted to do. It was what she needed to do if she ever wanted to become an independent person and a grown-up woman. If she was being selfish, so be it—she felt entitled to have a self!

On the day Betsy actually moved out, her father, saddened by his loss, openly wept and pleaded with her to stay. He tried to manipulate her and "pulled out all the stops." He said he and her brothers couldn't make it without her. He said it reminded him of the day her mother moved out. She told him, "I'm not your wife, Dad! I'm your daughter and it's time for me to move out." I had warned Betsy she was not going to get her father's blessings and to expect "change back!" responses until he realized she was serious about changing. She held her ground, letting him know she was not moving back, but that she was not cutting off contact either.

Betsy was unsure what she owed her father, but she was sure that it wasn't an obligation to sacrifice her future for him. She could take care of herself, or she could take care of him. It was an either/or choice—she could not do both. Quitting her long-time role of surrogate spouse ("Daddy's Little Princess") broke the family trance. Her father became so depressed that he sought professional help and, at last report, was resolving a lifetime of losses and doing much better. By differentiating a self, Betsy finally had a self to esteem. Free of her father's expectations and a role that was emotionally incestuous, Betsy traded her shame-based identity for one that was based on self-esteem. She had formed a self-affirming identity.

Step Five: Confronting Your Shame-Inducing Parents

Zen Master Thich Nhat Hanh, who integrates Buddhism and psychotherapy, tells a teaching tale called "The Man Who Thought He Was A Grain of Corn" (in Simpkinson, 1989, p.20). It is a story that instructs us that healing does not occur in a vacuum, but in the relationship between the person with the symptom and the persons who affect the symptom.

"The story takes place in a Vietnamese mental hospital that was near farm land, chickens, ponds, and ducks. A patient in the hospital was a man who appeared quite normal. He ate like other people, spoke like other people, and was fond of jogging. His only abnormality was his belief that he was a grain of corn. He was therefore terrified of being eaten by a chicken and would run away whenever he saw one. The nurses in the hospital couldn't catch him because he was running for his life.

When the nurses reported this to his doctor, the doctor attempted to counsel the patient. He told him, 'You know, my friend, you are not a grain of corn, you are a human being! You have a human body with arms and legs, and a human face with two eyes, a nose, and a mouth. Do you not agree?' 'Yes, yes, I agree,' said the man. Given that they agreed, the doctor pre-scribed that the patient repeat this sentence 300 to 400 times a day: 'I am a human being; I am not a grain of corn!' He was also asked to write the same sentence down until he filled 100 sheets of blank paper. The man was very motivated to get well and repeated the sentence faithfully as prescribed. He wrote it down in every spare moment.

Several months passed and the doctor asked the nurses how the patient was doing. They told the doctor that the man had been most compliant and appeared to be cured of his false belief. So the doctor met with his patient and asked, 'How are things going?' The man smiled at the doctor and said, 'I know very well that I am a human being. I am not a grain of corn!' The doctor was delighted with his patient's progress, and his treatment plan. He said, 'Well, I think we can let you go home in a couple of days. Come to the office with me and we will start the paperwork.'

On the way to the office, they came upon a chicken, and the man ran for his life. The doctor was very disappointed. Once hour later, a nurse brought the man back to the doctor's office. The doctor looked at him reproachfully, not saying anything at first. Finally he said, 'Well, you told me that you knew you were a human being and not a grain of corn. So why did you run away when you saw the chicken?' The patient answered, 'I do know that I am a human being and not a grain of corn. But how could the chicken know?'

If the doctor is intelligent and learns from his patient, he will change his way of practicing.

A client can change the false idea that he or she is a "grain of corn," or a "bad person," or any other shame-based core belief about the self. However, if the parents who induced the shame continue to relate in ways that reinforce a shamed sense of self, and the client continues to take it in, there is no healing. It doesn't matter how well he or she is doing in psychotherapy, the work will not hold up if shame is still being internalized. Core beliefs can be countered, basic rights can be affirmed, and dysfunctional roles can be discarded, but unless the client relates from a position of equality and demands respect, the process of healing is incomplete. Either the shaming parent has to stop mistreating the client, or the client has to stop the relationship as it is. The "chicken" must be confronted and told that the client is no longer a "grain of corn."

This is the purpose of a confrontation—to state the truth, stand up to the parent, tell them what you object to, and set limits on their shaming behavior. "Confrontation is merely a statement of facts and feelings...to resolve or bring closure to the relationships that plague you most" (Engel, 1989, p.109). The purpose is not to shame them, get even, dump repressed rage, or change them into the parents you always wanted. If you are confronting for the wrong reasons, you are most likely stuck in the position of an angry or dependent child. If you are stuck in blame, you are stuck in shame. However, when you truly understand that the "badness" was theirs (for shaming you), and not yours (for feeling ashamed), your self-esteem will take a quantum leap!

Confrontation is a way of checking out how effectively you have completed steps one through four in the healing process. Timing is everything and confrontation works best toward the latter stages of therapy. I discourage my clients from confronting shaming parents until they have progressed in the following ways: (1) they understand how shame was induced and no longer blame themselves for being molested, battered, or whatever; (2) they have released enough shame, rage, and grief that they can maintain a reasonably grown-up position in the face of an intimidating parent; (3) they are able to maintain positive self-esteem in the face of more rejection, abandonment, belittlement, crazymaking, etc.; and (4) they are intellectually and emotionally prepared for a worst possible scenario with a desperate parent seeking to preserve the status quo.

Susan Forward refers to confrontation as "the road to independence" and the "most empowering act that you will ever perform" (1989, p.236). She pushes her clients "very hard" to confront their "toxic parents" because it establishes equal power and puts a stop to the process of displacing fear, guilt, and anger onto one's children or partner—"What you don't hand back, you pass on" (p.238). Her definition of a "toxic" parent as one who traumatizes, abuses, or denigrates his children (p.6) is very close to our definition of a shame-inducing parent. And shame is clearly induced by "toxic" parenting, as indicated by her statement, "Whether adult children of toxic parents were beaten when little or left alone too much, sexually abused or treated like fools, overprotected or overburdened by guilt, they almost all suffer similar symptoms: damaged self-esteem, leading to self-destructive behavior" (p.6).

There are three modes of confrontation—maximum, minimum, and limit setting. A maximum confrontation puts all the cards on the table—past, present, and future. It is done either face to face with the shame-inducing parent or by writing them a letter. Forward is an advocate of the maximum confrontation, provided her client is strong enough to handle any negative consequences from it, has a sufficient support system, has adequately rehearsed what to say, and holds the parents responsible for childhood trauma as opposed to blaming themselves (p.241). She suggests signaling the confrontation by beginning with, "I'm going to say some things to you I have never said before" (p.242). Adapting her model for our purposes, the client then covers four major issues:

1. This is how you shamed me

2. This is how I reacted to the shaming messages, rules, and/or roles.

3. This is how it made me feel about myself, e.g., core beliefs

4. This is how I expect to be treated from now on.

Here is an example of a maximum confrontation letter sent by a client who was battered, terrorized, and abandoned as a child. When the shaming environment is extreme as in this case, it is difficult to confront without being accused of "parent bashing." The intention is not to bash them, but to stop protecting them, break the "no expression" rule, and tell the truth. This gets the unfinished business out in the open where it can be dealt with.

Jim, the man who wrote this letter, was almost forty and had been in weekly individual therapy for one and a half years. He had released much of his shame and rage and was able to confront his parents in a fairly detached way, i.e., he was not retaliating. On the contrary, he had a sincere desire to resolve unfinished business and move on. Writing this letter was risky because he had never broken the "no separation" rule and, in the past, his parents had threatened to disown him for making feeble attempts to separate, e.g., changing his name.

Dear Mom and Dad,

I have wanted to write this letter for quite some time but have never found the courage to do so until now. I am writing now because your requests for me to move close to you require a response.

It is true that I am far away. I have chosen to live in the Pacific Northwest because I love this part of the country. But I have also chosen to live here because it would be too painful for me to live close to you. The more contact I have with you, the more I feel criticized, manipulated, and pulled into your marital problem. So I have chosen to keep my distance. In your last letter you said you can't understand why I seem so angry. Let me tell you why.

(This is how you shamed me.)

As a child, I was beaten frequently with a belt, stick, or whatever else was handy. You beat me on my bare bottom until welts came up and bled. I was a victim of child abuse. This is a fact, whether you acknowledge it or not. Dad, your temper terrified me. The times you were drunk, and drove recklessly on back roads, I feared for my life. I cried, and begged you to slow down, but you never listened. You didn't seem to care that I was being traumatized, and that hurt bad.

Mom, you did nothing to protect me and Susie (Jim's younger sister) from dad's alcoholism and violent temper. Worse, you encouraged the physical abuse by telling dad to punish us for misbehaving, knowing that he would beat us. You said things like, "Wait until your father gets home!"—and we waited in terror. I felt abandoned at a time when I was dependent on you for comfort and protection. You wanted me to be the adult and reversed roles with me. I was supposed to take care of you when you were depressed and lonely. You confided in me about how unhappy you were with dad, and I was caught in the middle. I tried to keep the peace, but I didn't know what to do and felt like a failure. When I didn't do exactly what you wanted, I got the silent treatment.

(This is how I reacted to the shaming messages, rules, and/or roles.)

I felt deeply shamed by the ways you treated me. Dad, when you beat me, I thought I was bad, really bad, like everything wrong was my fault. I lived in fear of the next beating, knowing I was helpless to defend myself. I felt enraged and wanted to get even. Mom, I felt so sad and alone, especially when you failed to protect me or withdrew from me. There was always a crisis and I had intense feelings, yet I was not allowed to express them. It wasn't safe—things would have only gotten worse for me if I had spoken up. I longed for a normal family and pretended that things weren't so bad. But they were!

(This is how it made me feel about myself.)

As a result of being beaten and abandoned, I thought I was a bad kid. I felt like I was worthless, or else you wouldn't have mistreated me the way you did. I tried to win your love, and when I failed it only made me feel more worthless. I tried to prove my worth, but deep down I knew I was pretending to be something I wasn't. I actually believed I deserved to be abused as a child, and that I deserved to be unhappy as an adult. I've made mistakes too—taking out my anger on my wife and kids, trying to control others with the threat of violence, treating people with contempt. This has reinforced the feeling that there is something terribly wrong with me, and at times I have hated myself.

(This is how I expect to be treated from now on.)

Now I'm more forgiving of myself and my self-esteem is mending. I want things to be different between us. I want to forgive you too, but there's a part of me that is having trouble letting go. It would be easier if you owned up to your mistakes. A sincere apology would help to heal our relationship. I love you very much and I would like to have a better relationship from here on. That means no more verbal attacks, no more attempts to put me in the middle of your marital problems, no more guilt trips because I'm not there to take care of you. I am not moving, so stop asking me to do so.

I hope you will read this letter over several times and be able to understand where I'm coming from. I expect you will be talking to Susie about the things I've said. I am sending her a copy of this letter so that she will know exactly what I said. It is my hope we can face up to our disappointments in one another and find a way to improve our relationship. I would appreciate it if you would write me back and respond to this letter.

Jim

Needless to say, a maximum confrontation of this kind is
anxiety-provoking and should never be insisted upon (as some
therapists do). If the client is pushed to confront, and unable to
do so for whatever reason, shame will be experienced for being
"wimpish." The affirming therapist challenges but never asks a
client to do anything that exceeds their limits. To do so communicates that they don't measure up, induces more shame, destroys trust in the therapist, and undermines the healing process.
Furthermore, if the confrontation is the therapist's agenda, the
client is giving away power and merely transferring a one-down
position from the powerful parent to the powerful therapist. The
client should dictate the pace, otherwise there is no safe place
and the story will be put off or not told at all. If it is the client's
agenda, a maximum confrontation is an effective way of resolving
unfinished business and reclaiming power from shaming parents.

These positives can also be achieved through the process of
minimum confrontation, which is less direct and intimidating. A
minimum confrontation puts only the present and future cards
on the table, and avoids some of the emotional intensity associated with the past. It therefore bypasses some parental denial,
excuse making, blaming, threatening, and other defensive strategies that escalate tensions. Because it does not ask the parent
to take responsibility for scenes they would like to forget, minimum confrontation is less anxiety arousing for both sides. This
is critically important in some situations, e.g., where the parent
has a history of violence or where the parent is elderly or seriously
ill.

This does not imply that a maximum confrontation is ruled out
with sick parents. A friend who was molested by her father
confronted him on his death bed. As he lay dying, she took his
hand and said, "Dad, there's something we've never talked
about." He was unable to open his eyes but squeezed her hand
and nodded slightly. She continued, "When I was thirteen, you
put your hand on my breast." He nodded again. "I want you to
know that it hurt me deeply, and for a long time I felt bad about
myself. But I've worked it out and I'm okay now. And I've
forgiven you." He heaved a sigh of relief and began to weep. By
lovingly confronting him before he died, my friend did her father,
and herself, a tremendous service. I believe this touching story

dispels once and for all the notion that confrontations must be antagonistic.

Many clients choose not to confront parents directly and opt for a minimum confrontation. It can be done in several ways. The first is to confront parents in fantasy in the safe space of the therapist's office. The client can use the "empty chair" technique, imagine his or her parents present, and confront them in accordance with the major issues—this is how you shamed me, how I reacted, how it made me feel about myself, how I expect to be treated now. Similarly, psychodramatic techniques (Moreno, 1972) such as role-playing allow therapist and client to enact the confrontation, thus ensuring that blocked emotions will be aroused and released.

A second way is for the client to write a "no holds barred," "let it all hang out" maximum confrontation letter, but not send it. The letter can instead be read in the safe haven of the psychotherapy session, as if the parents were present, listening, and accountable for their behavior. It is most effective to write each parent separately because the major issues are usually different. Some clients prefer to make an audiotape letter to each parent, which is then listened to during the therapy hour. Either way works.

Both maximum and minimum confrontations are optional. The third type of confrontation is not an option if the client is committed to completing the process of healing shame. It is essential. The client is not pressured to use it, but the therapist makes clear that the work is incomplete without it. It involves setting limits on the parent's behavior so that no new shame wounds are inflicted. This is considered the least you can do for yourself if you are going to maintain self-esteem. This mode of confrontation is done directly with the real life parent in response to any shaming behavior. This willingness to confront communicates a message that asserts, "I demand respect!" and "I expect to be treated as an equal!" Limit setting signals an adult-to-adult way of relating. "If adulthood has any meaning, it must lie in attaining equal power in relation to...one's family of origin" (Kaufman, 1989, p.237).

Let's consider some examples of setting limits with parents who are still shaming their adult children. The following parent comments and behaviors are taken from actual cases; the client responses are what we came up with in session to confront the parent and set limits. It is a good idea to anticipate the parent's shaming behaviors and rehearse responses, because in the heat of the moment it is hard to think clearly. As my former Gestalt therapy trainer Bob Resnick explained it, "It's easier to answer the quiz show questions when you're at home watching television."

—To the belittling parent who says, "You never were very smart. I'm not surprised you lost your job." Client response: "Dad, you've been putting me down for as long as I can remember. If you're going to insult me, keep it to yourself. I've had enough!"

—To the scornful parent who says, "My God you've gained weight! Don't you have any self-respect?" Client response: "Mom, I'm working on regaining my self-respect. You can help by being less judgmental. Otherwise, I'm not going to come over."

—To the molesting parent who "accidentally on purpose" walked into the bathroom while my thirty-six-year-old client was bathing. Client response: "Get the hell out of here! If you ever do anything like this again, I swear to God I'll call the police and report you!"

—To the engulfing parent who says, "If you really loved me, you'd phone me more than once or twice a month." Client response: "Mom, I really do love you, but I'm an adult and I'm in charge of my life. I'll phone you when I want to talk with you."

—To the brainwashing parent who says, "Why don't you attend church any more? Your father and I are ashamed of you!" Client response: "I'm sorry you have a problem with that. I don't. But, I won't discuss religion with you, and that's non-negotiable!"

—To the confusing parent who says, "You have no reason to be upset with your mother." Client response: "Listen dad, you can't talk me out of my feelings any more. They're my feelings and they're valid. Besides, this is between me and mother so please stay out of it."

This mode of confrontation is startling to parents who are used to intimidating their adult children and being one-up in terms of power. Their child, regardless of age, feels intimidated because of the threat that has always been there; namely, rejection, abandonment, battering, or any other response that will inflict more shame and restore the parent to power. Some clients, who claim they could never confront their parents, say..."It would kill them!" The thought of challenging the parent's power and relating as an equal is experienced as murderous. This is a sure sign that they are still under the spell of the family trance. The client who believes their parent is that vulnerable is always being controlled.

According to Donald Williamson, a family therapist who writes about terminating the boundary between adult clients and older parents, "parental vulnerability may be the ultimate intimidation" (1981, p.442). He calls for a radical change in the balance of power between generations, and sees equal power as the prerequisite of "psychological adulthood and ... personal authority in living" (pp.441-442).

Confronting by setting limits is a way of reclaiming power and asserting a peer relationship to one's parents. This mode of confrontation is very effective in most cases, but it must be done consistently if parents are to learn that you are serious about demanding a change, i.e., "Don't believe in one-trial learning." Parents will seldom relinquish power without a fight, so change is likely to be gradual and take some time. Keep drawing the line, most parents will eventually get it because most parents want to be respectful.

Those parents who choose to honor limits, convey respect and send a new message that says, "I take you seriously." This marks a new beginning in the relationship, one that recognizes the worth of the adult child.

Although the purpose of confrontation is to benefit the client, the parent who begins to show respect is also benefitted. Potter-Efron and Potter-Efron state, "...relationships built around shame damage the participants, even those who seem to gain power and control" (1989, p.164). As they become more aware of how they have inflicted shame, parents have the opportunity to make amends. The habitual shamer typically feels alienated from his or her children and this intensifies self-hatred.

Learning to respect one's children requires parents to contain their shame. It is only from this position that parents can own it and begin their own healing process. Since the majority of shaming parents are unaware of what they have done or are still doing, the awareness that they have damaged someone they love becomes a strong motive toward self-improvement. Their own self-esteem improves by containing their shame and showing respect.

However, many shaming parents are unwilling to grant equal power to their once dependent children, not only because it represents a loss of control, but also because they are afraid of losing face. To give up power and honor a limit that has been set feels like defeat. They resist any changes in the power structure of the family by invalidating or attacking their children's position. Such parents say, "You're being oversensitive!," or "Don't talk to me in that tone of voice!" Another common scenario is for the parent to simply ignore the limit and continue to behave disrespectfully. It is not that the limit was not clearly stated, or that it was misunderstood, it is simply that the shame-based parent is locked into certain patterns of behavior and is unwilling to change.

When limit setting has no impact, the client must up the ante by resetting the limit and adding on an ultimatum. To illustrate, one client set a limit with an alcoholic mother, insisting that she not telephone at times when she had been drinking. The mother ignored the limit so the client issued the following ultimatum: "If you continue to call when you're drunk, I will not only hang up the phone, but get an unlisted phone number. Then you will not be able to call at all!" The ultimatum worked and her mother only called when she was sober, a change that was better for both parties.

I discourage clients from issuing an ultimatum unless they are committed to carrying it out. If it is not carried out as soon as the parent oversteps the limit, the client loses credibility and is taken even less seriously than before. This would undermine the goal of gaining equal power and reinforce the parents' one-up position in the family hierarchy. The client again feels like a helpless child with a shamed sense of self.

If the ultimatum is carried out but has no impact, i.e., the parent continues to behave in ways that shame, then the client has no choice but to consider a temporary or permanent cutoff. This decision should be made by a grown-up part of the personality, not an angry, vindictive inner child part. A temporary cutoff is considered when contact with parents keeps reopening old shame wounds and slows the process of healing. Time apart gives the client a chance to gain perspective on family relationships, and time to try out new ways of being without pressure to "change back!" It also sends a message to the parents that they had better be ready to be more respectful if they want to maintain the relationship.

Stacy

Stacy decided to cut off temporarily from her mother because whenever they got together she felt controlled. She tried limit setting, but as Stacy put it, "It was like trying to stop a freight train with a rope." Her engulfing mother saw Stacy's new assertiveness as evidence that therapy was bad for her, and pressured her to quit. Finally, Stacy wrote her mother, "I'm trying to sort some things out, and until I do, I don't want to have any contact. As it is, I lose myself when we're together and it's too big a price to pay. A 'time out' will give us both time to think about how we are going to relate to each other when we resume contact. This decision is non-negotiable so don't even try to argue with me."

After several months of no contact, Stacy wanted to try again. As she explained it, "Mom still wants to control me, but she's more subtle because she knows I mean business. It's okay now because I see what she's doing and I'm not so reactive to it. Instead of getting hooked, I find myself thinking—'that's mom,' and I tell her to back off. And she does."

Permanent cutoff runs the risk that the client may begin to re-enact childhood shame scenes with someone else. It should therefore be considered carefully, and is rarely a good idea unless the parents in question are the worst kind of shamers, e.g., child molesters in denial, batterers who remain violent, terrorizers who continue to threaten. In such cases, stopping all contact indefinitely may be the only way to protect oneself. If maintaining the relationship only brings more shame and suffering, and the client has given up hope that the parents will change and show respect, permanent cutoff is a legitimate solution.

Janet

After nearly two years of psychotherapy, Janet brought in her incestuous father and collusive mother for a confrontation. Like most molesting fathers and their dependent wives, this couple were masters of denial. He claimed, "I must have been drunk," and she said, "I never saw it, so how do I know she's telling the truth?" Collectively, they attacked Janet's story and implied that she must be "crazy." Afterwards, Janet realized they were not going to change and that they consistently attacked her self-esteem. She wrote each parent a letter explaining why she would no longer see them. Shortly thereafter, she ended therapy. I ran into Janet about two years later and asked about the cutoff. She said, "It was a loss just like you said it would be, but I've never regretted doing it. Nothing good would have come from continuing the relationship, and a lot of good has come from ending it." "Like what?" I asked. She smiled, "Like my sanity and self-esteem."

Step Six: Forgiving or Letting Go

The process of confrontation is one of resolving unfinished business with shaming parents. It is a step that must be taken if the client is to attain equal power and psychological adulthood. The willingness to confront, set limits, and relate as a peer signals the end of the one-down way of a child relating to a parent. "If the parent is still the psychological parent then the offspring is psychologically a child, as far as that relational system is concerned. By definition, an 'adult' cannot have 'parents' in an emotional sense" (Williamson, 1981, p.444). Being an adult implies giving up the wish or need to be parented and "leaving home." Mother and father become "former parents" (pp.444-445). Leaving the parental home means no longer seeking validation, no longer being controlled, and "no longer being programmed by the transgenerational script" (p.445). In other words, "leaving home" means breaking the family trance and taking responsibility for one's own life. Only from this position of emotional independence can the client be free of the messages, rules, and roles that were shaming.

The process of releasing shame and confronting in order to resolve the past makes forgiveness and letting go possible. This is the final step in the healing process, and should not be undertaken before completing the previous steps. To prematurely forgive or let go means that the client will remain stuck with a laundry list of negative emotions, particularly shame and resentment. The forgiveness issue is one about which there is a great deal of confusion in the helping professions. Understanding the distinction between forgiving and letting go clears things up and makes this sixth and final step much easier.

One cannot forgive without letting go, but one can let go without forgiving. This means that when you forgive a parent, you also let go of your resentment for having been harmed. However, you can let go of your resentful feelings without actually forgiving the shamer. This distinction is an important one because some parents have done unforgivable things and understandably, some clients cannot forgive them. This would mean being unable to complete the healing process except for the fact that the same clients who cannot forgive are perfectly capable of letting go. Thus, it is not necessary to forgive to complete the healing process, only to let go. Let's examine each of these concepts carefully.

Several authors have done an excellent job defining what forgiveness is and isn't (Smedes, 1984; Simon and Simon, 1990). First of all, forgiving and forgetting are not the same. They are right next to one another in the dictionary, but worlds apart in reality. Forgiveness is not "celestial amnesia" as a well-known New Age psychiatrist would have it. As children, we forget shame scenes in order to protect our vulnerable selves. Once we have remembered such scenes, it is not a good idea to forget them again. To do so would be to go back into denial and undo a lot of hard work and learning.

To forgive is not to avoid confrontation and pretend all is forgiven when the wounds are in fact unhealed. Nor is it to overlook, justify, or make excuses for parental behaviors that induced shame. Because your parents were battered as children does not make it okay that they battered you. It may help explain their abusiveness, but it certainly does not excuse it. There is no excuse for abusing children! Forgiveness does not "let them off the hook" and absolve them of the responsibility for their actions

(Simon and Simon, p.16). I believe one could truly forgive a parent and, at the same time, sue them for damages (I have seen this happen in a case involving incest).

Forgiveness is not rationalizing. Rationalizing is a defense whereby we come up with a reassuring but incorrect explanation for the parent's behavior. I am aware of several well-known authors and lecturers who confuse this point. Speaking of parents who molested their children, they say things like, "They did the best they could with what they knew at the time," or "If they could have done better, they would have." I couldn't disagree more strongly with this viewpoint. It is utterly wrong! The parent who molests his or her own child is not doing their best when they are exploiting and betraying a powerless victim. They are doing their best when they are not molesting, not giving in to their needs for power and sex, not transferring shame. They are responsible for their behavior, just as we are if we choose to bring helpless children into the world. To hold that they are less responsible because of their own childhood, or stress, or whatever, is to rationalize. This may appeal to the little kid part who still wants to believe in the good parent, but it encourages the idea that the victim was somehow responsible and bad. It is a carryover from the suggestible child self that took the bad qualities of the parents into the self in order to preserve the illusion that they were good.

What forgiveness is, is the process of giving up the resentment toward and reconciling with the shaming parent. The release of shame and indignant anger for having been wounded makes possible a reconciliation wherein the forgiving client extends a friendly attitude toward the forgiven parent. "To forgive one's parent is an act of reunion, just as to forgive oneself is an act of reunion with oneself" (Kaufman, 1989, p.238). The great Protestant theologian, Paul Tillich, agreed with this view of forgiveness. He wrote, "genuine forgiveness is participation, reunion overcoming the power of estrangement" (in Smedes, p.48). True forgiveness takes place when estranged people come together again and participate in a renewed relationship, i.e., they take part and share in the relationship.

Forgiveness is more likely to occur if the client really gets to know the as yet unforgiven parent. Williamson writes, "Children do not 'know' parents except as 'parents,' and have no direct knowledge of the inner world of experience of the man and woman who used to be 'mommy' and 'daddy'" (1981, p.446). Having a more complete and intimate picture of the man and woman behind the parental roles facilitates both the acts of forgiveness and letting go. I therefore ask clients to interview their parents, but only after confronting them as outlined in step five. This is because adults shamed as children survived by making excuses for their parents' behavior, and getting a family history will tempt them to let the parent "off the hook," e.g., "He was abused much worse than I ever was, how can I fault him for what he did?"

This habit of excusing parental mistreatment is another example of trance logic. It argues that the parent is not accountable because he or she had a difficult childhood (a belief typically presented by the parent to avoid shame). With this logic we could excuse Attila the Hun, Hitler, and the next serial killer. Remember, there is no justification for repeatedly shaming a child. Adults are accountable to their children for their behavior that affects their children. Nevertheless, understanding how each parent was treated as a child, what rules and roles they adopted, and whether they ever "left home" makes the client less emotionally reactive to their "former parents." As the client elicits their personal story, including how they related to their own parents and siblings, and how they connected as a couple to start the family, a new perspective is gained—one that is conducive to forgiving.

It should be obvious that the act of forgiveness is much easier if the parent is willing to meet the client half way. They must understand that they inflicted a deep wound, they must validate and feel your pain, they must be willing to be confronted and really listen, they must promise never to wound you again—"This is the truthfulness those you forgive must bring with them as their entree back into your life"(Smedes, pp.51-54).

In other words, the shaming parent can encourage a more forgiving attitude by owning up to their shaming ways and doing what they can to repair the damage. For example, I treated one client whose molesting father offered to pay for her treatment, and to seek help himself, both of which he did. In another case, a woman I had seen for over a year for depression disclosed that she had molested her son. At my suggestion, she reported herself to Child Protective Services. Of her own free will, she continued in therapy and paid for therapy (individual and family) for her son. She did whatever she could to repair the damage. She became accountable. By taking responsibility for their shame-inducing actions, such parents do their children and themselves a service that helps to heal the wounds.

However healing forgiveness can be, and it can, telling a client that they have to forgive their parents is disrespectful, if not insulting. This is especially true in relation to the parent who does not take responsibility for their faulty parenting. Forgiveness is the client's decision to make, and theirs alone, and it is well nigh impossible for those who endured the worst kinds of shaming experiences. A client who was raped by her father as a helpless and innocent child should not be expected to reconcile with someone who brutalized her. Even suggesting that she should feel friendly or close adds insult to injury. The implication that she should be able to forgive him is likely to reinforce the belief that she is not entitled to her feelings, that there is something wrong with her.

Kaufman (1989) states, "Clients should not be pressured or admonished into forgiving their parents. That is tantamount to shaming them for still resenting and not forgiving the parent" (p.238). I remember using a sentence completion technique with a woman who had been a battered child. I said, "The one thing I never want you to say to me is..." and she answered, "That I have to forgive my father!" The affirming therapist never imposes his or her agenda, and seeks to validate the client's emotional experience.

For clients who cannot honestly forgive, there is the alternative of letting go. Letting go is different from forgiveness in that it does not imply reunion and reconciliation. Whereas forgiveness brings the shamer and the shamed back together, letting go does not. Both release the trapped emotional energy that feeds into feelings of bitter hurt over having been mistreated, but only forgiveness calls for participation in a relationship with the shaming parent. Both free up energy that can be used elsewhere, but only forgiveness asks for that energy to be reinvested in the relationship. Both forgiving and letting go imply giving up the urge to get even, but only letting go allows the client to remain estranged from the shaming parent. To let go is to release the intense feelings that were once associated with childhood without necessarily reconciling with the shaming parent.

A client who cannot bring himself or herself to forgive, can complete the healing process by letting go. Painful shame scenes may be remembered, but only by choice, and after they have been purged of the intense feelings they once contained. Letting go means that the once powerful and shaming parent loses their previous stimulus value. He or she can no longer stir up feelings from the past, because those feelings are released and gone. They cannot inflict new shame wounds because the client has awakened from the family trance and become a psychological adult. The shaming parent cannot be controlled or changed, but the client understands the parent's ways of relating and is ready to confront or set limits accordingly. If acknowledging shame can be thought of as taking hold of your childhood reality, then letting go is moving on.

Some clients resist the idea of either forgiving or letting go. There are several reasons they would rather nurse their grievances. First, by holding on to the idea that shaming parents deserve to be punished, the child within feels validated. To explain, if something is damaged, then punishing the responsible party is appropriate because it affirms that whatever was damaged has value. To fail to punish the shamer would be to betray the child part of the self by implying that nothing of value was damaged. Not forgiving holds the shaming parent accountable by saying, in effect, "You damaged something valuable and now you must pay the price!"

Second, refusing to forgive or let go allows us to hang on to some aspect of our identity, even if it is shame-based. Holding on becomes a way of maintaining the self that we have come to know, e.g., incest victim, Adult Child of Alcoholic (ACOA), "Bad Seed," etc. This can be a means of avoiding change or postponing growing up and taking responsibility for one's life. At the same time, it may be a way of indicting one's parents for their "crimes." To illustrate, one adult client told his parents, "It's not my fault I can't hold a job. I'm a drug addict. That's just the way I am." Still enraged with his parents for neglecting him, his failure in life shamed them just as they once shamed him (David Calof refers to this as "holding your parents hostage").

Third, not forgiving or letting go feels self-protective. It creates the illusion that by staying resentful, we will have the power to ward off further rejection, abandonment, molestation, or any other shame-inducing behavior. The angry energy serves as a buffer that allows the client to feel more in control and less vulnerable. In a short story by Audra Adelberger (1990), a woman named Kirstin imagines a dialogue with her dying father, a tyrant who battered and belittled her as a child. The story begins with her saying to him: "It seems almost safer to forgive you after you're dead than to open myself to it before you die. You may walk right in and hurt me again. At least if I don't forgive you I am closed against you. Yes, it's safer to wait until you can no longer hurt me." She believes that withholding forgiveness makes her less vulnerable to further shame wounds.

Finally, some clients won't forgive or let go for fear that it would validate their parents' denial or condone the mistreatment they dished out during childhood. "If I forgive her, it will be like telling her it's okay to be alcoholic, that it had no effect on me." Or, "If I stop hating him, it would be like agreeing that he didn't molest me, that I made it up." Holding on to grievances reminds the parent that his or her shaming behavior really happened and that it hurt bad.

At first glance, these are powerful reasons that stand in the way of forgiving or letting go. However, nursing grievances and holding on to resentment is bad for you—bad for your mind, body, and spirit. Without forgiving or letting go you can never have peace of mind, never be in harmony with the world around you. Forgiving your parents or letting go of your indignation is something you do to heal, something you do for your own benefit, not theirs. As we define a separate and powerful self, we eliminate the need for our shame-based identities. We replace the old identity with a new one that is based on pride for whom we uniquely are. We have no need to hold on so that we can call ourselves ACOA's or codependents, or any other label that ties us to the past. Labels are for jars. We don't need to hold on to protect ourselves because we have better ways to do it. We can affirm our rights, express ourselves, confront shaming behaviors, set limits, and either temporarily or permanently cutoff. We have real power! Finally, forgiving or letting go does not collude with their denial or minimize the effects of what parents did or didn't do. It has nothing to do with forgetting or condoning their faulty parenting. It is an internal process and a sign of wellness and positive self-esteem (Simon and Simon, p.18). Not to forgive or let go ultimately hurts the client far more than the shaming parent.

Adults who were shamed as children feel ashamed about feeling shame; that is why they feel so uncomfortable exposing themselves in therapy. They feel humiliated for having been mistreated, and for not having the kind of parents every child wants. They feel embarrassed about the survival tools they used to protect themselves, e.g., denying reality, pretending to like being molested, developing eating disorders, becoming "people pleasers," etc. They feel guilty about the things they did in childhood and adolescence to get even, e.g., lying, failing academically, drugging, engaging in promiscuous sex, etc. They feel ashamed for being self-destructive adults and for the ways they have become like their parents, e.g., for addictions or for sending the same shaming messages to their own children.

As clients learn they were not responsible for their own mistreatment, and understand the things they did as a result of internalizing shame, self-blame is replaced by self-compassion and feelings of worth. These are the first stirrings of self-forgiveness. Somewhere in the process of forgiving or letting go the issue of self-forgiveness emerges and becomes foremost in awareness. By this time the client has internalized a forgiving parent in the person of the affirming therapist. Now, when confronted with the mistakes they have made and the limitations they have, past and present, the client is able to be more self-accepting. The critical and shaming parent voice is replaced by a forgiving and affirming parent voice.

Forgiving your parents is optional. Forgiving yourself is not—it is essential to completing the healing process. This means you must forgive your child self for being vulnerable, weak, and unable to protect you any better than he or she did. You must forgive yourself for being suggestible—for taking in negative messages and forming core beliefs that convinced you of being bad and unlovable. You must forgive yourself for adopting rules and roles that necessitated a false self and led to an identity based on shame. You must forgive yourself for the compulsions that enabled you to maintain denial and anesthetize pain—booze, drugs, overeating, overworking, indiscriminate sex, whatever.

You must forgive yourself for re-enacting shame scenes by mis-treating yourself or others, or by connecting with someone who mistreated you the way your parents did. In short, you must forgive yourself for being shamed as a child, for making mistakes as a result of being shamed, and for not taking responsibility sooner.

To forgive yourself is the culmination of the healing process and the destination on the journey to self-esteem. It is an accom-plishment that comes from acknowledging and releasing shame in the context of an affirming relationship. Self-forgiveness is a gift to yourself that becomes possible after affirming your right to make mistakes and giving rebirth to your true self. It is to enter into a positive relationship with your child within, and to make a lifelong commitment to love and care for that child. To forgive yourself is to be delighted with who you have become, feeling full of pride and self-respect. It is the essential outcome that signals the completion of the process of healing shame.

Conclusion

Healing Family Wounds to Self-Esteem

Approximately fifteen years ago, while working on my doctorate in clinical psychology, I had the opportunity to train with the late Dr. Arnold Beisser. Arnie had been a force in the Gestalt Therapy Institute of Los Angeles since its inception, leading groups of student trainees. He has written several books, including a masterpiece—*Flying Without Wings: Personal Reflections on Loss, Disability, and Healing* (1988). At age twenty-four, Arnie had completed medical school and was a national tennis champion. He was seemingly on top of the world. Then, he developed a fever, and in a matter of hours, polio so ravaged his body that he was left permanently paralyzed from the neck down, unable to breathe outside an iron lung. His coming to terms with, and rising above his disability is a triumph of the human spirit. He is an inspiration to all who have known him. I feel privileged to have been his student.

Our Gestalt therapy training group met at Arnie's home, a few minutes from the University of California at Los Angeles where he was a clinical professor of psychiatry. Our group had been together for two years, changing trainers every half-year to introduce us to different therapeutic styles. We had come together as strangers, faced our shame, and affirmed one another. Healing shame in this group setting was one of the most rewarding personal and professional experiences of my life. I grieved when the time came for the group to dissolve. It had been an intensely emotional experience, and we were all saddened at the thought of saying goodbye.

There was total silence for the first half-hour of our final meeting. I don't know why the others chose not to speak. I said nothing because I could not find the words to express either my sense of appreciation or loss. Finally, Arnie broke the silence. To compensate for his limited breathing capacity, he conserved energy by not wasting words. When Arnie spoke, we listened! I have never forgotten what he said, and I can quote him verbatim. He said, "You know, we all pretty much want the same thing. We want to be loved! But...if we don't think we are worthy of love, we want to be appreciated. But...if we don't think we are worthy of appreciation, we want to be respected. But...if we don't think we are worthy of respect, we want to be feared. But...if we don't think we are worthy of fear, we want to be hated." The implication was clear—what we want from others, and therefore what we are likely to get, depends on how worthy we see ourselves.

Children want to be loved! But, those who internalize too much shame develop core beliefs that they are not worthy of love. Depending on the degree to which they were shamed, they will settle for less than they need and deserve. As parents, adults who were shamed as children feel compelled to re-enact shame scenes from their own childhoods. Despite good intentions, they are often incapable of affirming their own sons and daughters. Parents who feel unworthy of love, especially those most deprived of self-esteem, are bound to mistreat their own children and induce too much shame.

As adults, we want to be loved! But, we settle for less if our parents' behavior communicated the message that we were worth less. This is the origin of our shame and low self-esteem. As children we took in negative messages that suggested we were not worthy of love—we were inadequate, unwanted, dirty, or whatever, depending on how we were shamed. Those most shamed feel least deserving; those less severely shamed still settle for less than they need. To the extent that we settle for less than love, and extend less than love to ourselves and others, we are burdened by shame.

What we all wanted was for our parents to love us unconditionally and convince us that we were worthy and prized. Those who were deprived of unconditional love often expect it from inappropriate sources, e.g., from our partners or children. Or, still needing to be parented, we may continue to seek it from our mothers and fathers. This too is inappropriate, and prevents us from becoming psychological adults. We must "leave home" and learn to parent ourselves. We mourn the loss of unconditional love in childhood, but as healed adults we extend it to the child within. We invest ourselves in affirming relationships that reinforce positive self-esteem. Perhaps the most important aspect of self-parenting is learning to accept our imperfections and practice self-forgiveness.

As a way of coping with parents whose failures induced shame, we developed a false self. This false self was based upon the belief that our true self was unacceptably bad, and the fantasy that by being the son or daughter our parents wanted, we could win their love. By erecting a false self and hiding our true self, we defended against further encounters with shame. In so doing, we held on to the illusion that our parents were emotionally available, when in reality we felt abandoned. We experienced false selfhood as a shamed sense of self—we felt inferior, inadequate, or defective. This shame, internalized in childhood, was carried into adulthood. Our false self, which has little to do with who we really are, became a part of our identity.

The six-step process presented in Chapter Five is a model for healing shame. Completing these steps will serve as a launching pad for reaching true selfhood—we rise above shame. To rise above shame means that we have awakened from the family trance and differentiated a separate and autonomous self. It means that we return to life unburdened by shame and in control of how we think, feel, and relate. Rising above shame emphasizes the active aspect of the healing process, the re-experiencing and releasing that takes place in the context of an affirming relationship. To be free of the past makes possible a more intimate way of relating to our partners, our parents, our children, ourselves.

Rising above shame allows us to reach our goal of authentic or true selfhood. We bring our true self out of hiding because another human being is emotionally warm and contactful. We tell our stories and "speak the unspeakable" because the affirming relationship feels safe. Feeling held, and trusting another person to get close, we complete a rebirthing process that produces emotional growth (becoming more of a person) and integration (becoming more of who we truly are). The healing process is corrective because it validates our life experiences and reverses our developmental failures. We restructure new core beliefs that enhance self-esteem, live by new rules that affirm our basic rights, and form a true personal identity based on healthy pride. We feel emotionally alive and expressive, we enjoy intimate relationships, we know how to care for ourselves. The once-wounded self has been affirmed and is, once and for all, experienced as worthy, whole, and free of disabling shame. Rising above shame means we have attained a higher level of awareness and a new perspective on life—it is to "fly without wings!"

References

American Psychiatric Association (1987). *Diagnostic and statistical manual of mental disorders* (3rd ed. rev.). Washington, D.C.: Author.

Anthony, E. J. (1987). Risk, vulnerability and resilience: An overview. In E. J. Anthony and B. J. Cohler (Eds.), *The invulnerable child*. New York: Guilford.

Bader, Ellyn, & Pearson (1988). *In quest of the mythical mate: A developmental approach to diagnosis and treatment in couples therapy*. New York: Bruner/Mazel.

Barlow, D. H. (1988). *Anxiety and its disorders*. New York: Guilford.

Bateson, G., Jackson, D., Haley, J., & Weakland, J. (1956). Toward a theory of schizophrenia. *Behavioral Science, 1*, 251-264.

Bass, E., & Davis, L. (1988). *The courage to heal*. New York: Harper and Row.

Beavers, W. R. (1982). Healthy, midrange and severely dysfunctional families. In F. Walsh (Ed.), *Normal family process* (pp. 45-66). New York: Guilford.

Beck, A. T., & Emery, G. (1985). *Anxiety disorders and phobias*. New York: Basic Books.

Bednar, R. L., Wells, M. G., & Peterson, S. R. (1989). *Self esteem: Paradoxes and innovations in clinical theory and practice*. Washington, D.C.: American Psychological Association.

Black, C. (1981). *It will never happen to me*. Denver, CO: M.A.C.

Blume, E. S. (1990). *Secret survivors: Uncovering incest and its aftereffects in women*. New York: Wiley and Sons.

Bowen, M. (1978). *Family therapy in clinical practice*. New York: Jason Aronson.

Bradshaw, J. (1988). *Bradshaw on: Healing the shame that binds you*. Deerfield Beach, FL: Health Communications.

Brown, S. (1985). *Treating the alcoholic: A developmental model of recovery*. New York: Wiley and Sons.

Brown, S. (1988). *Treating adult children of alcoholics: A developmental perspective*. New York: Wiley and Sons.

Calof, D. L. (1989). Adult survivors of incest and child abuse. *Network Symposium*.

Cantwell, H. B. (1986). Psychiatric implications of child neglect. *Harvard Medical School Mental Health Letter, 3*(6), 5-6.

Courtois, C. A. (1988). *Healing the incest wound: Adult survivors in therapy.* New York: W. W. Norton.

Davis L. (1990) *The courage to heal workbook.* New York: Harper and Row.

Elkhaim, M. (1986). A systematic approach to couple therapy. *Family Process, 25,* 35-42.

Engel B. (1989). *The right to innocence: Healing the trauma of childhood sexual abuse.* Los Angeles: Jeremy P. Tarcher.

Epstein, N. B., Bishop, D. S., & Baldwin, L. M. (1982). McMaster model of family functioning: A view of the normal family. In Walsh & Froma (Eds.), *Normal family processes.* New York: Guilford.

Erickson, E. H. (1950). *Childhood and society.* New York: W. W. Norton.

Finkelhor, D., & Browne, A. (1985). The traumatic aspect of child sexual abuse: A conceptualization. *American Journal of Orthopsychiatry, 55,* 530-541.

Forward, S. (1989). *Toxic parents: Overcoming their hurtful legacy and reclaiming your life.* New York: Bantam.

Fossum, M. & Mason, M. (1986). *Facing shame: Families in recovery.* New York: W. W. Norton.

Framo, J. (1982). *Explorations in marital and family therapy.* New York: Springer.

Freeman, L. and Strean, H. S. (1986). *Guilt: Letting go.* New York: Wiley and Sons.

Freud, A. (1966). *The ego and the mechanisms of defense.* New York: International Universities Press.

Friedman, M. S. (1985). *The healing dialogue in psychotherapy.* Northvale, NJ: Jason Aronson.

Friel, J. & Friel, L. (1988). *Adult children: The secrets of dysfunctional families.* Pompano Beach, FL: Health Communications.

Garbarino, J., Guttmann, E., & Seeley, J. W. (1986). *The psychologically battered child.* San Francisco: Jossey-Bass.

Gaylin, W. (1979). *Feelings.* New York: Ballantine.

Gelles, R. J. & Connell, C. P. (1985). *Intimate violence in families.* Beverly Hills: Sage.

Gendlin, E. T. (1986). *Let your body interpret your dreams.* Wilmette, IL: Chiron.

Goldberg, J. (Ed.). *Psychotherapeutic treatment of cancer patients*. New York: Free Press.

Greenberg L. S., & Safran, J. D. (1987). *Emotion in psychotherapy*. New York: Guilford.

Halpern, H. M. (1976). *Cutting loose*. New York: Bantam.

Hare, R. D. (1986). Twenty years of experience with the Cleckley psychopath. In W. H. Reid, D. Dorr, J. I. Walker, & J. W. Bonner III (Eds.), *Unmasking the psychopath*. New York: W. W. Norton.

Harper, J. M., & Hoopes, M. H. (1990). *Uncovering shame: An approach integrating individuals and their family systems*. New York: W. W. Norton.

Hinsie, L. E., & Campbell, R. J. (1970). *Psychiatric dictionary* (4th Ed.). New York: Oxford University Press.

Jehu, D. (1988). *Beyond sexual abuse: Therapy with women who were childhood victims*. New York: Wiley and Sons.

Johnson, S. M. (1985). *Characterological transformation: The hard work miracle*. New York: W. W. Norton.

Justice, B., & Justice R. (1979). *The broken taboo: Sex in the family*. New York: Human Sciences.

Kaufman, G. (1989). *The psychology of shame: Theory and treatment of shame-based syndromes*. New York: Springer.

Kerr, M. E. (1981). In A. S. Gurman, & D. P. Kniskern (Eds.), *Handbook of family therapy* (pp. 226-264). New York: Bruner/Mazel.

Kerr, M., & Bowen, M. (1988). *Family evaluation: An approach based on Bowen therapy*. New York: Norton.

Kluft, R. P. (1985). *Childhood antecedents of multiple personality*. Washington D.C.: American Psychiatric Press.

Kramer, J. R. (1985). *Family interfaces: Transgenerational patterns*. New York: Bruner/Mazel.

Kritsberg, W. (1985). *The adult children of alcoholics syndrome*. Pomnpano Beach, FL: Health Communications.

Kroger, W. S., & Fezler, W. D. (1976). *Hypnosis and behavior modification*. Philadelphia: J.B. Lippincott.

L'Abate, L. (1985). *The handbook of family psychology and psychotherapy: Vol. II*. Homewood IL: The Dorsey Press.

Lansky, M. R. (1984). Violence, shame, and the family. *International Journal of Family Psychiatry, 5*, 21-40.

Lerner, H. G. (1985). *The dance of anger*. New York: Harper and Row.

Lerner, R. (1985). *Daily affirmations for adult children of alcoholics.* Deerfield Beach, FL: Health Communications.

Mahler, M., Pine F., & Bergman, A. (1975). *The psychological birth of the human infant: Symbiosis and individuation.* New York: Basic Books.

Masterson, J. F. (1981). *The narcissistic and borderline disorders.* New York: Bruner/Mazel.

Mathias, B. (1986). Lifting the shade on family violence. *Family Therapy Networker, May-June,* 20-29.

McArthur, D. S. (1988). *Birth of a self in adulthood.* Northvale, NJ: Jason Aronson.

McConnell, P. (1986). *A workbook for healing: Adult children of alcoholics.* San Francisco: Harper and Row.

McFarland, B., & Baker-Baumann, T. (1990). *Shame and body image: Culture and the compulsive eater.* Deerfield Beach, FL: Health Communications.

McMullin, R. E. (1986). *Handbook of cognitive therapy techniques.* New York: W. W. Norton.

Melnick, J. (1978). Starting therapy—assumptions and expectations. *The Gestalt Journal, I*(1), 74-82.

Middelton-Moz, J. (1989). *Children of trauma: Rediscovering your discarded self.* Deerfield Beach, FL: Health Communications.

Middelton-Moz, J. (1990). *Shame and guilt: The masters of disguise.* Deerfield Beach, FL: Health Communications.

Middelton-Moz, J., & Dwinell, L. (1986). *After the tears: reclaiming the personal losses of childhood.* Deerfield Beach, FL: Health Communications.

Miller, A. (1981). *The drama of the gifted child.* New York: Basic Books.

Minuchin, S. (1974). *Families and family therapy.* Cambridge, MA: Harvard University Press.

Moreno, J. L. (1972). *Psychodrama.* Beacon, NY: Beacon House.

Morawetz, A, & Walker, G. (1984). *Brief therapy with single parent families.* New York: Bruner/Mazel.

Morrison, A. P. (1978). The eye turned inward: Shame and the self. In D. L. Nathanson (Ed.), *The many faces of shame.* New York: Guilford.

Murphy, L. B., & Moriarty, A. (1976). *Vulnerability, coping and growth: From infancy to adolescence.* New Haven, CT: Yale University Press.

Napier, N. J. (1990). *Recreating your self: Help for adult children of dysfunctional families.* New York: W. W. Norton.

Nathanson, D. L. (Ed.). (1987). *The many faces of shame*. New York: Guilford.

Nichols, M. (1984). *Family therapy, concepts and methods*. New York: Gardne.

Norwood, R. (1985). *Women who love too much*. Los Angeles: Jeremy P. Tarcher.

Pierce, R. A., Nichols, M. P., & DuBrin, J. R. (1983). *Emotional expression in psychotherapy*. New York: Gardner.

Polster, E. and Polster, M. (1973). *Gestalt therapy integrated*. New York: Bruner/Mazel.

Potter-Efron, R., & Potter-Efron, P. (1989). *Letting go of shame*. San Francisco: Harper & Row.

Putnam, F. W. (1989). *Diagnosis and treatment of multiple personality disorder*. New York: Guilford.

Russell, D. E. H. (1986). *The secret trauma: Incest in the lives of girls and women*. New York: Basic Books.

Schaefer, C. E., Briesmeister, J. M., & Fitton, M. E. (1984). *Family therapy techniques for problem behaviors of children and teenagers*. San Francisco: Jossey-Bass.

Scharff, D. E., & Scharff, J. S. (1987). *Object relations family therapy*. Northvale, NJ: Jason Aronson.

Seinfeld, J. (1990). *The bad object: Handling the negative therapeutic reaction in psychotherapy*. Northvale, NJ: Jason Aronson.

Seligman, M.E.P. (1981). A learned helplessness point of view. In L. P. Rehm (Ed.), *Behavior therapy for depression*. New York: Academic Press.

Seixas, J. H., & Youcha, G. (1985). *Children of alcoholism*. New York: Harper and Row.

Simon, S. B., & Simon, S. (1990). *Forgiveness*. New York: Warner Books.

Simpkonson, A. (1989). The man who thought he was a grain of corn. *Common Boundry, 20*.

Smedes, L. B. (1984). *Forgive and forget*. New York: Pocket Books.

Stein, R. (1973). *Incest and Human Love*. Dallas, TX: Spring.

Steinglass, P. (1987). *The alcoholic family*. New York: Basic Books.

Subby, R. (1987). *Lost in the shuffle*. Pompano Beach, FL: Health Communications.

Sullivan, H. S. (1953). *The Interpersonal theory of psychiatry*. New York: W. W. Norton.

Trask, R. (1989). God's phone number, repairing the effects of religious fanaticism. *U.S. Journal: Conference on adult children of alcoholics*, July 27, 1989.

Twentyman, C. T., Rohrbeck, C. A., & Amish, P. (1985). In L. L'Abate (Ed.), *The handbook of family psychology and therapy* (Vol. II pp. 909-910). Dorsey.

Valentine, R. J. (1987). Freedom of choice versus honoring commitment. In P. Titelman (Ed.), *The therapist's own family*. Northvale, NJ: Jason Aronson.

Van Dusen, W. (1972). *The natural depth in man*. New York: Harper and Row.

World Publishing Co. (1970). *Webster's new world dictionary of the american language*. New York: Author.

Wechsler, H. J. (1990). *What's so bad about guilt?* New York: Simon and Schuster.

Wegscheider, S. (1981). *Another chance: Hope and health for the alcoholic family*. Palo Alto, CA: Science and Behavior Books.

Whitfield, C. L. (1987). *Healing the child within*. Pompano Beach, FL: Health Communications.

Williamson, D. S. (1981). Personal authority via termination of the intergenerational hierarchical boundary: A "New" stage in the family life cycle. *Journal of Marital and Family Therapy, October*, 441-452.

Williamson, D. S. (1982). Personal authority via termination of the intergenerational hierarchical boundary: Part II—The consultation process and the therapeutic method. *Journal of Marital and Family Therapy, April*, 23-37.

Wood, B. L. (1987). *Children of alcoholism*. New York: New York University Press.

Wurmser, L. (1987). Shame: The veiled companion of narcissism. In D. L. Nathanson (Ed.), *The many faces of shame*. New York: Guilford.